D0882936

WALRAS' ECONOMICS
A PURE THEORY OF CAPITAL
AND MONEY

Michio Morishima

WALRAS' ECONOMICS

A PURE THEORY
OF CAPITAL AND MONEY

CAMBRIDGE UNIVERSITY PRESS

CAMBRIDGE

LONDON · NEW YORK · MELBOURNE

Published by the Syndics of the Cambridge University Press
The Pitt Building, Trumpington Street, Cambridge CB2 1RP
Bentley House, 200 Euston Road, London NW1 2DB
32 East 57th Street, New York, NY 10022, USA
296 Beaconsfield Parade, Middle Park, Melbourne 3206, Australia

© Cambridge University Press 1977

First published 1977

Printed in Great Britain at the
University Press, Cambridge

Library of Congress Cataloguing in Publication Data

Morishima, Michio, 1923–
Walras' economics.
1. Walras, Leon, 1834–1910. 2. Economics – History. I. Title.
HB105.W3M67   330'.092'4   76-40833
ISBN 0 521 21487 4

HB105
W3
M67

Contents

Preface

In this book I have refrained from recapitulating the full story of Walras' economics and have contented myself with reviewing only its theoretical kernel. Such a restriction will not, I hope, give the reader a distorted view of Walras as perhaps the similar restriction in my previous book on Marx's economics might have given of Marx. In the case of Marx, pure economic analysis was not dominant even in the three volumes of *Capital*.

In Walras, according to his original schedule, his work was expected to be enormous. The existing definitive edition of *Eléments d'économie politique pure* which William Jaffé translated into English is no more than Book One of a treatise on the elements of political and social economy that he was intending to write. The treatise was supposed to be made up of three Books; the other two were entitled 'Elements of Applied Economics or the Theory of Agricultural, Industrial, and Commercial Production of Wealth' and 'Elements of Social Economics or the Theory of the Distribution of Wealth via Property and Taxation'. Unfortunately, however, he could only publish two volumes of collected papers, *Etudes d'économie sociale*, 1896, and *Etudes d'économie politique appliquée*, 1898, instead of the planned Book Two and Book Three. The restricted view which I maintain in this book has naturally resulted in my entirely ignoring Walras' applied economics or social economics, but this will not have serious effects, although I believe that we can only judge the full value of his pure economics by considering it in the context of his original farsighted scheme.

Recent studies of Walras' economics have been mainly devoted to making his general equilibrium theory of exchange and production mathematically rigorous, so that his theory has been completely sterilized. Such work should of course be welcomed, unless it is done to excess. It is, however, neither wise nor consistent with the Walrasian law of the optimum to spend increasing mathematical efforts on a subject of decreasing marginal economic significance. In my opinion, Walras' theory of exchange and production is not the end and aim of his study but an overture to his general equilibrium theory of capital formation and circulation. Therefore, what we have to do first of all is to elaborate in economic, rather than mathematical terms his theory of growth and money, which in Walras' work was not complete. In reconsidering Walras from such a point of view, he appears as an economist who was comparable with Marx and who anticipated Keynes.

Walras' economics contains various weak points, but I gather all of my major criticisms in the final chapters of the book. In the other chapters, although I criticize him internally on a number of points, I concentrate mainly on revising his economic model and bringing it to completion as Walras' theory. The most important revision is concerned with his four-class view of society, according to which the capitalist society is considered as consisting of four independent classes, workers, landowners, capitalists and entrepreneurs, so that decisions to invest are made by entrepreneurs independently from decisions to save by capitalists. Walras emphasized this view in various places of his book but was unable to construct a mathematical model reflecting this view. One of the main aims of this volume is to present such a model – a microscopic counterpart of Keynes' economy where investment and savings are decided independently and, hence, where Say's law does not prevail.

As any modern student of Walras must, I acknowledge Jaffé's definitive edition: Leon Walras, *Elements of Pure Economics or the Theory of Social Wealth* (a translation by W. Jaffé of the Edition Définitive (1926) of the *Eléments d'économie politique pure*), published by Richard D. Irwin Inc., Homewood, Illinois (1954). I also thank the publishers for permission to quote. A substantial part of this book is based on my articles, 'Short lectures on Leon Walras', *Economic Notes*, Vol. II, No. 2, Siena, 1973 and 'Leon Walras and money' in J. M. Parkin and A. R. Nobay (eds.), *Current Economic Problems*, Cambridge University Press, 1975. The latter was read at an annual conference of the Association of University Teachers of Economics held at Manchester, 1974, while its original version was written in January 1964, at All Souls College, Oxford. I started to write the manuscript of the book in the summer of 1974, at Queen's University, Canada. I have benefited from a number of helpful comments and suggestions from participants in the seminars in numerous universities in Britain, Belgium, Canada, Italy, Japan and the Netherlands where I was given the opportunity to read some chapters of the book, as well as from those students who attended my lectures at the London School of Economics. Finally I am greatly indebted to Ms Jo Bradley for stylistic improvement.

M.M.

January 1977

Introduction

Having written in my *Marx's Economics* that Marx should be ranked as high as Walras in the history of mathematical economics, I was almost bound to write a companion book about Walras. I consider it worth writing because I believe that Walras is misunderstood by most students, including those fellow economists who specialize in the so-called Walrasian theory of general equilibrium. There are only a few exceptions; I believe that even Walras himself probably did not perfectly understand the significance and implications of his own contributions.

There are two distinct views of Walras, one originating with Schumpeter and the other with Jaffé. Schumpeter writes about Walras:[1]

The simple greatness which lies in unconditional surrender to one task is what strikes us when we look back on this scholarly life. Its inherent logic, inevitability, and power impress us as a natural event. Exclusive meditation on the problems of pure economics formed its content. Nothing else.

The course of his studies shows the thinker's unfitness for practical matters: failures such as we should expect of one who prepared for the École Polytechnique by studying Descartes and Newton; lack of enthusiasm for outworn paths such as every searching mind experiences.

[A]lready...in 1859...he was convinced that economic theory could be treated mathematically. From that moment on he knew what he wanted, from that moment on his whole strength was dedicated to *one* end. Here – in the method and not in any specific problems – is the origin of his work. [Schumpeter's italics]

[1] Schumpeter, J. A., *Ten Great Economists from Marx to Keynes* (George Allen & Unwin, London, 1952), pp. 74–9.

He walked a solitary path without the moral support to which the practical man as well as the scientist is usually accustomed. Thus his portrait shows all the characteristics which distinguish the truly creative mind from those that are created.

William Jaffé, on the other hand, describes Walras as follows:[2]

[H]is mathematical attainments proved insufficient to enable him to gain entrance to the École Polytechnique...With Bohemian insouciance he neglected his engineering studies, which he found distasteful, and turned to literature... Realizing that he was not meant for a literary career, he promised his father in the summer of 1858 that he would devote his life to economics.

He tried his hand at journalism but was soon discharged because of the independence of his opinions...

In a series of public lectures delivered in Paris during 1867–1868...Walras expounded his philosophy of social reform based on the methaphysical ideas of Victor Cousin and Étienne Vacherot, calling for a conciliation of interests. Ideological as his position was, he resisted the efforts of his Saint-Simonian friends to enrol him among their number, because their socialism was 'unscientific'. He always thought of himself as a 'scientific' socialist...

Whether only out of caution or out of sheer intellectual curiosity, he initially concentrated upon pure economics, which then became his dominant passion.

This was the achievement of Walras, a lonely, cantankerous savant, often in straitened circumstances, plagued with hypochondria and a paranoid temperament, plodding doggedly through hostile, uncharted territory to discover a fresh vantage point from which subsequent generations of economists could set out to make their own discoveries.

Despite these diverse, if not inconsistent, characterizations of Walras' life and personality, there are no significant differences between Schumpeter and Jaffé in their appraisal of his academic achievements. They seem to agree in considering that Parts II–VI of the *Elements of Pure Economics* are the richest and most important part of all Walras' three main volumes on pure economics, applied economics and social economics.[3] In these parts Walras developed four models of general equilibrium, (i) of exchange (of two and then of more than two commodities), (ii) of production, (iii) of capital accumulation or economic growth, and (iv) of money and circulation. He derived demands for commodities, aggregate savings, and the desired cash balance as functions of prices and the rate of interest, from the single principle of maximum ultility. He also discussed, not rigorously but rather intuitively or heuristically, the existence and stability of the general equilibrium solutions to each system. He used such novel concepts as '*numéraire*', '*tâtonnement*', '*rareté*', '*coefficients de fabrication*', '*revenu net perpetuel*', '*encaisse désirée*', and so on, all of which were later found to be basic to general equilibrium analysis. Both Schumpeter and Jaffé show a high appreciation of these contributions. They pay them uniform tribute and none is singled out for more praise than the others.

This evaluation of Walras by Schumpeter and Jaffé differs greatly from Blaug's. He writes: 'Walrasian economics is thin in substance, stressing form at the expense of content. We have... seen one example of this in his treatment of capital theory... [H]is monetary theory would supply additional evidence of formalism...Walras' contributions to substantive economics [are] almost solely confined to the theory of consumer behaviour, where he did see much further and more clearly than his contemporaries.'[4] Blaug also writes: 'In contrast to the thousands of pages that Böhm-Bawerk and Wicksell lavished on the subject, Walras takes exactly 40 pages in the *Elements* to show how the rate of interest is determined. The Walrasian theory is formally impeccable; but what is its substance?'[5] Similarly, if the number of pages of a work reflects its academic quality (!), we should point out that Walras' general equilibrium theory of

[3] Léon Walras, *Elements of Pure Economics or the Theory of Social Wealth*, a translation by W. Jaffé of the Edition Définitive (1926) of the *Eléments d'économie politique pure*, annotated and collated with the previous editions (Richard D. Irwin, Inc., Homewood, Illinois, 1954); *Études d'économie politique appliquée* (*Théorie de la production de la richesse sociale*), 2nd edn (Rouge, Lausanne, 1936; originally 1898); *Études d'économie sociale* (*Théorie de la répartition de la richesse sociale*), 2nd edn (Rouge, Lausanne, 1936; originally 1896).

[4] Blaug, M., *Economic Theory in Retrospect*, 2nd edn (Heinemann Educational Books, London, 1973), p. 587.

[5] *Op. cit.*, p. 585.

money occupies only 20 pages; and the whole money section of the *Elements*, including chapters dealing with the problems, then current, of bimetallism and bank notes and a chapter on foreign exchange, is no more than a 60-page work. Nevertheless, Schumpeter regards Walras' treatment of bimetallism as 'nothing short of classic' and 'definitive for a long time to come', and Jaffé describes it as 'a complete theory of the bimetallist standard'.[6]

Although I know that Blaug's view of Walras is a popular one, I feel that it must be rejected entirely. It is, first of all, completely wrong to confuse Walras with the present-day Walrasians, just as it is to confuse Marx with Marxists. Walras was not only interested in the rigorousness and elegance of the theory. On the basis of his capital theory, Walras proposed the nationalization of a number of private properties (land, natural monopolies, railways, etc.), which led to a tax reform, and his monetary theory provided the basis for a money reform. Moreover, he was not an author who wanted to inflate the number of pages of his writings; he avoided repetition and verbiage as much as possible. For him, there was no reason to make Part v of the *Elements*, on capital theory, and Part vi, on money theory, longer than they actually were; the earlier parts of the book had already provided sufficient explanation of many of the necessary concepts and behavioural assumptions of the theories.

In fact, in my opinion, the ultimate aim of the book was to construct a model, by the use of which we can examine how the capitalist system works. The model is first presented, in Parts ii and iii, in its simplest form, by neglecting production, capital accumulation and money, and concentrating attention on exchange. It is then successively made more general and realistic, so as to allow for production in Part iv, then saving and investment in Part v, and finally money transactions and money holding in Part vi. Thus these parts should not have the equal weight that Schumpeter and Jaffé gave them, but should be regarded as indispensable components of an organic unity. In particular, the relationship of Parts v and vi to Parts ii, iii and iv is one of an edifice to its foundations. Blaug appreciates only the foundations, whereas I judge that it is great because the edifice built on them is great, though Walras himself thought

---

[6] Schumpeter, *op. cit.*, p. 29; Jaffé, *op. cit.*, p. 451.

for many years that his prime contribution to economic theory lay in his marginal utility theory. As much of the groundwork for Parts v and vi had been laid in the earlier parts, it was sufficient to allocate a rather small number of pages to them; it is clear that their shortness has nothing to do with their significance.

Neither Schumpeter, Jaffé nor Blaug recognizes the importance of Part vii, entitled 'Conditions and Consequences of Economic Progress: Critique of Systems of Pure Economics'. Among them Blaug, who complains of Walras' formalism, explicitly criticizes him for not being able to derive the laws of change of the capitalist economy from his systems of general equilibrium. As Blaug points out, Hicks expresses a similar complaint in *Value and Capital*.[7] The neglected Part vii of the *Elements*, however, includes chapters entitled 'The Continuous Market' and 'The Marginal Productivity Theorem'. The former is concerned with economic fluctuations taking place in an economy with a permanent market which is open at all times. The latter, with the subtitle 'The Law of General Price Movements in a Progressing Economy', clearly derives several laws of the working of the whole system, among which the most important is stated by Walras as: '*In a progressive economy, the price of labour (wages) remaining substantially unchanged, the price of land-services (rent) will rise appreciably and. . .the rate of net income* [the rate of profit or the rate of interest] *will fall appreciably.*'[8]

By obtaining this apparently Ricardo-like (or Marx-like) conclusion, Walras was led to an examination of Ricardian theory. The rest of Part vii is mainly devoted to critical exposition of the English classical school. Walras writes: 'The efforts of the English School to develop a theory of rent, wages and interest were far more sustained and thorough than those of the various French schools that came into existence after the Physiocrats.' He praises Ricardo as 'the founder of pure economics in England'.[9] Among other things he considered Ricardo's price–cost equations as constituents of his general equilibrium system and critically examined their working in relation to other components of the system.

Although Walras and Marx were ignorant of each other's

<hr />

[7] Hicks, J. R., *Value and Capital*, 2nd edn (The Clarendon Press, Oxford, 1946), p. 61.

[8] Walras, *Elements*, pp. 390–1. Walras' italics.   [9] *op. cit.*, p. 398.

work, their relationship becomes clear once we agree to legitimize Walras as a Ricardian. It is true that Marx established his theory on the basis of the labour theory of value, while Walras used the scarcity theory of value. In spite of this difference, I believe that Marx would have been happy to accept the principal conclusion of Walras quoted above. Moreover, both Walras and Marx founded their respective scientific socialisms on their economics – in the case of Walras, on his pure economics and, in the case of Marx, on his scientific economics. We may say, therefore, that Marx would have held Walras in as much respect as he did Ricardo. It is not right to assume that Marx and Walras would have been completely antagonistic towards each other, as many contemporary economists believe. They were the two greatest disciples – or critics – of Ricardo.

Let us next consider the relationship between Walras and Keynes. One topic in economic theory now enjoying popularity is the provision of a micro-economic foundation for Keynesian economics. This is usually done by using Hicks' model in *Value and Capital* as a foundation on which Keynesian buildings are to be erected. However, this approach is not wise or, at least, not efficient. There is an important difference between Keynes and Hicks: Keynes eliminates the demand–supply equation for bonds, keeping the investment–savings equation within the system, while Hicks presents a model in which there is no explicit place for the investment–savings equation. Walras differs from Hicks in this respect; his system is exactly the same as Keynes', retaining the aggregate equation between investment and savings, instead of the bond equation. From the point of view of traditional general equilibrium theory Walras' system of capital accumulation is rather difficult to understand. In conventional theory, a market is assumed behind each equation of the system, while there is no specific market behind the Walrasian equation between aggregate savings and aggregate investment. It is a macroeconomic equilibrium condition which reflects equilibrium in many markets. It is clear from a reading of Walras' *Elements* what great efforts he expended in interpreting that equation. One can compare them with the efforts which the first-generation Keynesians made to understand the same Keynesian equation immediately after the publication of Keynes' *General Theory*.

Moreover, there is an additional similarity at a deeper level between Walras and Keynes. In the usual theory of general equilibrium after Hicks, the economy consists of firms and households, the latter not being classified. In contrast, Walras' economy has clear class distinctions. It consists of workers, landowners, capitalists and entrepreneurs. Savings are made by the first three classes. As savings by the working and landowning classes are negligible, the major part of aggregate savings comes from capitalists. On the other hand, entrepreneurs decide on production and investment. At the early stages of development of capitalist society, capitalists and entrepreneurs were identical, so there was no great inconsistency between investment and savings. In subsequent stages some capitalists are no longer entrepreneurs and entrepreneurs are not necessarily capitalists. Therefore savings and investment become independent of each other and the inconsistency between them becomes a major issue in the economy. Keynes pursued the consequences which arise from this independence. On the other hand, Walras insisted on his four-class view of society and noticed the independence of entrepreneurs from capitalists, but he did not clarify its economic implications. Besides, the mathematical model he actually formulated is a classical one, based on the identity of entrepreneurs with capitalists, so that there is a big gap between Walras' sociological view and his mathematical model. If we could revise the latter so as to make it consistent with the former, we would have a model which could be equivalent to Keynes' model.

However, it would be rather difficult to obtain as many results from this model as Keynes derived from his macroeconomic one. Hicks ascribed the sterility of Walras' analysis to the lack of comparative statics or laws of motion of the economy. This is not precisely correct, as I have already mentioned. In Part VII of the *Elements* Walras obtained several laws from his model, but they are not sufficient to satisfy us. In my opinion the reason for this sterility is not the one deduced by Hicks, but that Walras constructed his theory of general equilibrium as a one-stage theory. As I wrote in my *Marx's Economics*, Marx first constructed a multi-sectoral, price-determination model and then reduced the corresponding output-determination model to a two-sector reproduction scheme to obtain fruitful results.

This kind of two-stage approach was later discovered independently by Hicks. He reduced his complex model, containing many variables, to a simple one, consisting of three equations for 'commodity', 'money' and 'securities', which in turn is reduced to the Keynesian *IS* and *LM* model by further eliminating the equation for 'securities'. In the same way, if we apply the two-stage approach to Walras' system we obtain a model which we can no longer accuse of sterility. In fact, when Walras derived the Ricardian-like conclusion which I quoted above he implicitly used the two-stage approach.

The theory of general equilibrium is a branch of economics in which great names have presented economic models which reflect their views about society. According to the usual view Walras emphasized consumer choice, inter-market relationships and the price mechanism; the Austrians and Wicksell, time preference and the structure of roundabout production; Marx, the exploitation of people by people; Schumpeter, entrepreneurship and innovations; Keynes, the economic role of the government and the central bank; Hicks, expectations, temporary equilibrium and perfect equilibrium over time; etc., etc. This tradition changed entirely after the Second World War; no new view of society has since been presented, although economists have continued to vie with each other in mathematical ability. It seems that general equilibrium theorists are now only interested in proving, re-proving or generalizing the theorems or laws discovered by their predecessors. The primary aim of this book is not to make contributions in this direction; instead I want to extract and gather together Walras' economic visions from various parts of his principal work, the *Elements*, and I want to reconstruct his mathematical economic models so as to fit his visions and to see how these models work.

The book can be outlined as follows: in Part I I make preparations for an explanation of Walras' theory of capital and his theory of money. With this aim his theory of exchange is examined for the existence and stability of an equilibrium in Chapters 1 and 2. Similar work will be done for the model of production in Chapters 3 and 4. I shall not simply reproduce Walras' theory; the reader will see how my understanding of it differs from the conventional one.

Part II deals with Walras' theory of capital accumulation. As

I have already pointed out, Walras had a four-class view of society (which I take as more advanced than Marx's two-class view) although he was unable to formulate a model in which entrepreneurs behave independently of capitalists. To realize Walras' intentions, Chapter 5 carefully revises his model. I refer to the case where investment is flexible and smoothly and quickly adjusts itself to savings, as in Say's world, and the other case, where investment is decided independently of savings, as in the Keynesian world. Chapters 6 and 7 investigate economic growth in Say's and in the Keynesian world respectively.

It is known that Walras frequently revised his theory of money, so that even the version in the definitive edition should not be regarded as his final word. It should be revised in various respects; it even contains mathematical slips. In Part III we try to reconstruct Walras' theory in his own spirit. In Walras the theory of money is not separable from the theory of growth. Chapter 8 includes a summary of the latter so as to make Part III self-contained. We propose a corrected version of the Walrasian money model. It is a very general system, so that we can discuss various alternative theories of interest so far presented within its framework (Chapter 10). The quantity theory of money, or the so-called classical dichotomy between the real and monetary theories, is the topic of Chapter 11. Say's law is again discussed in Chapter 12 for an economy with money.

Part IV contains only Chapter 13, in which I criticise Walras. The main points of criticism are (i) that Walras does not distinguish between new and old capital goods except in allowing for depreciation of the latter, so that no attention is paid to obsolescence, the age composition of capital, and so on ; (ii) that he ignores the production period and always assumes instantaneous production; and (iii) that he does not discuss the period of circulation of money satisfactorily. To remove these weak points I propose to extend Walras' model to produce the one which I call the Walras–von Neumann model. This is a proposal exactly parallel to that which I made for Marx in my *Marx's Economics*. As I have already pointed out, both were Ricardians. Their thinking thus flowed from a common source and formed two tributaries, until they finally converged again with von Neumann at the critical point in the history of the development of economic analysis when the von Neuman revolution was brought about. Von Neumann himself could not go far into the investigation of his model, except to establish the existence of a balanced growth path. I have shown in my *Theory of Economic Growth*[10] that the von Neumann model has a temporary equilibrium at each point of time and the sequence of these equilibria traces out a path which may be examined for efficiency and optimality. Production and consumption turnpike theorems have also been discussed within the von Neumann framework, but many things remain to be done in order to achieve a complete theory of motion of the capitalist society.

[10] Morishima, M., *Theory of Economic Growth* (The Clarendon Press, Oxford, 1969).

PART I

Exchange and Production

CHAPTER I

Arbitrage and exchange equilibrium

In *Capital* Marx began his investigation of capitalist production by analysing how a particular kind of commodity becomes the *numéraire* in terms of which all other commodities uniformly express their value. He wrote: 'Every one knows, if he knows nothing else, that commodities have a value-form common to them all, and presenting a marked contrast with the varied bodily forms of their use-values. I mean their money-form. Here, however, a task is set us, the performance of which has never yet even been attempted by *bourgeois* economy, the task of tracing the genesis of this money-form, of developing the expression of value implied in the value-relation of commodities, from its simplest, almost imperceptible outline, to the dazzling money-form. By doing this we shall, at the same time, solve the riddle presented by money.'[1] In the first part of his *Elements*[2] Walras was concerned with more or less similar problems. Of course, their methods of analysis were completely different; they saw different entities behind the system of prices: Marx saw abstract human labour, and Walras *rareté*. But they both thought that it was of basic importance to clarify the problem of the *numéraire*, before launching into detailed examinations of the working of the capitalist economy.

Although Walras was greatly helped by his father's theory of social wealth and Cournot's theory of arbitrage, he began a truly original study of free competition. It was deep, rigorous and revolutionary. In addition, he should be congratulated on his success in his campaign for the mathematization of the social sciences. He wrote: 'The twentieth century, which is not far off, will feel the need...of entrusting the social sciences to men of general culture who are accustomed to thinking both inductively

[1] Marx, K., *Capital*, Vol. I (Progress Publishers, Moscow, 1963), pp. 47–8, Marx's italics.

[2] *Elements*, Part II and Part III, pp. 83–207.

and deductively and who are familiar with reason as well as experience. The mathematical economics will rank with the mathematical sciences of astronomy and mechanics; and on that day justice will be done to our work.'[3] We have indeed done exactly as he expected!

From the viewpoint of our contemporary level of economic analysis, however, one might allege that Walras was crude in a number of respects. First, he gave the subjective equilibrium conditions, i.e. the conditions of individuals' maximum satisfaction, in the form of equations stating that for each individual the ratio of the marginal utilities between any two commodities equals the ratio of their prices, rather than in the more advanced Kuhn–Tucker inequality form, which allows for the possibility of a corner maximum. Secondly, he gave the objective equilibrium conditions, i.e. the conditions of clearing markets, in the form of demand–supply equations, not in the more elaborate inequality form which allows for some goods to be abundant and to be sold at a zero price. Thirdly, Walras did not rigorously prove that his system of equations of general equilibrium has a solution, although he showed that it contained exactly as many independent equations as unknowns to be determined.

After a cursory reading of the *Elements*, one might admit all these criticisms to be valid. But more careful study makes it clear that Walras was not so shallow; he was profound and meticulous in his economic reasoning. We should not take Walras' system of equations as being self-contained. In fact, because of his mathematical limitations he could not state every condition of general equilibrium in a correct mathematical way, so that he had to supplement his equations with verbal explanations and qualifications.

In the light of Walras' various remarks and comments in the parts of the *Elements* which deal with the general equilibrium of exchange, I believe that the following is not a farfetched interpretation of his theory. Obviously Walras was concerned with an exchange economy where all individuals are price takers. Let p be a price vector, $p = (p_1, p_2, ..., p_n)$. Each individual is provided with certain quantities of the n commodities, $\bar{x}_1, \bar{x}_2, ..., \bar{x}_n$, before trade, and wishes to convert them into $x_1, x_2, ..., x_n$ through

[3] *op. cit.*, p. 48.

exchange so as to maximize his utility function:

$$u = u(x_1, x_2, ..., x_n). \tag{1}$$

He will maximize it subject to his budget equation:

$$\Sigma p_i x_i = \Sigma p_i \bar{x}_i. \tag{2}$$

In addition, the stocks of commodities he holds after trade should be non-negative:

$$x_i \geqq 0 \quad (i = 1, ..., n). \tag{3}$$

For our contemporaries, this problem of maximization is not difficult; we can apply the famous Kuhn–Tucker theorem[4] and obtain the first-order conditions for u to be a conditional maximum:

$$u_i \leqq \lambda p_i \quad (i = 1, ..., n), \tag{4}$$

where u_i is the partial derivative of u with respect to x_i and λ the Lagrangean. If conditions (4) hold with strict inequality ‘ < ’ for some i, then the corresponding x_is should take on zero value at the maximum; otherwise $x_i \geqq 0$. I venture to say, in spite of the fact that Walras put the maximum conditions not in the inequality form but in the equation form, that he obtained virtually the same conditions as our (4) above. Also, while inequalities (3) are not to be found anywhere in his book, he took account in his argument of the constraint that non-negative stocks of commodities would be held after exchange.

The following quotations will justify this claim. For an economy with two commodities Walras wrote: ‘*Given two commodities in a market, each holder attains maximum satisfaction of wants, or maximum effective utility, when the ratio of the intensities of the last wants satisfied, or the ratio of their raretés* [i.e. marginal utilities], *is equal to the price*...It is possible, of course, that a party to the exchange may find it to his advantage to offer the entire amount of whichever one of the two commodities he possesses to start with [i.e. to have $x_i = 0$ for commodity i with $\bar{x}_i > 0$] or to demand none at all of the other commodity [i.e. to have $x_i = 0$ for i with $\bar{x}_i = 0$].’[5] For the latter case he concluded: ‘ *The quantity demanded of one of the two commodities by a holder of the other commodity*

---

[4] We assume that u traces out indifference curves which are convex to the origin everywhere.

[5] *Elements*, p. 125; Walras’ italics.

becomes zero, whenever the price of the commodity demanded is equal to or greater than the ratio of the intensity of his maximum want for it to the intensity of the last want which can be satisfied by the quantity possessed of the commodity offered [i.e. the ratio of their marginal utilities].'[6] For the former: ' *The holder of one of the two commodities will offer all he possesses of that commodity whenever the price of the commodity demanded in exchange is equal to or less than the ratio of the intensity of the last want which can be satisfied by the commodity demanded to the intensity of the maximum want satisfied by the commodity to be offered.*'[7] From these quotations it is evident that for the two-commodity case Walras obtained the subjective equilibrium conditions (4), rather than the simple equations, $u_i = \lambda p_i, i = 1, ..., n$. Nothing will be altered when several commodities are exchanged. Walras obviously knew this fact.[8]

Next, although it has often been said that a rigorous analysis of free goods was first made by such German-speaking economists as Zeuthen, Neisser, von Stackelberg, etc., the concept of scarcity, which is in opposition to the concept of freeness of goods, is fundamental to Walras' theory of value. Walras accepted neither the British labour theory of value nor the French utility theory, because neither gave proper consideration to scarcity. In more detail, against the labour theory of value he wrote: 'Surely, if labour has value and is exchangeable, it is because it is both useful and limited in quantity, that is to say it is scarce. Value, thus, comes from scarcity. Things other than labour, provided they are scarce, have value and are exchangeable just like labour itself.'[9] Against the utility theory he wrote: 'Utility...is not sufficient to create value. Besides being useful, a thing must be scarce, i.e. it must not exist in unlimited quantities ...The air we breathe, the wind that fills the sails at sea or turns windmills on land, the sun that gives us light and heat and ripens our harvests, water and steam from heated water, these and many other forces of nature are not only useful, but indispensable. And yet they have no value. Why? Because they are unlimited in quantity and everyone can obtain all he wants of them, whenever they are present at all, without giving up anything or making any sacrifice in return.'[10]

The main aim of Walras' theory of exchange was to verify the

---

[6] *op. cit.*, p. 132; his italics.   [7] *op. cit.*, p. 133; his italics.
[8] See *Elements*, p. 175.   [9] *op. cit.*, p. 202.   [10] *op. cit.*, p. 202.

view that all valuable and exchangeable things are useful and at the same time limited in quantity, and *vice versa*. For this purpose he paid particular attention to the quantity of a commodity which is demanded by an individual when its price is zero. He called this quantity the 'extensive utility' of that commodity and assumed that it is ordinarily finite.[11] He concluded: '[T]he intensity of the last want satisfied would be zero if a commodity which possessed a utility curve were so plentiful that its quantity exceeded its extensive utility, as would be the case, for example, if it were unlimited in quantity... If [a commodity] became useless, or, though useful, became unlimited in quantity, that commodity would no longer be scarce and would cease to have value in exchange.'[12]

The total extensive utility of commodity i is the sum of the individual extensive utilities. It is the total quantity of i which individuals want to retain when its price is zero; in other words, it is the sum of x_is over all individuals at $p_i = 0$. As each x_i depends not only on p_i but also on the other prices, the total X_i is a function of all prices, so that the total extensive utility, i.e. X_i at $p_i = 0$, may fluctuate if the prices of other commodities change. We may then interpret the above-quoted statements of Walras as follows. Let $p_1^0, ..., p_n^0$ be the general equilibrium values of the prices. Let $X_i(p_1^0, ..., p_{i-1}^0, 0, p_{i+1}^0, ..., p_n^0)$ be the particular total extensive utility of commodity i which is obtained when equilibrium prices prevail in all other markets. Then the equilibrium price of commodity i is zero, i.e. $p_i^0 = 0$, if the 'total extensive utility' of i falls short of the quantity possessed, i.e.

$$X_i(p_1^0, ..., p_{i-1}^0, 0, p_{i+1}^0, ..., p_n^0) < \bar{X}_i,$$

where $\bar{X}_i$ denotes the total quantity of commodity i originally held, i.e. the sum of $\bar{x}_i$ over all individuals. This rule of pricing is exactly the same as that which we now call the rule of free goods.

For an individual let us write

$$d_i = x_i - \bar{x}_i$$

if his x_i exceeds his $\bar{x}_i$, and

$$s_j = \bar{x}_j - x_j$$

[11] See *Elements*, p. 98, p. 115 and p. 132.   [12] *op. cit.*, p. 145.

if his $\bar{x}_j$ exceeds his x_j. The individual will buy the amount d_i of commodity i from other persons and sell the amount s_j of commodity j to other persons. In the market the total demand for commodity i amounts to the sum of d_is over all individuals and the total supply to the sum of s_is. They are denoted by

$$D_i(p_1, ..., p_n) \quad \text{and} \quad S_i(p_1, ..., p_n),$$

respectively, since they depend on prices. The sum of the budget equation (2) over all individuals can then be written in the form

$$\Sigma p_i D_i(p_1, ..., p_n) = \Sigma p_i S_i(p_1, ..., p_n), \tag{5}$$

which is usually referred to as Walras' law. General equilibrium is then defined as a state of the economy where no excess demand is present in any market; that is to say,

$$D_i(p_1, ..., p_n) \leq S_i(p_1, ..., p_n) \quad \text{for all } i. \tag{6}$$

As prices are all non-negative, it follows from (5) and (6) together that

$$D_i(p_1, ..., p_n) < S_i(p_1, ..., p_n) \quad \text{implies } p_i = 0, \tag{7}$$

because otherwise we have

$$\Sigma p_i D_i(p_1, ..., p_n) < \Sigma p_i S_i(p_1, ..., p_n)$$

if there is an excess supply in some markets; this contradicts Walras' law (5).

By definition it is clear that excess demand, $D_i - S_i$, is identical with $X_i - \bar{X}_i$. Walras' law and the equilibrium conditions may then be written, in terms of X_is, as

$$\Sigma p_i X_i(p_1, ..., p_n) = \Sigma p_i \bar{X}_i \tag{5'}$$

and $\qquad\qquad X_i(p_1, ..., p_n) \leq \bar{X}_i \quad \text{for all } i, \tag{6'}$

respectively. In the state of equilibrium, if there is a commodity in excess supply, then (7) holds; that is, for the equilibrium prices, $p_1, ..., p_n$, that satisfy (6'), we have the rule

$$X_i(p_1, ..., p_n) < \bar{X}_i \quad \text{implies } p_i = 0. \tag{7'}$$

Thus the equilibrium prices are determined so as to obey the rule of free goods.

Is there any price set that satisfies conditions (6) or (6')? This problem of the existence of equilibrium was discussed by Walras quite rigorously for the case of exchange between two goods ((A) and (B)). Taking either, say (B), as the *numéraire*, he assumed that demands D_a, D_b and supplies S_a, S_b are continuous functions of the price of (A) in terms of (B). Then, as will be seen in Chapter 2 below, the excess demand functions satisfy all the conditions necessary for applying Brouwer's fixed-point theorem to find a solution to

$$D_a(p_a, 1) \leqq S_a(p_a, 1) \quad \text{and} \quad D_b(p_a, 1) \leqq S_b(p_a, 1), \quad (8)$$

where p_b is set at 1 because (B) is taken as the *numéraire*. Therefore, as such economists as Arrow, Debreu and others have seen, there must be at least one solution which satisfies (8).

In spite of this general conclusion, Walras asserted that there would be no solution to (8) in the following peculiar case: '[A]t any price of (A) in terms of (B) below A_p, ...there would be a number of demanders of (A) offering (B) in exchange, but no one would demand (B) in exchange for (A). Also, at any price...of (A) in terms of (B) above A_p, there would be a number of demanders of (B) offering (A) in exchange, but no one would demand (A) in exchange for (B).'[13] In fact, in this case, there would be no demanders and no suppliers of (A) and (B) at $p_a = A_p$, so that inequalities (8) are satisfied with 0 = 0 at that price. This solution was regarded by Arrow, Debreu and others as an exchange equilibrium, but since there is no exchange in that state, Walras concluded that it was not an equilibrium exchange.

Whereas present-day economists examine the existence of a general exchange equilibrium defined as a state establishing (6) or (6'), Walras was concerned with whether there is an equilibrium exchange that is a solution to (6) or (6') with $D_i = S_i > 0$ for at least one commodity i. An equilibrium exchange is an exchange equilibrium, of course, but not *vice versa*. If we call the former an essential exchange equilibrium, we may say that what Walras wanted to discover is whether the Arrow–Debreu equilibrium is essential or not; his answer to this question was negative, as it should be unless additional conditions are imposed.

[13] *op. cit.*, p. 108.

The problem of the essentiality of equilibrium is not peculiar to the exchange economy. For the production economy it may be asked whether at least one commodity is really produced in the state of equilibrium; if no commodity at all is produced, the equilibrium involving production is reduced to an exchange equilibrium. Similarly, the equilibrium involving capital accumulation is not essential if no net investment is made in any good, and neither is the monetary equilibrium if the price of money is zero, because in these cases they are reduced to a simple production and a real economic equilibrium, respectively. Among these four essentiality problems, only the last is famous, as the Hahn problem.[14] However, as has been seen above, the existence problem was first posed by Walras as the problem of whether there is an essential equilibrium.

Next, Walras was concerned with finding a solution to (6) or (6') for the general case involving more than two commodities. In tackling this problem, he used a distinctive approach. If there are n commodities, we have $\frac{1}{2}n(n-1)$ pairs of commodities to be possibly exchanged with each other. An equilibrium will be found for each pair in the same way as Walras solved the exchange equations of the two-commodity economy. '[Thus the] problem of the exchange of several commodities for one another now appears to be solved. Actually, [however,] it is only half solved. Under the conditions described above, there would indeed be a certain equilibrium in the market so far as the prices of commodities taken two at a time were concerned; but that equilibrium would be an imperfect equilibrium. *We do not have* perfect *or general market equilibrium unless the price of one of any two commodities in terms of the other is equal to the ratio of the prices of these two commodities in terms of any third commodity.* This remains to be proved.'[15]

In order to show how a general equilibrium will be established throughout multiple markets, Walras used the theory of arbitrage which had been developed by Cournot.[16] But he was not successful in this venture; it did not result in any rigorous mathematical

[14] Hahn, F. H., 'On Some Problems of Proving the Existence of an Equilibrium in a Monetary Economy', in F. H. Hahn and F. P. R. Brechling (eds.), *The Theory of Interest Rates* (London: Macmillan, 1965).

[15] *op. cit.*, p. 157. Walras' italics.

[16] *Elements*, pp. 153–65.

proof of the existence theorem. Moreover, it poses a more funda-mental problem for us, which Walras was also unable to solve. On the one hand, as we have seen above, he used an exchange model consisting of the individuals who behave as price takers. In this model the prices of commodities, in terms of some fixed *numéraire*, are proposed and adjusted by auctioneers. On the other hand, in the arbitrage model there is no auctioneer; a bargain is struck directly between two individuals, and the price between any two commodities, say the price of commodity i in terms of commodity j, is an *ex post* exchange ratio between i and j. Thus the two models are based on different concepts of prices. It is not entirely clear whether the two models produce the same general equilibrium; so we have to ask the following three questions: Is there a general equilibrium for (i) the model with auctioneers or (ii) the model of arbitrages? If both these are answered in the affirmative, are the two general equilibria identical with each other?

Walras could not give a complete answer to any of these, except in the trivial case of the two-commodity economy. However, he had a fairly clear programme. To solve the first problem he provided an economic theory, the celebrated theory of *tâtonnement*, which explains how equilibrium prices are empirically determined in the market with auctioneers by the mechanism of free competition; while to solve the second problem he proposed an analytical method, according to which each of the $\frac{1}{2}n(n-1)$ bilateral exchange equations is solved mathematically, by specifying the algebraic or analytical form of the demand and supply functions, and the partial equilibrium solutions thus obtained are adjusted so as to satisfy the conditions of complete arbitrage. Walras' success with the first problem was probably greater than with the second, though it was far from complete. However, if we could solve the third problem, i.e. if we could show that the equilibrium brought about by *tâtonnement* is identical with that achieved by arbitrage, on the assumption of their existence, we would not need to prove the existence of a general equilibrium by both methods. We shall discuss a revised and completed version of Walras' theory of *tâtonnement* in the next chapter; in the rest of this chapter we confine ourselves to verifying the 'identity' thesis. Then no arbitrage-theoretic proof of the existence of general equilibrium is needed.

For the two-commodity economy, the identity of the two equilibria, one being *tâtonnement*-theoretic and the other arbitrage-theoretic, can be shown in the following way. Let p_a be the price of commodity (A) in terms of (B). In order to acquire D_a units of (A), the individuals must supply, in exchange, commodity (B) in the amount

$$S_b = p_a D_a. \tag{9}$$

Similarly, when they supply S_a units of (A), they acquire (B) in the amount

$$D_b = p_a S_a. \tag{10}$$

Exchange is made between (A) and (B), with the exchange ratio, p_a, so that

$$S_b = p_a S_a. \tag{11}$$

The equilibrium condition (11) determines only *the exchange ratio*; the absolute magnitude of the exchange is left undetermined. Also, we know only that each individual will be at least as well off after trade as he was before it; we do not know whether each occupies the best possible position after trade. In order for each individual to be able to choose his best position, he has to be permitted to divide the exchange of his d_a of (A) for his s_b of (B) into a number of piecemeal exchanges of equal size.[17] We assume that each and every piecemeal exchange transaction is made as far as it is advantageous, and that the process of transaction finally stops when no advantage is gained by an additional transaction. Hence, at the point at which every individual ceases to make any further transactions, everybody in the market is satisfied, so that the aggregate demands and supplies are on the respective demand and supply curves; that is to say,

$$\begin{aligned} D_a &= D_a(p_a, 1), \quad S_a = S_a(p_a, 1), \\ D_b &= D_b(p_a, 1), \quad S_b = S_b(p_a, 1). \end{aligned} \tag{12}$$

The solutions to the equations (9)–(12) give the equilibrium price and the equilibrium transaction quantities by the theory of arbitrage. (In the two-commodity case the arbitrage theory is trivial, because there is, of course, no arbitrage *via* a third commodity.)

---

[17] For the piecemeal transaction, see *Elements*, pp. 122–5.

In this system, if (A) is not free, p_a is positive; considering (9), (10) and (12), we have from (11):

$$D_a(p_a, 1) = S_a(p_a, 1), \quad D_b(p_a, 1) = S_b(p_a, 1). \tag{13}$$

On the other hand, if (A) is free, that is, $D_a \leqq S_a$, with $p_a = 0$, we have $D_b = S_b = 0$ from (10) and (11). Thus,

$$D_a(p_a, 1) \leqq S_a(p_a, 1), \quad D_b(p_a, 1) = S_b(p_a, 1). \tag{13'}$$

Conditions (13) or $(13')$ give a general equilibrium which an auctioneer would establish in the competitive market by adjusting the price. It is now seen that the bilateral bargain equilibrium is identical with the *tâtonnement* equilibrium, provided that any transaction can be divided into infinitesimally small pieces.

Let us next extend the above identity thesis to the case of the exchange of many commodities with one another. Suppose there are m individuals and n goods. Throughout the rest of this chapter indices h and i are used to represent individuals and j and k to represent goods. The individual i has his initial endowment $\bar{x}_i = (\bar{x}_{1i}, ..., \bar{x}_{ni})$ and his utility function $u_i(x_i)$, which is a differentiable and strictly quasi-concave function of the quantities of goods, $x_i = (x_{1i}, ..., x_{ni})$, which he wants to retain after trade.[18]

Let us now call x_i an allocation to individual i, which is compared with another possible allocation x_i'. If i prefers x_i to x_i', or weakly prefers x_i to x_i' (that is to say, either x_i is preferred or the individual is indifferent between x_i and x_i'), we write $x_i \succ x_i'$, or $x_i \succcurlyeq x_i'$, respectively. The outcome of exchange is an allocation $x = (x_1, ..., x_i, ..., x_m)$, or simply (x_i), which is a redistribution of the initial endowments $(\bar{x}_i)$, so that

$$\sum_i x_i = \sum_i \bar{x}_i, \tag{14}$$

which is assumed for all xs below.

We now specify the rules of exchange as follows. First, it is assumed that the individuals reject a proposed reallocation

---

[18] A function u is said to be strictly quasi-concave if $u(tx + (1-t) x^0) > u(x)$ for all t such that $0 < t < 1$ and all non-negative x and x^0 such that $u(x) \leqq u(x^0)$.

$x^1 = (x_i^1)$ of the initial allocation $\bar{x} = (\bar{x}_i)$ unless

$$x_i^1 \geqslant \bar{x}_i \quad \text{(for all } i\text{)} \quad \text{and} \quad x_i^1 > \bar{x}_i \quad \text{(for some } i\text{)}.$$

An eligible allocation x^1 is further compared with another x^2; if $x_i^2 \geqslant x_i^1$ for all i and $x_i^2 > x_i^1$ for some i, x^1 will be replaced by x^2 which will in turn be compared with another possible allocation. This process of monotonic replacement of x^1 by x^2, x^2 by x^3, and so on, will finally settle at a Pareto-optimum allocation x,[19] so that x has no other x' such that

$$x_i' \geqslant x_i \quad \text{(for all } i\text{)} \quad \text{and} \quad x_i' > x_i \quad \text{(for some } i\text{)}.$$

At the start of the process x^1 is socially preferred to $\bar{x}$ unless $x^1 = \bar{x}$, and the process is monotonic. Therefore, if the preferences are assumed to be transitive, the final allocation x must dominate the initial endowment $\bar{x}$; thus, unless $x = \bar{x}$, we have

$$x_i \geqslant \bar{x}_i \quad \text{(for all } i\text{)} \quad \text{and} \quad x_i > \bar{x}_i \quad \text{(for some } i\text{)}.$$

Secondly we follow Walras (and Cournot) in assuming that individuals do not agree to the final allocation unless the price, i.e. the exchange ratio of one of any two commodities in terms of the other, is equal to the ratio of the prices of these two commodities in terms of any third commodity. For if this chain rule of exchange ratios is violated by some groups of three goods, then a direct exchange of one against another will be replaced by an indirect exchange through the third. Moreover, the rule tacitly presupposes that the prices or exchange ratios should be independent of the individuals involved. Otherwise, all buyers (or sellers) will rush to the most generous sellers (or buyers).

Let $x_{ji,kh}$ be the quantity of good j which i acquires from h in exchange for good k. The quantities of goods which an individual *offers* to another are taken as negative, so that

$$x_{ji,kh} = -x_{jh,ki}. \tag{15}$$

Also, we have identities

$$x_{ji} = \bar{x}_{ji} + \sum_{h \neq i} \sum_{k} x_{ji,kh} \quad \text{(for all } j \text{ and all } i\text{)}. \tag{16}$$

---

[19] An allocation x is said to be a Pareto-optimum if it is impossible at x to make some person better off, keeping everyone else at least as well off as before.

Now let p_{kj} be the quantity of good j acquired in exchange for one unit of good k, which is independent of the individuals involved, so that

$$p_{kj} = \frac{x_{jh,\,ki}}{x_{ki,\,jh}} \quad \text{(for all } h \text{ and all } i).$$

This, together with (15), implies

$$x_{jh,\,ki} + p_{kj}x_{kh,\,ji} = 0,$$

which may be put in the form,

$$p_{jl}x_{jh,\,ki} + p_{kl}x_{kh,\,ji} = 0,$$

because the Cournot–Walras condition of no further arbitrage requires

$$p_{kj} = \frac{p_{kl}}{p_{jl}},$$

provided that good l is not a free good. (If p_{kj} is larger (or smaller) than p_{kl}/p_{jl}, then a direct exchange between goods k and j is more (or less) beneficial to the supplier of k than a roundabout exchange through good l.) Hence,

$$\sum_j \sum_{h\neq i} \sum_k p_{jl}x_{jh,\,ki} + \sum_j \sum_{h\neq i} \sum_k p_{kl}x_{kh,\,ji} = 0. \tag{17}$$

Since the first term on the left-hand side of this expression is identical with the second term, (17) implies that

$$2\sum_j p_{jl}\left(\sum_{h\neq i} \sum_k x_{jh,\,ki}\right) = 0,$$

so that we obtain from (15) and (16)

$$\sum_j p_{jl}x_{ji} = \sum_j p_{jl}\bar{x}_{ji} \quad \text{(for all } i); \tag{18}$$

that is to say, in any state where no further arbitrage is possible, goods are allocated so that the budget equation holds for each individual.

The third rule is stated as follows. Let x_i be the final allocation to individual i; it satisfies (16). When each i carries out only t (where $t \leqslant 1$) of those transactions which bring him from $\bar{x}_i$ to x_i, his allocation after trade will be $x_i(t)$, with components,

$$x_{ji}(t) = \bar{x}_{ji} + t\left(\sum_{h\neq i} \sum_k x_{ji,\,kh}\right) \quad \text{(for all } j \text{ and all } i).$$

Obviously,

$$x_i(t) = tx_i + (1-t)\bar{x}_i \quad \text{(for all } i)$$

and
$$\sum_j p_{jl} x_{ji}(t) = \sum_j p_{jl} \bar{x}_{ji} \quad \text{(for all } i).$$

As the utility function of each individual is strictly quasi-concave, and x_i is at worst equally preferable to $\bar{x}_i$, we find that

$$x_i(t) \geqslant \bar{x}_i \quad \text{(for all } i),$$

so that all individuals prefer to the initial allocation $\bar{x}$ an allocation, $x(t) = [x_i(t)]$, which lies on the way from $\bar{x}$ to x. This holds for all positive t less than one. But it does not necessarily imply that they prefer the final allocation x to $x(t)$. The third rule required in order for the transition from $\bar{x}$ to x not to be obstructed states that

$$x_i \geqslant x_i(t) \quad \text{(for all } i) \quad \text{and} \quad x_i > x_i(t) \quad \text{(for some } i),$$

for all values of t between 0 and 1; otherwise someone would not agree, at some point on the way from $\bar{x}$ to x, to carry out any further exchange. In Walras' own words, this rule implies that 'all of the piecemeal exchange transactions, without exception and including the final one however small that may be, are advantageous, though the advantage diminishes progressively from the first to the [final] transaction'.[20]

Let us now prove the identity theorem, that the final allocation satisfying the above three rules is identical with the general competitive exchange equilibrium which is established when individuals maximize their own utilities subject to the respective budget equations, by taking prices as given. For the sake of simplicity we prove the theorem on the assumption that each individual retains some quantity of every good after the transactions. The proof holds true *mutatis mutandis* without this assumption, though it becomes more complicated.

As the final allocation $x = (x_i)$ is a Pareto-optimum by Rule 1, the individuals' indifference surfaces are tangential to each other at x. Suppose now that they are not all tangential to their budget planes; that is to say, there is an individual whose budget plane cuts his indifference surface. If it cuts from below for individual i, we have

$$x_i(t) < x_i < x_i(t') \quad\quad\quad (19)$$

[20] *op. cit.*, p. 124.

for all t and t' sufficiently close to 1 from below and above respectively. If
$$x_h(t') \geqslant x_h \quad \text{(for all } h \neq i\text{),}$$

for the same t', then the x cannot be a Pareto-optimum; it is dominated by $x(t')$. This is a contradiction, so that there must be an individual r for whom

$$x_r(t') \prec x_r \quad \text{for all } t' \text{ sufficiently close to 1 from above.} \quad (20)$$

Also, if we have $x_r \leqslant x_r(t)$ for some $t < 1$, then by virtue of the strict quasi-concavity of the utility function, we have $x_r \prec x_r(t'')$ for some t'' such that $t < t'' < 1$. Then individual r would not agree to those transactions which result in x_r, but would only partly carry them out, because of Rule 3. This is a contradiction; hence $x_r \succ x_r(t)$ for all $t < 1$.

This, together with (20), implies that $u_r(x_r)$ takes on a maximum at x_r subject to individual r's budget equation; therefore r's indifference curve is tangential to his budget equation. Under the simplifying assumption that each individual retains positive amounts of all goods, we can show that once an individual's indifference surface is tangential to his budget plane at the final allocation, which is a Pareto-optimum, the same is true for all other persons.[21] Hence, the indifference surfaces of all individuals are tangential to their respective budget planes; this obviously contradicts the assumption that individual i's budget plane cuts his indifference surface from below.

Therefore, if a person's budget plane cuts his indifference surface, it should do so from above; that is,

$$x_i(t) \succ x_i \succ x_i(t')$$

for all $t < 1$ and $t' > 1$, both being sufficiently close to 1. In this case this person i does not carry out all the transactions that result in x_i, because he reaches before x_i an $x_i(t)$ which is preferable to x_i; thus Rule 3 is violated. Hence we have a contradiction in any case, unless we accept that at the final allocation, x, all individuals' indifference surfaces are tangential to their respective budget planes.

We have thus seen that at the allocation x each $u_i(x_i)$ is maximized subject to the budget equation (18). Moreover, we

[21] It is so because at any Pareto-optimum the marginal rates of substitution between commodities are equalized through all individuals.

have (14), which means that the total demand for each commodity equals its total supply at the same x. Therefore, the final allocation x satisfying our three rules is a competitive exchange equilibrium.[22] By this identity theorem we may characterize the competitive equilibrium as a Pareto-optimum allocation of commodities which is reached by arbitrage operations and piecemeal exchange transactions.

[22] However, this equilibrium may not be essential. To show $x \neq \bar{x}$. We require that $\bar{x}$ is not a Pareto-optimum.

CHAPTER 2

The tâtonnement

Without giving a complete proof, we have discussed whether there is a competitive equilibrium of exchange. If we grant its existence (which is demonstrated later in this chapter), the next step will be to see how an equilibrium is reached in the real world, or, in Walras' words, 'in what way this problem of the exchange of several commodities for one another...is empirically solved in the market by the mechanism of competition'.[1] To tackle this problem, Walras assumed that for each and every commodity there was a perfectly organized market. It is, of course, true that in the actual economy many commodities lack such a market, even though they may have a poorly organized one. But this assumption is a kind of abstraction which scientists often make for the sake of finding the laws of motion that work in the ideal frictionless world.

Walras' aim was to clarify the process of competitive trading. This was a new subject for him, while the theory of monopoly and monopsony had already been dealt with by Cournot, with whose work Walras began his study of economics. He minimized monopoly elements throughout his book, justifying this confining of his scope to the analysis of competitive trading as follows: 'The markets which are best organized from the competitive standpoint are those in which purchases and sales are made by auction, through the instrumentality of stockbrokers, commercial brokers or criers acting as agents who centralize transactions in such a way that the terms of every exchange are openly announced and an opportunity is given to sellers to lower their prices and to buyers to raise their bids. This is the way business is done in the stock exchange, commercial markets, grain markets, fish markets, etc. Besides these markets, there are others, such as the fruit, vegetable and poultry markets, where competition, though not so well organized, functions fairly

---

[1] Walras, *The Elements*, p. 169.

effectively and satisfactorily. City streets with their stores and shops of all kinds – baker's, butcher's, grocer's, tailor's, shoe-maker's, etc. – are markets where competition, though poorly organized, nevertheless operates quite adequately. Unquestion-ably competition is also the primary force in setting the value of the doctor's and the lawyer's consultations, of the musician's and the singer's recitals, etc.'[2] Moreover, '[w]hat is bought and sold in [the stock exchange of a large investment centre like Paris or London] are titles to property in shares of very important kinds of social wealth, such as fractions of State and municipal loans or shares of railways, canals, metallurgical plants, etc.'.[3] Thus most important commodities have their own well organized markets, while many others, though not so well organized as to be able to find competitive equilibrium accurately, are under the pressure of competition, so that prices cannot deviate far from equilibrium values. Therefore, the Walrasian idealization can serve as a first approximation to reality. 'What physicist would deliberately pick cloudy weather for astronomical obser-vations instead of taking advantage of a cloudless night?'[4]

How does competition work in a well organized market? There are at least two methods of competitive trading. According to the usual one, all trades are provisional and not effective as long as excess supply or demand remains in the market. The quantities of goods individuals own do not change through the process of *tâtonnement* (or groping) towards a set of equilibrium prices, until they are finally discovered. Let $\bar{x}_i = (\bar{x}_{1i}, ..., \bar{x}_{ni})$ be the initial endowment of individual i. With prices $p = (p_1, ..., p_n)$, his purchasing power is

$$M = \sum_j p_j \bar{x}_{ji},$$

where prices p prevail. If he is a price taker, the amounts of commodities, $x_i = (x_{1i}, ..., x_{ni})$, which he wants to hold are determined so as to maximize his utility function $u_i(x_i)$ subject to the budget equation:

$$\sum_j p_j x_{ji} = \sum_j p_j \bar{x}_{ji}. \tag{1}$$

If the x_{ji} determined in this way exceeds (or falls short of) the amount, $\bar{x}_{ji}$, which he holds, then he will demand (or supply) commodity j in the amount $x_{ji} - \bar{x}_{ji}$ (or $\bar{x}_{ji} - x_{ji}$) on the market.

[2] *op. cit.*, pp. 83–4.   [3] *op. cit.*, p. 84.   [4] *op. cit.*, p. 86.

However, such individual demands (or supplies) are *all* ineffective unless the total demand for each commodity equals its total supply, or in other words, the equation

$$\sum_i x_{ji} = \sum_i \bar{x}_{ji}, \qquad (2)$$

holds for all commodities $j = 1, ..., n$. Thus, as long as there is excess demand for at least one commodity, no trade will be made; so individuals remain in the market, holding the same amounts of commodities as they had at the beginning of *tâtonnement*. When equilibrium prices are finally established, so that equation (2) holds for all j, transactions will be made and individuals will go home with the amounts of commodities, x_i, which they want.

According to the second method of *tâtonnement*, agreements to trade may be made between any pair of traders at any point of time during the process of *tâtonnement*, even though equation (2) does not hold for some or all commodities. These contracts are all effective, so that the amounts of commodities which individuals hold fluctuate from time to time. However, the trade contracted during the process of *tâtonnement* is not carried out at the respective prices which were being called in the market when the agreements were made, but at the equilibrium prices established when all excess demand is finally cleared from the market. When prices change during the course of *tâtonnement*, the amounts of commodities which an individual wants to sell or buy will change; he can, however, always cancel an agreement made under a different price, by redeeming or reselling the appropriate commodities from or to someone else.

Let $x_i^* = (x_{1i}^*, ..., x_{ni}^*)$ be the amounts of commodities held by individual i at some point of time t^* in the course of *tâtonnement*. Let $p = (p_1, ..., p_n)$ be the prices at the same time. Individual i began the *tâtonnement* with $\bar{x}_i$, so that he has so far bought commodity j in the amount $(x_{ji}^* - \bar{x}_{ji})$, if $x_{ji}^* > \bar{x}_{ji}$, or sold it in the amount $(\bar{x}_{ji} - x_{ji}^*)$, if $x_{ji}^* < \bar{x}_{ji}$, up to the point of time t^*. If the current prices p are the equilibrium ones, he has to pay the net amount $\sum_j p_j(x_{ji}^* - \bar{x}_{ji})$, which is equal to the expenditure for purchases minus the amount acquired from sales. On the other hand, he has stocks in kind, $x_{1i}^*, ..., x_{ni}^*$, which are evaluated at

$\sum_j p_j x_{ji}^*$. Therefore, his total purchasing power at t^* amounts to

$$\sum_j p_j x_{ji}^* - \sum_j p_j(x_{ji}^* - \bar{x}_{ji}), \tag{3}$$

subject to which the individual decides his new purchasing–selling plan. That is to say, at t^*, he determines the amounts of commodities $x_i = (x_{1i}, ..., x_{ni})$ which he wants to hold, in such a way that his utility $u_i(x_i)$ is maximized subject to the condition that the total value of x_i at p equals his purchasing power (3). Obviously, (3) is equal to $\sum_j p_j \bar{x}_{ji}$, so that the budget equation at t^* is identical with (1), the budget equation which prevails under the first kind of competitive trading. Thus, under the second method, an individual behaving as a price-taker responds to a given set of prices exactly as he does under the first (so that there is no difference between them in his demand and supply), in spite of the fact that in the course of *tâtonnement* transactions actually take place between individuals according to the second method, whereas according to the first they do not.

It is thus seen that in either method of competitive trading an individual's holdings of goods, $x_{1i}, ..., x_{ni}$, depend on the current prices p and the current value of the initial endowments, $\sum_j p_j \bar{x}_{ji}$, and are independent of the progress of his transaction agreements during the process of *tâtonnement*. As $\bar{x}_{ji}$s are constant, x_{ji}s depend on p only, so that the individual's excess demand functions are written as

$$x_{ji}(p_1, ..., p_n) - \bar{x}_{ji} \quad (j = 1, ..., n) \tag{4}$$

in the case of the first method of competitive trading, and as

$$x_{ji}(p_1, ..., p_n) - x_{ji}^* \quad (j = 1, ..., n) \tag{4'}$$

at time t^*, in the case of the second method. Since there is neither entry nor exit of traders during the process, the total amount of goods existing in the market remains unchanged, so that we have

$$\sum_i x_{ji}^* = \sum_i \bar{x}_{ji}$$

for each good $j = 1, ..., n$. Therefore, with either trading method, the total excess demand for good j in the market is given as

$$E_j(p_1, ..., p_n) = \sum_i x_{ji}(p_1, ..., p_n) - \sum_i \bar{x}_{ji},$$

which is a function of prices only.

Now let $p(t) = [p_1(t), p_2(t), ..., p_n(t)]$ be the prices shouted out by the price caller on the market at time t during one session of competitive trading, and $E_j(t)$ the excess demand for commodity j corresponding with these prices, i.e. $E_j[p(t)]$. We assume that, if the demand for commodity j exceeds (or falls short of) its supply at time t, the caller raises (or lowers) its price in proportion to its positive (or negative) excess demand. The proportionality factor, which Lange called the degree of price flexibility[5] may be generally different from commodity to commodity, but in the following analysis we assume for the sake of simplicity that it is the same for all commodities. Moreover, we assume that the degree of price flexibility is proportional to the level of prices, so that if a unit of excess demand induces a price increase of v pence at the price level of £1 it will increase the price by v pounds at a level of £100. Thus the degree of price flexibility is given by $v \sum_k p_k(t)$, where v is a positive constant common to all commodities. Then the price-adjustment equation for commodity j may be written as

$$p_j(t+1) - p_j(t) = v[\sum_k p_k(t)] E_j(t) \quad (j = 1, ..., n). \quad (5)$$

In this simple formula, however, no consideration is given to the non-negativeness of the price $p_j(t+1)$ to be proposed; in fact, if $E_j(t)$ takes on a negative value for a sufficiently small positive value of $p_j(t)$, then the above formula will give us a negative value of $p_j(t+1)$. To avoid this, we assume that (5) is valid only so far as it gives a non-negative price at $t+1$; otherwise, the caller would probably shout out a price of zero instead of throwing the market into an unnecessary state of confusion by calling out a negative price calculated according to the formula. We express the operation of comparing the $p_j(t+1)$ obtained by the formula (that is, $p_j(t) + F_j(t)$, where $F_j(t)$ represents the right-hand side of (5)) with 0 and taking the larger by $\max[p_j(t) + F_j(t), 0]$. Then the caller, who avoids negative prices, will proceed with *tâtonnement* according to the revised formula:

$$p_j(t+1) = \max\{p_j(t) + v[\sum_k p_k(t)] E_j(t), 0\} \quad (j = 1, ..., n). \quad (6)$$

We have not so far concerned ourselves with normalization of

[5] Lange, O., *Price Flexibility and Employment* (Bloomington, Indiana: The Principia Press, 1944).

prices. As has been seen in Chapter 1, however, prices are exchange ratios between commodities; in the presence of perfect arbitration, they are exchange ratios of commodities against the *numéraire*. What commodity can play the role of *numéraire*? It should be a non-free good; it is, in fact, impossible and meaningless to evaluate commodities in terms of a free good. Which commodity is not free? We can answer this question only after having carried out the whole *tâtonnement* process. But we need a *numéraire* at the outset of the process.

To avoid this *prima facie* paradox, we consider a composite commodity made up of one unit of every existing commodity and take it as the standard commodity (*numéraire*). We may safely assume that it is definitely non-free, because there will always be at least some components of this composite commodity which are not free. If all components are free, there is no scarce good in the economy, so that economic problems disappear.

The value of a unit of the composite commodity is equal to the sum of the prices of the components; that is $\sum_k p_k(t)$. A unit of commodity j is exchanged with $p_j(t)/\sum_k p_k(t)$ units of the composite commodity because they are equivalent. This exchange ratio,

$$q_j(t) = p_j(t)/\sum_k p_k(t), \tag{7}$$

gives the price of commodity j, at time t, in terms of the *numéraire* so chosen, and

$$q_j(t+1) = p_j(t+1)/\sum_k p_k(t+1) \tag{8}$$

gives the corresponding price at $t+1$. Dividing the numerator and the denominator on the right-hand side of (8) by $\sum_k p_k(t)$, substituting (6) into (8) and taking (7) into account, we then obtain

$$q_j(t+1) = \frac{\max\left[q_j(t)+vE_j(t), 0\right]}{\sum_k \max\left[q_k(t)+vE_k(t), 0\right]} \quad (j=1,...,n). \tag{9}$$

In this formula for determining normalized prices at $t+1$, the excess market demands, $E_j(t)$, $j=1,...,n$, are the sums of individual excess demands, (4) or (4'), over all individuals which are obtained by maximizing $u_i(x_i)$ subject to the budget equation (1). It is obvious that the maximum point is unaffected, even though we divide (1) by $\sum_k p_k$, i.e. we replace (1) by the normalized budget equation

$$\sum_j q_j x_{ji} = \sum_j q_j \bar{x}_{ji}. \tag{1'}$$

Hence we can see that the excess demands are functions of relative prices; namely,

$$E_j(t) = E_j[q_1(t), ..., q_n(t)]. \tag{10}$$

Evidently, the equations of price adjustment (9) which transform $q(t)$ into $q(t+1)$ satisfy (i) the condition for normalization of prices, whereby the sum of $q_j(t+1)$s is identically equal to one, and (ii) the condition for non-negativeness, whereby prices will fall no further than zero even if there exists an enormous excess supply. Also, in view of the definition of the excess demand functions, we have from (1')

$$\sum_j q_j E_j(q) = 0, \tag{11}$$

which holds identically for all possible qs and is referred to as the 'Walras law'.

If $q(t) \neq q(t+1)$, there is a movement of prices from time t to $t+1$. A point at which $q(t) = q(t+1)$ is said to be a fixed point or a stationary price system. Mathematical economists have established a theorem to the effect that there is at least one fixed point, provided that excess demand functions are all continuous.[6] Let q be such a fixed point; then we have from (9)

$$q_j = \frac{\max[q_j + vE_j(q), 0]}{c} \quad (j = 1, ..., n), \tag{12}$$

where

$$c = \sum_k \max[q_k + vE_k(q), 0].$$

[6] See, for example, my *The Economic Theory of Modern Society* (Cambridge University Press, 1976). To obtain the result we use usually Brouwer's fixed-point theorem, or its extension, Kakutani's theorem. The former may be stated as follows: If a set S is non-empty, closed, bounded and convex, a continuous transformation f of S into itself has a fixed point, i.e. a point $x \in S$ such that $x = f(x)$.

As c is shown to be positive,[7] it follows from (12) that if $q_j > 0$, then $q_j + vE_j(q) > 0$, so that $E_j(q) = (c-1) q_j/v$. Also, from (12), $E_j(q) \leqq 0$ if $q_j = 0$. Thus we find

$$E_j(q) \begin{cases} = (c-1) \, q_j/v & \text{if} \quad q_j > 0, \\ \leqq 0 & \text{if} \quad q_j = 0. \end{cases}$$

It is evident that such excess demand functions do not satisfy the Walras law unless $c = 1$. Hence,

$$E_j(q) \begin{cases} = 0 & \text{if} \quad q_j > 0, \\ \leqq 0 & \text{if} \quad q_j = 0. \end{cases}$$

In other words, we find that at the fixed point where prices cease to move, (i) there is neither excess demand nor excess supply of any scarce commodity (with a positive price), and (ii) an excess supply may occur for a free good (whose price is zero), while it has no possibility of excess demand. Thus the fixed point of the *tâtonnement* process gives an equilibrium price system which is the set of prices equating demand with the corresponding supplies, except for free goods. The existence of an exchange equilibrium is established.[8]

Let us now discuss the stability of the equilibrium prices. Walras' own analysis was not based on our adjustment equations (9). In his discussion of stability, he first of all ruled out free goods, so that he could take any of the remaining n goods, say the nth, as the *numéraire*. There was no need for him to conceive of a composite *numéraire* commodity. Next, in developing his stability analysis of competitive trading, Walras benefited from the work of Cournot, who had taught mechanics at Lyon, so that it was easy for him to discuss the stability of equilibrium from the proper dynamic point of view. Walras, in fact, wrote: 'Such an equilibrium [a stable one] is exactly similar to that of a suspended body of which the centre of gravity lies directly beneath the point of suspension, so that if this centre of gravity were displaced

---

[7] Suppose the contrary, i.e. $q_k + vE_k(q) \leqq 0$ for all k. As $q_k \geqq 0$, we have $\sum\limits_k q_k^2 + v \sum\limits_k q_k E_k(q) \leqq 0$. By the Walras law the second term is zero, while the first must be positive because $q_k \geqq 0$ and $\sum\limits_k q_k = 1$. Thus we have $0 < 0$, a contradiction.

[8] The equilibrium thus found may not be 'essential'.

from the vertical line beneath the point of suspension, it would automatically return to its original position through the force of gravitation. This equilibrium is, therefore, *stable*.'[9] He also wrote: 'This equilibrium [an unstable one] is exactly similar to that of a suspended body of which the point of suspension lies directly beneath the centre of gravity, so that if this centre of gravity once leaves the vertical line above the point of suspension, it does not return automatically but keeps on moving farther and farther away until through the force of gravitation it reaches the position vertically beneath the point of suspension. Such an equilibrium is *unstable*.'[10] Thus, thanks to Cournot, economists could, from the outset, discuss the stability of economic equilibrium as a dynamic problem of whether a forced displacement from an equilibrium position will generate a movement so as to restore equilibrium eventually.

Thirdly, Walras discussed the stability of equilibrium in the framework of a many-goods economy. In spite of this fact, many economists credit Hicks with the first attempt to generalize to any number of markets the stability condition of a single market. Lange, for example, explicitly wrote: 'Walras...formulated it [i.e. the stability condition] in a way which limits its applicability to partial-equilibrium analysis. Within the framework of general-equilibrium theory the stability conditions must take into account the repercussions of the change in price of a good upon the prices of other goods as well as the dependence of excess demand (or excess supply) of a good on the prices of the other goods in the system. This has been done by Professor Hicks.'[11]

There is, however, a dissimilarity between Walras and Hicks in their stability analysis. This is associated with the above-mentioned second characteristic of Walras' stability analysis; that is to say, Walras was apparently concerned with the dynamic movement of prices, while Hicks did not explicitly derive his stability conditions from a dynamic model. Suppose $p_1(t), ...,$ $p_{n-1}(t)$ are not equilibrium prices, so that

$$E_1[p_1(t), ..., p_{n-1}(t), 1] \neq 0. \qquad (13)$$

Then $p_1(t)$ will change to $p_1(t+1)$, so as to establish a partial

[9] Walras, *Elements*, p. 109. Walras' italics.
[10] *ibid.*, p. 112. Walras' italics.
[11] Lange, *op. cit.*, p. 91.

equilibrium in the market for commodity 1; this is,

$$E_1[p_1(t+1), p_2(t), ..., p_{n-1}(t), 1] = 0. \tag{14}$$

In his treatment of the repercussions of the change in the price of commodity 1 on the prices of other commodities, Walras also differed from Hicks. Unlike Hicks, he arranged the markets in a definite order and assumed that the repercussions proceed in the following way. First, the change in the price of commodity 1 disturbs the market for commodity 2, so that its price is changed to $p_2(t+1)$, in such a way that supply and demand are equated in that market, given the price of commodity 1 at $p_1(t+1)$ and the remaining prices at $p_3(t), ..., p_{n-1}(t)$; that is,

$$E_2[p_1(t+1), p_2(t+1), p_3(t), ..., p_{n-1}(t), 1] = 0.$$

Then, in the same way, the price of commodity 3 is adjusted so as to establish

$$E_3[p_1(t+1), p_2(t+1), p_3(t+1), p_4(t), ..., p_{n-1}(t), 1] = 0,$$

and so forth. After these adjustments have all been made, we have

$$E_1(p_1(t+1), p_2(t+1), ..., p_{n-1}(t+1), 1) \neq 0, \tag{15}$$

since equation (14) is violated, because prices $p_2(t), ..., p_{n-1}(t)$ have changed to $p_2(t+1), ..., p_{n-1}(t+1)$, respectively. The inequality (15) at $t+1$ is closer to equality than the inequality (13) if the condition,

$$|E_1[p_1(t+1), ..., p_{n-1}(t+1), 1]| < |E_1[p_1(t), ..., p_{n-1}(t), 1]|, \tag{16}$$

is satisfied. Walras said: 'This [condition] will appear probable if we remember that the change from $[p_1(t)$ to $p_1(t+1)]$, which reduced the above inequality $[(13)]$ to an equality, exerted a direct influence that was invariably in the direction of equality at least so far as the demand for [commodity 1] was concerned; while the [consequent–Jaffé] changes from $[p_2(t)$ to $p_2(t+1)$, $p_3(t)$ to $p_3(t+1)]$, ..., which moved the foregoing inequality farther away from equality, exerted indirect influences, some in the direction of equality and some in the opposite direction, at least so far as the demand for [commodity 1] was concerned, so that up to a certain point they cancelled each other out. Hence, the new system of prices $[p_1(t+1), ..., p_{n-1}(t+1)]$ is closer to equilibrium than the old system of prices $[p_1(t), ..., p_{n-1}(t)]$; and it is only necessary to continue this process along the same lines for the system to move closer and closer to equilibrium.'[12]

Let us now assume that if excess demand for some commodity is positive (or negative), a partial equilibrium of the market for that commodity is established by raising (or lowering) its price. Then we find that $p_1(t+1) \gtrless p_1(t)$ according as

$$E_1[p_1(t), ..., p_{n-1}(t), 1] \gtrless 0.$$

On the other hand, (16) implies

$$E_1[p_1(t+1), ..., p_{n-1}(t+1), 1] - E_1[p_1(t), ..., p_{n-1}(t), 1] \lessgtr 0$$

according as $E_1(p_1(t), ..., p_{n-1}(t), 1) \gtrless 0$. Therefore, Walras' stability condition implies

$$\frac{E_1[p_1(t+1), ..., p_{n-1}(t+1), 1] - E_1[p_1(t), ..., p_{n-1}(t), 1]}{p_1(t+1) - p_1(t)} < 0. \quad (17)$$

That is to say, it requires that a change in the price of commodity 1 induces a change in its excess demand in the opposite direction after all prices have been adjusted. Putting Walras' stability condition in this form, we may find that it is very similar to the condition obtained by Hicks, in spite of the apparent dissimilarities between their approaches.[13] It is interesting to see that, in his stability condition (16), Walras was taking the absolute value of the excess demand $E_1(t)$ as a Liapounoff function, though his method was crude; in this respect, he was closer to post-war economists such as Arrow, Hurwicz, etc., than to Hicks, who did not explicitly deal with the dynamic movement of prices, or Samuelson, who, instead of using the Liapounoff method, solved dynamic equations of price adjustment in order to examine whether prices will eventually approach their respective equilibrium values.

---

[12] Walras, *Elements*, p. 172.

[13] Hicks, J. R., *Value and Capital* (Clarendon Press, 1946), pp. 66–73 and p. 315. If one does not like Walras' arrangement of the markets in a definite order, one may follow Hicks and assume that when the price of commodity 1 changes from $p_1(t)$ to $p_1(t+1)$, the prices of all the other commodities are adjusted so as to establish equilibrium in their markets simultaneously, i.e.

$$E_j(p_1(t+1), p_2(t+1), ..., p_{n-1}(t+1), 1) = 0 \quad (j = 2, ..., n-1).$$

For $p_1(t+1), ..., p_{n-1}(t+1)$ thus determined, calculate $E_1(t+1)$. Then (16) and (17) follow *mutatis mutandis*.

Finally we return to our original *tâtonnement* process, formulated as (9). At the outset of the process, $t = 0$, initial prices $q(0)$ are quoted by the caller. The only requirements imposed upon them are (i) that they are non-negative and (ii) that they add up to unity; otherwise, they are arbitrary. The formula (9) determines $q(1)$ on the basis of $q(0)$, then $q(2)$ on $q(1)$, and so on. Each term of the infinite sequence $\{q(t)\}$, $t = 1, 2, \ldots$ *ad inf.*, generated in this way satisfies the above two requirements; that is to say, $q_j(t), j = 1, \ldots, n$, are non-negative and $\sum_j q_j(t)$ equals unity for all t. This means that each $q(t)$ is bounded, so that by the Bolzano–Weierstrass theorem the sequence $\{q(t)\}$ has at least one limiting point, say q^0.[14]

Consider now a new sequence $\{q^t\}$, starting from q^0:

$$q^1 = f(q^0),$$
$$q^2 = f(q^1),$$
$$\ldots\ldots\ldots\ldots,$$

where $f(q)$ represents $[f_1(q), f_2(q), \ldots, f_n(q)]$, and $f_j(q)$ the right-hand side of (9). Under the conditions given in footnote 15 we can show that $\{q^t\}$ must sooner or later return to q^0.[15] We thus have

$$q^1 = f(q^0), \quad q^2 = f(q^1), \quad \ldots, \quad q^0 = f(q^{r-1}), \tag{18}$$

[14] The Bolzano–Weierstrass theorem states that a bounded set containing many points has a limit point, i.e., in our case, a point that is the limit of a subsequence of $\{q(t)\}$.

[15] Let $\{q(t_i)\}$, $i = 1, 2, \ldots$ be a subsequence of $\{q(t)\}$ which converges to q^0 as i tends to infinity. Define $z(t_i)$ as $q(t_i) = q^0 + z(t_i)$; so that $\lim_{i \to \infty} z(t_i) = 0$. In view of (9), we obtain

$$q(t_i + 1) = f[q(t_i)] = f[q^0 + z(t_i)].$$

Therefore, $\lim_{i \to \infty} q(t_i + 1) = f(q^0) = q^1$. Similarly, $\lim_{t \to \infty} q(t_i + 2) = f(q^1) = q^2$, and so on.

To obtain (18) we assume that f generates $q(t_i)$, $q(t_i + 1)$, $q(t_i + 2)$, $\ldots$ which uniformly converge to $q^0, q^1, q^2, \ldots$, respectively; so for any $\epsilon > 0$, there can be found a k such that $|q(t_i + s) - q^s| < \epsilon$ for all s, when $i > k$.

Suppose now the contrary of the assertion in the text is true; namely, the sequence $[q^t]$ started from q^0 never returns to q^0, so that $q^t \neq q^0$ for all t. Let d^t be the distance between q^t and q^0 and $\epsilon(q^t)$ an ϵ neighbourhood of q^t, $t = 0, 1, 2, \ldots$ by the supposition $d_t > 0$ for all t. Assume that we may take a positive number d such that $d_t \geqq d$ for all t. Then we may take ϵ so small that $\epsilon(q^0)$ is distinct from each of $\epsilon(q^t)$, $t = 1, 2, \ldots$. For a sufficiently large i, both $q(t_i)$ and $q(t_{i+1})$

where $q^t \neq q^0, t = 1, 2, ..., r - 1$. If $r = 1$, we have $q^0 = f(q^0)$, so that q^0 is an equilibrium price set and the *tâtonnement* path $q(t)$ converges with q^0. If $r > 1$, it converges with the limit cycle $q^0 q^1 ... q^{r-1} q^0$ and never approaches an equilibrium price set.

Thus the necessary and sufficient condition for stability is that r be equal to 1. In order to consider this mathematical condition in more intuitively understandable economic terminology, it is convenient to extend the concept of a fixed point so as to include those of higher orders. Let us consider a cycle of length r defined by (18), from which we obtain, by substitution,

$$q^0 = f\langle f\{...f[f(q^0)]...\}\rangle.$$

Denoting r times the transformation f by F_r, we find that q^0 is a fixed point of F_r, which we call a fixed point of order r. Similarly, $q^1, q^2, ..., q^{r-1}$ are fixed points of the same order. In other words, $q^i = F_r(q^i)$, $i = 0, 1, 2, ..., r - 1$. In addition to these, it is certain that there is one more fixed point of order r, that is the fixed point of order one, q^*, satisfying $q^* = f(q^*)$. It can, in fact, easily be seen that q^* is also a fixed point of any higher order:

$$q^* = f\langle f\{...f[f(q^*)]...\}\rangle.$$

Distinguishing from q^*, the points q^i, which are starting points of a path which returns for the first time to the start after r periods, are called *proper* fixed points of order r; they are stationary points in the system where r elemental periods are consolidated into one comprehensive period. We can now see that the stability condition, $r = 1$, that we have obtained for the process (9) is satisfied if there are no proper stationary points of any higher order; the path has then to approach some equilibrium point which is a fixed point of order 1. Therefore, if the fixed point of order 1 is unique and it is the sole fixed point of any order, then all cycles

are in $\epsilon(q^0)$. Let $t_{i+1} = t_i + s$. Then, as has been seen above, $q(t_i + s)$ is in $\epsilon(q^s)$. Thus $q(t_{i+1})$ is in both $\epsilon(q^0)$ and $\epsilon(q^s)$, which are distinct from each other. This is impossible; hence d should be zero.

This implies that q^0 is a limiting point of $\{q^t\}$. That is to say, there is a subsequence $\{q^{t_i}\}$ such that $\lim_{i \to \infty} q^{t_i} = q^0$. Then, by the same reasoning as above $\lim_{i \to \infty} q^{t_i+1} = q^1$, $\lim_{i \to \infty} q^{t_i+2} = q^2$, and so on. In particular, $\lim_{i \to \infty} q^{t_i-1} = q^v$ for some positive number v. As $\lim_{i \to \infty} q^{t_i} = f(\lim_{i \to \infty} q^{t_i-1})$, we have $q^0 = f(q^v)$. On the other hand, $f(q^v) = q^{v+1}$ and $q^0 \neq q^{v+1}$ since $d_{v+1} > 0$ by assumption. This is a contradiction; therefore, the supposition that $d_t > 0$ for all t is denied; so that $d_t = 0$ for some t.

are ruled out and the equilibrium given by the fixed point is globally stable.

Thus the uniqueness of the fixed point of any order is a sufficient condition for stability. But the uniqueness of the fixed point of order 1 only does not necessarily imply stability. This is shown by an example with market excess demand functions satisfying the weak axiom of revealed preference. Although this axiom is very restrictive for market excess demand functions (while it is natural and plausible for individuals' excess demand functions), the example is interesting, because it illustrates that the unique equilibrium (guaranteed by the axiom) is not necessarily stable. Contrary to the well known result that the axiom is sufficient to show that the equilibrium is globally stable,[16] the path will not approach an equilibrium, but some cycle with length $r > 1$, if it starts from an unspecified initial point, while it may approach an equilibrium, i.e. r may take on the value 1, if it commence at some particular initial point. Whether a path converges with a cycle or an equilibrium, or with which cycle or which equilibrium it converges, depend entirely on the initial position from which it starts.

Let us now present an example. Consider a two-goods economy with market excess demand functions:

$$E_1 = (-p_1 + \tfrac{5}{3}p_2)/(\sum_j p_j),$$
$$E_2 = -(p_1/p_2)(-p_1 + \tfrac{5}{3}p_2)/(\sum_j p_j). \qquad (19)$$

These satisfy Walras' law: $p_1 E_1 + p_2 E_2 = 0$. By normalizing p_1 and p_2 so that $p_1 + p_2 = 1$, we have

$$E_1 = \tfrac{5}{3} - \tfrac{8}{3}p_1, \quad E_2 = \frac{-p_1}{1 - p_1}(\tfrac{5}{3} - \tfrac{8}{3}p_1), \qquad (19')$$

so that the equilibrium prices are

$$p_1^* = \tfrac{5}{8}, \quad p_2^* = \tfrac{3}{8} \qquad (20)$$

at which $E_1^* = 0$ and $E_2^* = 0$.

Now we show that the weak axiom of revealed preference holds between $p^* = (p_1^*, p_2^*)$ and any other normalized price set $p = (p_1, p_2)$. As $p_1 E_1^* + p_2 E_2^* = 0$, the equilibrium demands and

---

[16] This is a theorem that has been established for usual systems with the price adjustment equations of the Samuelson–Arrow–Hurwicz type.

supplies are feasible in the sense that they satisfy the budget condition. Nevertheless, excess demands $E_1(p)$ and $E_2(p)$ are chosen at p, so that $[E_1(p), E_2(p)]$ is preferred to (E_1^*, E_2^*). The weak axiom requires that $E_1(p)$ and $E_2(p)$ are not feasible at p^*; otherwise $[E_1(p), E_2(p)]$ would be chosen. The required infeasibility implies

$$p_1^* E_1(p) + p_2^* E_2(p) > 0. \tag{21}$$

Substituting (19′) and (20) into the left-hand side of this expression, we obtain

$$p_1^* E_1(p) + p_2^* E_2(p) = \frac{(5 - 8p_1)^2}{24(1 - p_1)},$$

which is definitely positive for all non-negative values of p_1 less than one. This shows that the inequality (21) of the weak axiom has to hold.

The weak axiom thus formulated implies the uniqueness of the equilibrium price set, because if there is another set of equilibrium prices p^{**} at which $E_1^{**} = 0$ and $E_2^{**} = 0$, it is evident that inequality (21) does not hold between p^* and p^{**}.[17] However, this does not necessarily imply the uniqueness of the fixed point of higher order; in fact, our excess demand functions (19′) have fixed points of order 2. Applying the formula (9) to (19′), we obtain

$$p(t+1) = (\tfrac{3}{4}, \tfrac{1}{4}), \quad p(t+2) = (\tfrac{1}{4}, \tfrac{3}{4}), \quad p(t+3) = (\tfrac{3}{4}, \tfrac{1}{4})$$

if we set $p(t)$ at $(\tfrac{1}{4}, \tfrac{3}{4})$. Therefore, both $(\tfrac{1}{4}, \tfrac{3}{4})$ and $(\tfrac{3}{4}, \tfrac{1}{4})$ are proper fixed points of order 2.

We can now calculate *tâtonnement* paths by the use of the adjustment equation

$$p_1(t+1) = \frac{1}{1 + \max\left[0.6 - \dfrac{p_1(t)}{[1 - p_1(t)]^2}[1 - 1.6p_1(t)], 0\right]},$$

which is obtained, from (9), by assuming $v = 1$ and substituting (19′) into it. The two paths which we have calculated are one starting from the initial position $p_1 = 0.62$ (which is very close to

---

[17] Here we exclude the corner maxima and presume that indifference curves have no kink. For more general cases where these are allowed, see Arrow, K. J. and L. Hurwicz, 'Some Remarks on the Equilibrium of Economic Systems', *Econometrica* (Vol. 28, 1960), pp. 640–6.

the equilibrium point $p_1^* = \frac{5}{8}$) and one from $p_1 = 0.24$ (which is very close to the fixed point of order 2, $p_1 = \frac{1}{4}$). The results are shown in Fig. 1, a and b. It is interesting to see that, in spite of the presence of the weak axiom of revealed preference, both the equilibrium point and the equilibrium cycle of order 2 are unstable. The figures clearly show that the calculated paths diverge from them and approach the same limit cycle of order 8. In fact, in the case of Fig. 1a, the path starting from $p_1 = 0.62$ is sufficiently near to the cycle at $t = 21$ and almost returns to the same point at $t = 29$, while it is seen from Fig. 1b that the path from 0.24 gradually diverges from the equilibrium cycle of order 2 [with the amplitude $(\frac{1}{4}, \frac{3}{4})$] towards the cycle of order 8. These instability conclusions are true for all initial points except $p_1 = 0$. It is curious that the equilibrium is stable only for $p_1 = 0$, the remotest possible initial position. In this case, we have $p_1(1) = \frac{5}{8}$ for $p_1(0) = 0$ and $p_1(t)$ stays at $\frac{5}{8}$ thereafter.

This is a disappointing conclusion: the *tâtonnement* formula (9) does not necessarily enable us to find any set of equilibrium prices, though some do exist. Nevertheless we may still believe that in the real world the *tâtonnement* method of finding equilibrium prices will work more powerfully and effectively than any mathematical theory of price adjustment. The caller always learns from experience and never reacts in the same way as he reacted in previous similar circumstances. He is not a robot, rigidly applying the same formula (9) with a constant degree of price flexibility, v, in all circumstances; he will change the value of v as soon as he finds that, with that value, (9) is generating undamped oscillations of prices. He will reduce the value of v and adjust prices more carefully.

We have so far been concerned with a system where the time interval required for one round of *tâtonnement* and the price adjustment coefficient are fixed at 1 and v, respectively. A more general system is possible, in which it takes h units of time for one round of *tâtonnement* and price adjustments during that time interval are proportional to the length of time, so that the adjustment coefficient takes on the value vh. Then we may rewrite (9) as

$$q_j(t+h) = \frac{\max\{q_j(t) + vhE_j[q(t)], 0\}}{\sum\limits_{k} \max\{q_k(t) + vhE_k[q(t)], 0\}} \qquad (j = 1, ..., n). \quad (22)$$

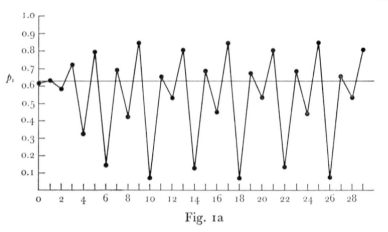

Fig. 1a

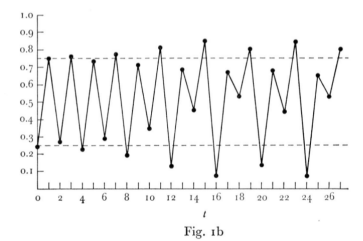

Fig. 1b

Defining, as usual, $\dot{q}_j(t) = \lim\limits_{h \to 0}[q_j(t+h) - q_j(t)]/h$, the modified process is converted into differential equations

$$\dot{q}_j = F_j(q) - q_j[\sum_k F_k(q)] \quad (j = 1, \ldots, n), \tag{9'}$$

where

$$F_j(q) = \lim_{h \to 0} \max\left[vE_j(q), -\frac{1}{h}q_j\right] = \begin{cases} vE_j(q) & \text{if } q_j > 0, \\ \max[vE_j(q), 0] & \text{if } q_j = 0. \end{cases} \tag{23}$$

We can show that this differential equation system is globally stable, provided that the excess demand functions fulfil the weak axiom of revealed preference.[18] In other words, granting the weak axiom, the continuous adjustment of prices enables us to remove all possibilities of limit cycles, which we cannot do in the case of discrete adjustment by the difference equations (9). As we approximate differential equations (9') by difference equations (22), by taking h sufficiently small, we may conclude that the weak axiom of revealed preference is a sufficient condition for stability, if the market is well organized in the sense that it has a price caller who can adjust price sufficiently frequently. Thus

[18] Differential equations (9') may be discontinuous at q with some $q_i = 0$. Similar discontinuities may happen for the differential equations in Chapter 4 below. The problems which this sort of discontinuity due to switching may cause, can be solved in the way discussed in my *Equilibrium, Stability and Growth* (Oxford, 1964), pp. 38–43.

The stability proof is outlined as follows.

(i) Consider an auxiliary non-normalized system

$$\dot{z}_j = F_j(z) \left(\sum_k z_k \right) \quad (j = 1, ..., n). \tag{24}$$

Defining $r_j = z_j / \sum_k z_k$, we obtain

$$\dot{r}_j = \left(\dot{z}_j \sum_k z_k - z_j \sum_k \dot{z}_k \right) \Big/ \left(\sum_k z_k \right)^2 = F_j(r) - r_j \left[\sum_k F_k(r) \right],$$

because each F_k is homogeneous of degree zero in z. Hence the path of r generated by (24) is identical with the path of q of the original system (9'), provided that both paths start from the same initial point. Therefore, if z converges to the equilibrium in the system (24), then q does so in the original one (9').

(ii) Let $D = \frac{1}{2} \sum_j z_j^2$. It remains constant because

$$\dot{D} = \sum_j \dot{z}_j z_j = v \left[\sum_j z_j E_j(z) \right] \left(\sum_k z_k \right) = 0$$

by (23), (24), and Walras' law. Fix w so as to have $D = \sum_k (w q_k^*)^2$.

(iii) Next define V as $V = \frac{1}{2} \sum (z_j - w q_j^*)^2$. Then,

$$\dot{V} = \left[\sum_j (z_j - w q_j^*) F_j(z) \right] \left(\sum_k z_k \right) \qquad \text{from (24)}$$

$$\leq v \left[\sum_j (z_j - w q_j^*) E_j(z) \right] \left(\sum_k z_k \right),$$

where the last weak inequality follows from the definition of $F_j(z)$. The Walras' law and the weak axiom of revealed preference imply that

$$\dot{V} < 0, \quad \text{unless } z = w q^*.$$

Hence z converges to $w q^*$ as t tends to infinity. This means that q converges to q^*.

the stability depends on the caller's ability as well as the shapes of the excess demand functions. (The conventional stability analysis in terms of differential equations implicitly assumes the required ability of the caller, so that economists have already assumed a certain measure of stability at the outset of their analysis when they decide to adopt the differential equation version of price adjustment equations.) In the actual economy, thanks to the caller's skill and good sense, traders usually agree to a set of equilibrium prices at the end of a session of *tâtonnement*, unless catastrophic circumstances occur in the market.[19]

[19] It should be noted that (9) or (9′) is the formula of *tâtonnement* for a ficticious, moneyless economy which is constructed for theoretical purposes. In the actual world money can serve as the *numéraire* except in some really exceptional cases. Though the possibility cannot be ruled out, there is practically no need for introducing the composite-commodity *numérarire*; so that we may examine stability with formula (6), taking p_js as prices in terms of money. However, we cannot do so at this point, because problems concerning money have not yet been discussed at all.

CHAPTER 3

Walras' law and production

'Any order of phenomena, however complicated, may be studied scientifically provided the rule of proceeding from the simple to the complex is always observed.'[1] Having formulated his mathematical theory of exchange, which ignored the fact that commodities are products which result from the combination of such factors of production as labour, land and capital goods, Walras was concerned with a more complicated problem, i.e. the probem of formation of a general equilibrium in an economy where production is simultaneous with exchange. In this economy, not only the prices of the commodities (products) to be exchanged, but also the prices of the factors to be used for production, are variables; and both outputs and inputs must be determined. Yet the system is not general enough, since production or reproduction of capital goods is completely ignored and only production of consumption goods is allowed for.

Walras discussed the reproduction of capital goods, separately from the simple production of consumption goods, in his 'Theory of Capital Formation and Credit', which is, of course, his growth theory, and which we will deal with in Part II. In this chapter, however, we confine ourselves to Walras' production theory, assuming that the available quantities of the factors of production are all given. The distinction between producible and non-producible factors disappears, so that in this abstract economy, constructed as a prelude to his main study of growth and money theory, there is no need to classify individuals as workers, landowners or capitalists. They all appear as owners of some factors of production.

Consequently, the economy has only two groups of goods and services: commodities and factors of production. There are a number of industries, or firms, each producing a single com-

[1] Walras, *Elements*, p. 211.

modity by means of commodities and factors, while factors are not produced. There are consumers who buy commodities with the income from the factors they own. However, there are no banks, no government and no international trade. Long-run dynamic factors, such as production periods and expectations, as well as investment, are all neglected.

Let us assume that there are n commodities and m factors. We denote output and consumption of good i by x_i and c_i, respectively, and supply of factor k by r_k, where $i = 1, ..., n$ and $k = 1, ..., m$. p_i represents the price of good i and v_k the price of factor k; p and v stand for the price sets $(p_1, ..., p_n)$ and $(v_1, ..., v_m)$, respectively. Each c_i is a continuous function of prices of goods and services, p and v, which is written as $c_i = c_i(p, v)$; similarly each r_k is a continuous function of the same variables:

$$r_k = r_k(p, v).$$

These functions are derived from the utility maximization of the individuals, so that they are homogeneous of degree zero in prices p and v, satisfying the budget identity:[2]

$$\sum_i p_i c_i(p, v) \equiv \sum_k v_k r_k(p, v). \tag{1}$$

Next we denote the quantity of good i required to produce one unit of good j by a_{ij} and the quantity of factor k employed per unit of production of good j by b_{kj}. As the industrial demand for commodity i amounts to $\sum_j a_{ij} x_j$ and the employment of factor k to $\sum_j b_{kj} x_j$, the conditions for general equilibrium of production may be given as: (i) the demand–supply conditions for commodities,

$$\sum_j a_{ij} x_j + c_i(p, v) \leqq x_i \quad (i = 1, ..., n), \tag{2}$$

(ii) the demand–supply conditions for factors,

$$\sum_j b_{kj} x_j \leqq r_k(p, v) \quad (j = 1, ..., m), \tag{3}$$

and (iii) the price-cost conditions for commodities,

$$p_j \leqq \sum_i a_{ij} p_i + \sum_k b_{kj} v_k \quad (j = 1, ..., n). \tag{4}$$

---

[2] This identity may be referred to as the budget identity at the market level, that is the sum of the individual's budget equations.

As will be seen later, if the demand–supply conditions, (2) or (3), hold with strict inequality for some good i or some factor k, then the corresponding price p_i or v_k is null; that is to say, a good which is over-produced or a factor which is not fully employed will be free (the rule of free goods), while if the price–cost condition, (4), holds with strict inequality for some industry j, then the corresponding output x_j is null; that is, an industry which is un-profitable will be closed (the rule of profitability).

In most economic models the budget identity at the market level is identical with Walras' law, so called, which requires that the total value of the excess demands for goods and services be identically zero. This is true for Walras' exchange model, but not for the above production model, which Walras himself constructed. In fact, defining excess demand functions of goods and factors as

$$E_i(p, v, x) = \sum_j a_{ij} x_j + c_j(p, v) - x_i \quad (i = 1, ..., n),$$

$$F_k(p, v, x) = \sum_j b_{kj} x_j - r_k(p, v) \quad (k = 1, ..., m),$$

where $x = (x_1, ..., x_n)$, the total value of the excess demands (or the aggregate excess demand) is given as

$$\sum_i p_i E_i(p, v, x) + \sum_k v_k F_k(p, v, x)$$
$$\equiv \left[\sum_i p_i c_i(p, v) - \sum_k v_k r_k(p, v) \right]$$
$$- \left[\sum_i p_i x_i - \sum_i \sum_j a_{ij} p_i x_j - \sum_k \sum_j b_{kj} v_k x_j \right]. \tag{5}$$

In this identity the part in the first pair of square brackets vanishes identically by virtue of the budget identity (1), while the part in the second pair which stands for the total excess profit or the total supernormal profit does not necessarily vanish, unless prices of goods are adjusted to their costs. Thus we find that Walras' law does not hold in the original system of general equilibrium of production due to Walras.

This rather paradoxical conclusion that Walras' system does not satisfy the Walras law is also true for his growth and money models, so that, strictly speaking, we must say that Walras did not know Walras' law. The identity which his three models of production, growth, and money alike satisfy is:

The aggregate excess demand

$$+ \text{the aggregate excess profit} \equiv 0, \quad (5')$$

which is no more than a restatement of (5).[3] Although this peculiar identity may look unreasonable at first sight, it is not difficult to understand why we have it. In Walras' own model, it is implicitly assumed that the aggregate excess profit (or supernormal profit) which may accrue in a positive or negative amount in the process of establishing an equilibrium is not distributed among individuals, so that the same amount is saved or dissaved by firms. Subtracting that amount from the total proceeds, $\sum_i p_i x_i$, the firms spend the rest on commodities and factors so as to acquire them in the quantities $\sum_j a_{ij} x_j$ and $\sum_j b_{kj} x_j$ respectively. Thus we have the budget equation of the firms:

$$\sum_i p_i x_i - \text{firms' savings (i.e. their aggregate excess profit)}$$
$$= \sum_i p_i (\sum_j a_{ij} x_j) + \sum_k v_k (\sum_j b_{kj} x_j).$$

This, together with the individuals' budget equation (1), yields the identity (5) in question.

In order to correct Walras' model so as to fulfil Walras' law, let us assume that the aggregate excess profit is distributed among individuals, say, in proportion to their ownership of capital goods. Then they earn extra income (positive or negative) in addition to the normal profit which is included in $\sum_k v_k r_k$. Consumption of goods and supply of factors now depend not only on their prices and the individuals' initial endowments, but also on the distributed aggregate excess profit, which in turn depends on the prices, p and v, and the levels of production of the various industries, x, so that we may write

$$c_i = c_i(p, v, x), \quad r_k = r_k(p, v, x).$$

[3] The left-hand side of (5) represents the aggregate excess demand, while the part in the second pair of brackets on the right-hand side stands for the aggregate excess profit. On the right-hand side there remains the part in the first pair, which is of course identically zero.

Defining A and B as the n by n and m by n matrices with elements a_{ij} and b_{kj}, respectively, and $c(p, v, x)$ and $r(p, v, x)$ as n- and m-dimensional column vectors with components $c_i(p, v, x)$ and $r_k(p, v, x)$, respectively, we find that these consumption and supply functions satisfy the new budget equation,

$$p'c(p, v, x) = v'r(p, v, x) + [p'(I - A) - v'B] x, \qquad (6)$$

where x represents the column output vector, p' the row commodity–price vector, v' the row factor-price vector, and I the identity matrix. Evidently, the second term on the right-hand side stands for the aggregate excess profit. Now equilibrium conditions are written as

$$Ax + c(p, v, x) \leq x \quad \text{(demand–supply for goods)}, \qquad (7)$$

$$Bx \leq r(p, v, x) \quad \text{(demand–supply for factors)}, \qquad (8)$$

$$p' \leq p'A + v'B \quad \text{(price–cost for goods)}. \qquad (9)$$

Excess demand functions are defined as

$$E(p, v, x) = Ax + c(p, v, x) - x,$$

$$F(p, v, x) = Bx - r(p, v, x).$$

In view of the revised budget equation (6), we can easily verify that these excess demand functions satisfy Walras' law,

$$p'E(p, v, x) + v'F(p, v, x) \equiv 0. \qquad (10)$$

There are a number of ways to show that the system (7)–(10) has non-negative solutions (p, v, x). Among them the following two are worth noticing. According to the first method, we reduce the production equilibrium system to an exchange equilibrium system and apply to it the Walrasian *tâtonnement* convention (which was explained in the previous chapter), to find an exchange equilibrium. The second method applies directly a newly invented *tâtonnement* formula to obtain a general equilibrium of production. Walras took the second approach without mentioning the possibility of the first, but in what follows we shall first give our attention to the first approach and then proceed to the second.

To begin with, let us reduce the system to one of exchange of factors of production. We assume that the matrix of input coefficients A is productive, so that $(I-A)^{-1}$ is non-negative and non-zero.[4] Putting

$$p' = v'B(I-A)^{-1} \quad \text{(Leontief's price solutions)}, \quad (11)$$

we find that the aggregate excess profit vanishes. That is to say, by adjusting prices of commodities to prices of factors in the way specified by the formula (11), we can keep the aggregate excess profit at the equilibrium level, i.e. at zero; so that no individual receives positive or negative extra income. The consumption of goods and the supply of factors are then independent of the outputs, x. As long as commodity prices are adjusted to factor prices in the proposed way, we may thus write

$$\left.\begin{array}{l} c(p,v,x) = c(v), \\ r(p,v,x) = r(v). \end{array}\right\} \quad (12)$$

Next we adjust outputs so as to equal

$$x = (I-A)^{-1}c(v) \quad \text{(Leontief's output solutions)}. \quad (13)$$

Substituting (12) and (13), we may rewrite the excess demand functions in the form:

$$F(v) = Bx - r(p,v,x) = B(I-A)^{-1}c(v) - r(v). \quad (14)$$

This represents the excess demands for factors which prevail in the market when p and x are instantaneously adjusted so that (11) and (13) hold. Also, by virtue of (11)–(14), we can rewrite (10) as

$$v'B(I-A)^{-1}c(v) - v'r(v) \equiv v'F(v) \equiv 0, \quad (15)$$

which says that Walras' law prevails in the factor market. It is evident that the equilibrium condition (7) holds at (13) with

[4] The matrix of input coefficients is said to be productive if it is feasible to produce outputs which are all greater than the corresponding inputs required. That is to say, A is productive if there is an output vector, say, $x^0 > 0$, such that $x^0 > Ax^0$. The productiveness implies $hx^0 \geq Ax^0$, for an h with $0 < h < 1$. As A is non-negative, we have $hAx^0 \geq A^2x^0$, the left-hand side of which is smaller than h^2x^0 because of the productiveness of A. Hence, $h^2x^0 \geq A^2x^0$. Repeating the same procedure we obtain $h^t x^0 \geq A^t x^0 \geq 0$ for all t. Since $0 < h < 1$, we have $\lim_{t\to\infty} A^t x^0 = 0$; since $x^0 > 0$, A^t must be convergent. Therefore,

$$(I-A)^{-1} = I + A + A^2 + \dots.$$

As A is non-negative, each term on the right-hand side is non-negative; hence, $(I-A)^{-1} \geq 0$.

equality; similarly (9) holds at (11) with equality. The remaining equilibrium condition (8) requires that

$$F(v) \leqq 0. \tag{16}$$

Thus the problem is reduced to that of finding a general equilibrium of exchange in the factor market, i.e., a set of factor prices which satisfy equilibrium condition (16).

A general equilibrium may now be found by the *tâtonnement* method discussed in Chapter 2. We take a composite commodity consisting of the unit of each factor of production as the *numéraire*, because we do not know which factors are not free and can serve as *numéraire*. Let $v_k(t)$ be the price of factor k in terms of the *numéraire* at the tth round of *tâtonnement*. Since the price of the composite commodity, that is, the sum of the prices of its components, should equal one, because it is the *numéraire*, we find that prices are normalized so that

$$\sum_k v_k(t) = 1, \quad \text{for all } t. \tag{17}$$

As we have seen in Chapter 2, prices at the $(t+1)$th round are determined according to the formula,

$$v_k(t+1) = \frac{\max\{v_k(t)+uF_k[v(t)], 0\}}{\sum_j \max\{v_j(t)+uF_j[v(t)], 0\}} \quad (k = 1, \ldots, m), \tag{18}$$

where u is a positive coefficient representing the degree of price flexibility. Equations (18) transform $v(t)$ into $v(t+1)$; if $v(t) \neq v(t+1)$, prices are changing at time t, while a point at which $v(t) = v(t+1)$ is a fixed point. The existence of a fixed point can be verified by Brouwer's fixed-point theorem,[5] provided $F_k[v(t)], k = 1, \ldots, m$, are continuous functions. We can also show that (16) holds at the fixed point, so that it is an equilibrium point. If the equilibrium point is globally stable, we may start the *tâtonnement* process from an arbitrary initial point $v(0)$. Formula (18) gives us subsequent price sets $v(1), v(2), \ldots$ which finally converge to the equilibrium point. This is a lucky case, and the *tâtonnement* approach is effective. But if the equilibrium point is not globally stable, then the path

---

[5] For the Brouwer fixed-point theorem, see footnote 2 of Chapter 2 above. In our present application, (18) gives a continuous transformation of S, a set of non-negative prices satisfying (17), into itself.

$v(t)$ may eventually converge to a limit cycle; the factor prices will oscillate endlessly and we shall not reach an equilibrium price set by this method, although its existence is mathematically assured by the fixed-point theorem.

So far so good; it seems that the *tâtonnement* in the factor market will probably finally enable us to find a general equilibrium of production. In a decentralized economy, however, it is rather unrealistic to assume that commodity prices instantaneously adjust themselves to factor prices in the way described by (11). Each industry knows only its own production coefficients, and because of lack of information no industry is able to calculate the exact price of its output which accords with formula (11). Similarly, no industry knows the value of its output which is consistent with current consumption, as formula (13) requires. Thus the bases on which the first method of *tâtonnement* becomes workable are not available in the actual economy.

Moreover, this method of reducing the model of production to a model of exchange of factors, by eliminating the variables concerning products, is inapplicable when there are alternative techniques of production and each industry has to choose one from among those available to it. In this more general case the input-coefficient matrix A is no longer a square matrix, so that we cannot conceive of the inverse $(I - A)^{-1}$, which is indispensable for elimination of the variables according to the first method. The second method of *tâtonnement* which Walras elaborated in the *Elements* is a device which enables us to solve simultaneously both the problem of determining commodity prices and outputs in a decentralized production system and the problem of choosing techniques.

In an economy which has n industries to produce n commodities with m factors, industry i can choose between k_i processes labelled $1_i, 2_i, ..., k_i$. Its material-input and factor-input coefficients are represented by matrices

$$A_i = \begin{pmatrix} a_{11_i} & \cdots & a_{1k_i} \\ a_{21_i} & \cdots & a_{2k_i} \\ \cdots\cdots\cdots\cdots\cdots \\ a_{n1_i} & \cdots & a_{nk_i} \end{pmatrix}, \quad B_i = \begin{pmatrix} b_{11_i} & \cdots & b_{1k_i} \\ b_{21_i} & \cdots & b_{2k_i} \\ \cdots\cdots\cdots\cdots\cdots \\ b_{m1_i} & \cdots & b_{mk_i} \end{pmatrix},$$

respectively. For the entire economy we have the material-input coefficient matrix A and the factor-input coefficient matrix B, which are the arrays of industrial input-coefficient matrices $(A_1, A_2, ..., A_n)$ and $(B_1, B_2, ..., B_n)$, respectively. The output matrix, I (the identity matrix), in the no-substitution economy is now extended into

$$J = \begin{pmatrix} \text{I} & \text{I} & \cdots & \text{I} & \text{O} & \cdots & \text{O} & \text{O} & \cdots & \text{O} \\ \text{O} & \text{O} & \cdots & \text{O} & \text{I} & \cdots & \text{I} & \text{O} & \cdots & \text{O} \\ \multicolumn{10}{c}{\cdots\cdots\cdots\cdots\cdots\cdots\cdots\cdots\cdots\cdots\cdots\cdots} \\ \text{O} & \text{O} & \cdots & \text{O} & \text{O} & \cdots & \text{O} & \text{I} & \cdots & \text{I} \end{pmatrix},$$

where the number of unities in the ith row equals the number of alternative techniques available to industry i, which is k_i. The output vector is, of course, $k_1 + k_2 + ... + k_n$ dimensional and denoted as

$$x' = (x_{1_1}, x_{2_1}, ..., x_{k_1}, x_{1_2}, ..., x_{k_2}, ..., x_{1_n}, ..., x_{k_n}),$$

with component x_{s_i} representing the quantity of good i produced by the s_ith method of production. In this expression of the output vector the prime signifies the transposition of the vector, so that x is a column vector. Walrasian equilibrium conditions are then given as

$$Ax + c(p, v, x) \leqq Jx, \tag{19}$$

$$Bx \leqq r(p, v, x), \tag{20}$$

$$p'J \leqq p'A + v'B. \tag{21}$$

This system is now solved by the method of *tâtonnement*, which is very similar to that for exchange equilibrium. As Walras appropriately warned us, however, there are complications, in the case of the *tâtonnement* in production, which did not arise in the case of exchange. First of all, in the exchange theory we assumed that traders can contract and recontract with each other without significant transaction costs. But in the production theory, it can hardly be assumed that production is freely reversible; obviously, unless we pay a heavy cost it is impossible to turn the production process around and obtain the factors used from the commodity produced by them. Secondly, production requires a certain lapse of time, which is different from product to product. Walras resolved the first difficulty by assuming that no production is done during the process of *tâtonnement* and that entrepreneurs use 'tickets' to represent outputs or inputs they want to produce or employ at the particular set of prices prevailing in the market. The number of tickets will be increased or decreased when circumstances change, the demand for each kind of ticket is equated with its supply when an equilibrium is established by *tâtonnement*. Entrepreneurs can decrease the number of tickets of any kind without any difficulty, because they can do so without this being accompanied by an actual process of production. After an equilibrium has been established, production is carried out. Walras got around the second difficulty, concerning the period of production by simply ignoring the time element.[6]

Walras assumed the following three rules of adjustment. (i) The price of a commodity p_i is raised or lowered according as the demand for it exceeds its supply or *vice versa*. (ii) Similarly, the price of a factor v_k is raised or lowered according as the demand for it exceeds its supply or *vice versa*. (iii) The output of commodity i is increased or decreased according as its price exceeds its cost of production or *vice versa*. These rules are mathematically formulated as

$$p_i(t+1) = \frac{\max[p_i(t) + uE_i(t), 0]}{M(t)} \quad (i = 1, ..., n), \quad (22)$$

$$v_k(t+1) = \frac{\max[v_k(t) + uF_k(t), 0]}{M(t)} \quad (k = 1, ..., m), \quad (23)$$

$$x_{s_i}(t+1) = \min[\bar{x}_{s_i}, \max(0, x_{s_i}(t) + wG_{s_i}(t))]$$
$$(s_i = 1_i, ..., k_i), (i = 1, ..., n), \quad (24)$$

where $E_i(t)$ represents the excess demand for commodity i, i.e. the difference between the two sides of the ith inequality of (19), $F_k(t)$ the excess demand for factor k, i.e. the difference between the two sides of the kth inequality of (20), and $G_{s_i}(t)$ the excess profit of the sth process of industry i, i.e. the difference between the two sides of the s_ith inequality of (21). All of them are the values at the tth round of the *tâtonnement* when $p(t)$, $v(t)$, $x(t)$ prevail. The coefficients u and w are positive and represent the price flexibility and the output flexibility, respectively; for the

---

[6] Walras, *Elements*, p. 242. See Chapter 13 below.

sake of simplicity, u is the same for all commodities and factors, while w is the same for all processes. Equations (22) and (23) have $M(t)$, that is the sum of their numerators, i.e.

$$M(t) = \sum_i \max[p_i(t) + uE_i(t), 0] + \sum_k \max[v_k(t) + uF_k(t), 0]. \quad (25)$$

On the right-hand side of equations (22) and (23), the max operation prevents prices, $p_i(t+1)$ and $v_k(t+1)$, from taking on negative values and $M(t)$ normalizes prices so that

$$\sum_i p_i(t+1) + \sum_k v_k(t+1) = 1.[7]$$

As for the output adjustment equations (24), $\bar{\bar{x}}_{s_i}$ is a sufficiently high production level of process s_i that it is infeasible, regardless of the production levels of other processes, because it results in a shortage of at least one factor of production.[8] The max operation of (24) prevents $x_{s_i}(t+1)$ from being negative, while the min operation of the same equation prevents it from exceeding $\bar{\bar{x}}_{s_i}$. The formula states that the output from process s_i increases or decreases in proportion to the excess profit within the range thus specified, $[0, \bar{\bar{x}}_{s_i}]$.

Assuming that the consumption functions $c(p, v, x)$ and the factor-supply functions $r(p, v, x)$ are continuous, we find that (22)–(24) transform $[p(t), v(t), x(t)]$ to $[p(t+1), v(t+1), x(t+1)]$ in a continuous way. Moreover, let S be a set of all possible combinations of p, v, x such that $p \geq 0$, $v \geq 0$ with $\sum_i p_i + \sum_k v_k = 1$ and $0 \leq x \leq \bar{\bar{x}}$, where $\bar{\bar{x}}$ is the vector with component $\bar{\bar{x}}_{s_i}$. Then the equations (22)–(24) give a transformation of S into itself. The requirements of the fixed-point theorem are thus completely satisfied, so that they have a fixed point (p^*, v^*, x^*) at which the values of p, v, x calculated by formulas (22)–(24) are equal to p^*, v^*, x^* themselves, on the basis of which the calculations are made. Furthermore, we can show that the denominator M of

[7] A detailed explanation of our price ajustment equations was given in Chapter 2 above.

[8] Suppose each process uses at least one factor, so that each s_i has a factor k with $b_{ks_i} > 0$. Then $\bar{\bar{x}}_{s_i}$ may be determined such that

$$b_{ks_i}\bar{\bar{x}}_{s_i} > \bar{r}_k \quad \text{for some } k,$$

where $\bar{r}_k$ is the total amount of factor k which exists in the economy.

(22) and (23) equals 1 at any fixed point.[9] Hence,

$$p_i^* = \max[p_i^* + uE_i^*, 0] = p_i^* + \max[uE_i^*, -p_i^*], \qquad (22')$$

$$v_k^* = \max[v_k^* + uF_k^*, 0] = v_k^* + \max[uF_k^*, -v_k^*], \qquad (23')$$

$$x_{s_i}^* = \min[\bar{\bar{x}}_s, \max(x_{s_i}^* + wG_{s_i}^*, 0)]$$

$$= x_{s_i}^* + \min[\bar{\bar{x}}_{s_i}^* - x_{s_i}^*, \max(wG_{s_i}^*, -x_{s_i}^*)], \qquad (24')$$

where E_i^*, F_k^*, $G_{s_i}^*$ denote the values of E_i, F_k, G_{s_i} at the fixed point. Hence we have

$$\max[uE_i^*, -p_i^*] = 0, \qquad (26)$$

$$\max[uF_k^*, -v_k^*] = 0, \qquad (27)$$

$$\min[\bar{\bar{x}}_{s_i} - x_{s_i}^*, \max(wG_{s_i}^*, -x_{s_i}^*)] = 0. \qquad (28)$$

As $p_i^* \geq 0$, (26) implies $E_i^* \leq 0$. Also we find from (26) that if $E_i^* < 0$, then $p_i^* = 0$; that is to say, the price of good i, p_i^*, is zero if its demand falls short of its supply (i.e. $E_i^* < 0$). In exactly the same way, (27) yields $F_k^* \leq 0, k = 1, ..., m$, and the rule of free goods does hold in all factor markets.

As $F_k^* \leq 0$, the demand for any factor k cannot be greater than its supply, which in turn cannot be greater than the total quantity existing in the economy. Then we find that each $x_{s_i}^*$ must be smaller than $\bar{\bar{x}}_{s_i}$, because if $x_{s_i}^* = \bar{\bar{x}}_{s_i}$ for some process s_i, then by the definition of $\bar{\bar{x}}_{s_i}$, the total demand for some factor k would exceed its availability, regardless of the production levels of the other processes; thus we have $F_k^* > 0$ for that k. This is a contradiction. Within the square brackets of the left-hand side of (28), therefore, the first element, $\bar{\bar{x}}_{s_i} - x_{s_i}^*$, is positive, so that (28) implies

$$\max(wG_{s_i}^*, -x_{s_i}^*) = 0, \qquad (28')$$

from which we have $G_{s_i}^* \leq 0$, because $x_{s_i}^* \geq 0$. In particular, if $G_{s_i}^* < 0$ in (28'), then $x_{s_i}^*$ must be zero; in other words, we have the rule of profitability, which states that if process s_i is unprofitable in the sense that the price of output p_i^* is smaller than the cost of production by that process, then it will not be adopted by industry i.

We have thus seen that, at the fixed point, demand does not exceed supply for each good and each factor, and price does not

[9] We can show $M = 1$ in the same way as we showed $c = 1$ in Chapter 2.

exceed cost for each process. This means that the fixed point is an equilibrium point satisfying (19)–(21). In addition, the rule of free goods and the rule of profitability hold at that point. In the state of equilibrium, therefore, (i) all factors of production are fully employed, except those which are free; (ii) industries adopt only those methods of production which are profitable; and (iii) the products are distributed among individuals, with no waste, unless they are free. Walras concluded that full employment of factors, efficient production and wasteless distribution of products were assured in competitive economies.

CHAPTER 4

The dual-adjustment rules: Walrasian and Keynesian

In the preceding chapter we discussed the Walrasian process of *tâtonnement* in production, which is based on the dual adjustment rules: (i) the price of a commodity (or factor) is raised or lowered whenever there is a positive or negative excess demand for that commodity (or factor); and (ii) the output of a commodity is expanded or reduced whenever the excess of its price over its cost of production is positive or negative. These cross dual-adjustments of prices according to quantities and *vice versa* are not the only way of groping for the equilibrium set of prices and outputs; there may be others. In fact, as is often observed in modern economies, quantities produced react on demand conditions in the market rather than price–cost relationships, and prices react on costs of production rather than demand conditions. We may conceive of an economy where prices and outputs are adjusted according to the following rules. (*a*) The price of a product is raised (or lowered) if its current price falls short of (or exceeds) its minimum cost of production. (*b*) Factor prices are rigid downwards; they remain unchanged in spite of an excess supply of factors, though they rise if there is excess demand. (*c*) Where there is an excess demand for (or supply of) the product of an industry, it increases (or reduces) its output. We shall refer to these rules of direct adjustments of prices on the basis of prices, and of quantities on the basis of quantities, as the Keynesian rules. In this chapter, we shall compare the Walrasian rules with the Keynesian ones with respect to the stability of equilibrium in production.

Keynesian economics is different from neoclassical theory of the Walrasian type in a number of respects. First, as has been stated above, the adjustment rules are different. Secondly, as will be seen below, Keynes distinguished the effective demands for commodities and factors arising from actual income from the notional demands assuming a state of full employment; Walras needed no such distinction, because the full employment of all factors (except free ones) was automatically established in his model and, hence, the notional demands were effective. Thirdly, Keynes did not accept Say's law, emphasizing the fact that investment and saving are independently decided by different groups of individuals, while Walras, although he also emphasized the same fact, paradoxically assumed a smooth adjustment of aggregate investment to aggregate saving. Of these three points, I take the final one as the most important distinction between Keynesians and neoclassicists; that is to say, an economist who believes Say's law can never be a Keynesian, and no neoclassical economist can deny the law. In spite of its crucial nature, however, we do not discuss Say's law at all in this part of the book. Here we examine equilibrium in simple production, so that the problem of capital accumulation does not arise, investment and saving being either ignored or given a minimum consideration. Say's law is a subject of growth theory and money theory. As the significance of the law will be discussed in detail later, especially in Chapters 7 and 12, we do not pay particular attention to it in this chapter, although we examine a Keynesian model for workability.

Let us begin by dealing with a neoclassical production model of the Walrasian type. Throughout the following, we confine ourselves to the case of the mth factor of production, say unskilled labour, being taken as the *numéraire*, so that in the Walrasian price adjustment equations (i.e. equations 22 and 23 of Chapter 3), we may ignore the terms (i.e. the denominators of those equations) which arose from the fact that we took as the *numéraire* the composite commodity consisting of one unit of each commodity and of each factor. Denoting the differentiation with respect to time by a dot above the relevant symbol, we formulate the Walrasian rules in terms of differential equations as

$$\dot{p}_i = u\xi_i \quad (i = 1, ..., n), \tag{1}$$

$$\dot{v}_k = u\eta_k \quad (k = 1, ..., m-1), \tag{2}$$

$$\dot{x}_{s_i} = w\zeta_{s_i} \quad (s_i = 1_i, ..., k_i), \; (i = 1, ..., n), \tag{3}$$

where
$$\xi_i = \begin{cases} E_i & \text{if} \quad p_i > 0, \\ \max\,(E_i, 0) & \text{if} \quad p_i = 0; \end{cases} \tag{4}$$

$$\eta_k = \begin{cases} F_k & \text{if} \quad v_k > 0, \\ \max\,(F_k, 0) & \text{if} \quad v_k = 0; \end{cases} \tag{5}$$

$$\zeta_{s_i} = \begin{cases} G_{s_i} & \text{if} \quad \bar{\bar{x}}_{s_i} > x_{s_i} > 0, \\ \min\,(G_{s_i}, 0) & \text{if} \quad x_{s_i} = \bar{\bar{x}}_{s_i} \\ \max\,(G_{s_i}, 0) & \text{if} \quad x_{s_i} = 0. \end{cases} \tag{6}$$

We use the same notation as we used in Chapter 3. That is, E_i is the excess demand function for commodity i; F_k the excess demand function for factor k; G_{s_i} the excess profit from process s_i (i.e. the s_ith process of industry i);[1] p_i and v_k the prices of commodity i and factor k, respectively; x_{s_i} the output produced by process s_i, $\bar{\bar{x}}_{s_i}$ an output of the same process which is so large that it is not producible, because it causes a shortage of some factors, regardless of the production levels of other processes; and u and w the coefficients of price and output flexibilities, respectively. Equations (2) do not include the equation for factor m, which is the *numéraire*, and v_m is always fixed at 1. The qualifications (4) and (5) state that where excess demand for a commodity (or factor) becomes negative when its price is zero, the price no longer diminishes but stays at the zero level; otherwise the prices of goods and factors increase (or decrease) if there is an excess demand (or supply) in the corresponding market. The qualification (6) implies that industry i no longer wants to increase the quantity it plans to produce by process s_i when its production reaches the infeasible level $\bar{\bar{x}}_{s_i}$, while it can no longer decrease the level of production once it reaches the level 0, even though the process is still unprofitable, i.e. $G_{s_i} < 0$. Otherwise the quantity produced by the s_ith process increases (or decreases) according as it yields a positive (or negative) excess profit.

We now ignore the effects of the distribution of income among individuals on demands for consumption goods and supplies of factors and simply assume that they are continuous functions of

---

[1] We may consider (3) to be an adjustment equation of the Marshallian type, because G_{s_i}, which determines x_{s_i}, gives an excess of the price (or demand price) of commodity i over its production cost (or supply price) by process s_i.

prices, p and v, and the aggregate income, Y. We write

$$c_i = c_i(p, v, Y) \quad \text{(the consumption function of good } i),$$

$$r_k = r_k(p, v, Y) \quad \text{(the supply function of factor } k).$$

The aggregate income is defined as

$$Y = v'\bar{r} + (p'Jx - p'Ax - v'Bx),$$

where the prime applied to a vector (p or v) represents the transposition of that vector and $\bar{r}$ is the vector of the endowments of the factors of production which the economy possesses. In this expression, the part in brackets stands for the aggregate excess profit, which vanishes in the state of equilibrium. J is the output coefficient matrix, while A and B are the material-input and factor-input coefficient matrices. As we assume that there are alternative processes of production, these matrices are rectangular.[2]

In equilibrium, no positive excess demand is present in any commodity or factor market, and no process can earn a positive excess profit, so that equilibrium conditions are

$$E \equiv Ax + c(p, v, Y) - Jx \leqq 0$$
$$\text{(demand–supply for commodities)}, \quad (7)$$

$$F \equiv Bx - r(p, v, Y) \leqq 0 \quad \text{(demand–supply for factors)}, \quad (8)$$

$$G \equiv p'J - p'A - v'B \leqq 0 \quad \text{(price–cost for processes)}, \quad (9)$$

We assume that they single out a unique equilibrium (p^*, v^*, x^*). Then its stability may be discussed in the following way.

Let us define the distance of the current state ($p(t), v(t), x(t)$) from the equilibrium state (p^*, v^*, x^*) as

$$D_1 = \frac{1}{2}\left\{\frac{1}{u}[p(t) - p^*]'[p(t) - p^*] + \frac{1}{u}[v(t) - v^*]' \right.$$
$$\left. \times [v(t) - v^*] + \frac{1}{w}[x(t) - x^*]'[x(t) - x^*]\right\}, \quad (10)$$

and the distance of the current speeds of adjustment [$\dot{p}(t), \dot{v}(t), \dot{x}(t)$] from the equilibrium speeds (0, 0, 0) as

$$D_2 = \frac{1}{2}\left[\frac{1}{u}\dot{p}'\dot{p} + \frac{1}{u}\dot{v}'\dot{v} + \frac{1}{w}\dot{x}'\dot{x}\right], \quad (11)$$

where $\tilde{v}'$ represents the ($m - 1$)-dimensional vector ($v_1, ..., v_{m-1}$);

[2] For their exact definitions see Chapter 3 above.

the vector $\tilde{r}'$ which will be used below is similarly defined as $(r_1, ..., r_{m-1})$. Evidently D_1 and D_2 are positive everywhere except at the equilibrium point, so that we may use them as Liapounoff functions of stability analysis.

Differentiating D_1 with respect to t and taking (4), (5) and (6) into account, we obtain[3]

$$\dot{D}_1 \leqq [p - p^*]'[c(p, v, Y) - c(p, v^*, Y^*)] \\ - [v - v^*]'[r(p, v, Y) - r(p^*, v^*, Y^*)], \qquad (12)$$

where $v_m = v_m^* = 1$. On the other hand, D_2 is differentiable with respect to t almost everywhere. Exceptional points are the switching points, at which some ξ_is are switched from E_is to 0, or some η_ks from F_ks to 0, or some ζ_{s_i}s from G_{s_i}s to 0, according to the switching rules (4), (5), and (6). At these points the value of D_2 decreases in a discontinuous way, and at all other points with $\xi = E$, $\eta = F$, and $\zeta = G$, we have

$$\dot{D}_2 = [\dot{p}', \dot{\tilde{v}}']\begin{bmatrix} \dfrac{\partial c}{\partial p} & \dfrac{\partial c}{\partial \tilde{v}} \\ -\dfrac{\partial \tilde{r}}{\partial p} & -\dfrac{\partial \tilde{r}}{\partial \tilde{v}} \end{bmatrix}\begin{bmatrix} \dot{p} \\ \dot{v} \end{bmatrix} + [\dot{p}', \dot{\tilde{v}}']\begin{bmatrix} \dfrac{\partial c}{\partial Y} \\ -\dfrac{\partial \tilde{r}}{\partial Y} \end{bmatrix}\dot{Y}. \quad (13)$$

Where income effects upon goods and non-*numéraire* factors are negligible,[4] we can show (i) that the right-hand side of (12) is negative unless $(p, v) = (p^*, v^*)$; (ii) that the first term on the right-hand side of (13) is also negative unless $(\dot{p}, \dot{\tilde{v}}) = 0$; and (iii) that the second term is negligible.[5] If $(p, v) = (p^*, v^*)$, then $G = G^*$, but if $x \neq x^*$, then $(\xi, \eta) \neq 0$, because (p, v, x) cannot be an equilibrium point, as it is assumed that the equilibrium point is unique. Hence $(\dot{p}, \dot{\tilde{v}}) \neq 0$ by (1) and (2). On the contrary, if $(\dot{p}, \dot{\tilde{v}}) = 0$ at a disequilibrium point, then we should have

[3] The equilibrium production vector x^* should be feasible, so that x^* is definitely smaller than the infeasible production vector $\bar{x}$. In deriving (12), we used this inequality, as well as the usual one requiring non-negativeness of the equilibrium point, $(p^*, v^*, x^*) \geqq 0$.

[4] This means that the partial derivatives of c_i, $i = 1, ..., n$, and r_k, $k = 1, ..., m-1$, with respect to Y are all negligible. Income effects are concentrated on the *numéraire* factor.

[5] In fact we can show that in the case where income effects are negligible, the Jacobean is negative quasi-definite; so we have (ii). Also, if it is negative quasi-definite everywhere, (i) is valid. For this result, see my *Equilibrium, Stability and Growth* (The Clarendon Press, Oxford, 1964), pp. 27–8. Finally, (iii) is obvious.

$\dot{x} \neq 0$, from which $(p, v) \neq (p^*, v^*)$ follows. Therefore, we find that while either D_1 or D_2 diminishes the other never increases; therefore, their sum is always diminishing, until the economy finally settles at the equilibrium point. It is now clear that D_1 and D_2, which take on positive values except at the equilibrium point, converge to zero. The stability is thus verified, independently of the technology (A, B, J), as long as substitution effects dominate over income effects in the households' demand–supply Jacobean:

$$\begin{bmatrix} \dfrac{\partial c}{\partial p} & \dfrac{\partial c}{\partial \tilde{v}} \\[2ex] -\dfrac{\partial \tilde{r}}{\partial p} & -\dfrac{\partial \tilde{r}}{\partial \tilde{v}} \end{bmatrix}.$$

It is important to note that the terms containing A, B and J disappear from the final formulae for $\dot{D}_1$ and $\dot{D}_2$, because it is assumed that (*a*) the price of a good is adjusted according to its excess demand and (*b*) the activity level of a process is adjusted according to the excess profit from the process. As will be seen below, as soon as these cross dual-adjustment rules (*a*) and (*b*) are abandoned, completely different stability conditions result.

We have so far assumed that households' demand and supply functions have been derived by the classical Walrasian procedure. That is to say, a household maximizes utility subject to the budget equation that the total expenditure on consumption goods plus the value of the reserved amounts of primary factors is equal to the total value of the endowments which the household has at that moment. Clower calls the demand for consumption goods and the supply (i.e. endowment minus reservation demand) of primary factors thus determined the notional demand and supply. Most traditional general equilibrium analyses are concerned with finding an equilibrium which is consistent with the notional demand and supply. However, as Clower emphasizes, the notional supplies of factors are not necessarily realized in Keynes' model. If some of the factors are unemployed for some reason, actual income is not equal to the notional full employment income, so that the households have to re-examine their consumption decisions, and the demands for consumption goods which are actually effective in the markets are different from the notional demands.

Let y_a^h be the actual income of household h and $u^h(c^h, s^h, d^h)$ its utility function, where c^h is a vector of the demands for consumption goods, s^h saving, and d^h a vector of the (voluntary plus involuntary) *actually* retained amounts of factors. In revising the consumption decision, d^h and y_a^h are given; u^h is maximized subject to the actual budget condition, $p'c^h + s^h = y_a^h$. We then have the active demand function $c^h = c^h(p, d^h, y_a^h)$ and the saving function $s^h = s^h(p, d^h, y_a^h)$. Taking this 'two-stage' decision rule explicitly into account, we may conceive of an economy in which prices and outputs are adjusted in the following ways: (a) the prices of commodities rise or fall according to whether they are lower or higher than the corresponding unit costs of production, and (b) outputs decrease or increase according to whether they exceed or fall short of the corresponding demands. For the sake of simplicity, we assume, in the rest of this chapter, that each industry is provided with a single production process.

Let us assume that the adjustment equations of the prices of outputs are of the type:

$$\dot{p}_i = \alpha_i[(p'A + v'B)_i - p_i] \quad (i = 1, \ldots, n), \tag{14}$$

where α_i is the adjustment coefficient, which is positive, and $(X)_i$ denotes the ith element of a vector X. (14) implies that p_i is raised if it is lower than the unit cost of production of good i and *vice versa*.

We take factor m as *numéraire*. For each of the other factors, we assume that its price is raised when its demand exceeds its notional supply and remains unchanged when the demand is less than the supply. An adjustment equation with this downwards rigidity property may be written as

$$\left. \begin{aligned} \dot{v}_k &= \beta_k \max[(Bx)_k - r_k(p, v, Y), 0] \quad (k = 1, \ldots, m-1), \\ \dot{v}_m &= 0, \end{aligned} \right\} \tag{15}$$

the adjustment coefficient β_k being obviously positive.

The actual employment of factor k cannot be greater than N_k, which is defined as

$$N_k = \min[(Bx)_k, r_k(p, v, Y)], \tag{16}$$

because of the lack of effective demand for it. This is true for all factors $k = 1, ..., m$, We define the aggregate actual income Y_a as

$$Y_a = v'N + \Pi_a, \qquad (17)$$

where Π_a represents the actual excess profit and N the column vector with components $N_1, ..., N_m$. Ignoring differences in the propensity to consume among households and effects of d^h, we have the aggregate actual consumption functions, $c = c(p, Y_a)$. We write the sum of investment, government expenditure, exports, etc. as Q, which is regarded as exogenous. (Q is a vector because our model is multi-sectoral.) Our adjustment rule for output is that x_i is increased (or decreased) if excess demand for commodity i is positive (or negative). This rule may be formulated as

$$\dot{x}_i = \gamma_i[Ax + c(p, Y_a) + Q - x]_i \quad (i = 1, ..., n), \qquad (18)$$

where γ_i is positive.

In the state of equilibrium, the speeds of the adjustment, $\dot{p}$, $\dot{v}$, $\dot{x}$, and the actual excess profit, Π_a, all vanish, but even so, full employment is not necessarily established, because in (15), the notional supply, $r_k(p, v, Y)$, may exceed industrial demand, $(Bx)_k$, for factors. Thus, like Keynes and unlike Walras, we may obtain an equilibrium with involuntary unemployment.

In this argument, obviously the two-stage decision rule plays a crucial role. But it must be noticed that the anti-Walrasian adjustment rules (14), (15) and (18) are also important. We may alternatively have, like Walras, $\dot{x}_i$ in (14) instead of $\dot{p}_i$, and $\dot{p}_i$ in (18) instead of $\dot{x}_i$;[6] this system may also produce an equilibrium with involuntary unemployment as long as the household behaves according to the two-stage decision rule and the factor prices are rigid downwards. It is recognized, however, that there is a big difference between the two systems. In the original system, if we start from an equilibrium state with unemployment, an increase in the autonomous demand for Q affects output x directly. If we assume that the new equilibrium to be established after the increase in Q is also an unemployment equilibrium, and that there is no bottleneck in any factor market on the path between the two equilibria, then wages and prices remain unchanged, so that we can easily find that an increase in Q results in an increased equilibrium output x. Therefore the total employment

---

[6] The switching rules to prevent p and x from becoming negative must be amended in an appropriate way.

Bx definitely increases, and hence unemployment definitely decreases.

The above argument assumes that the new equilibrium is stable. If there are no bottlenecks in the factor markets along the way, the stability condition is very simple, because all prices are kept constant throughout. If we assume, for the sake of simplicity, that the active consumption functions $c(p, Y_a)$ are linear with respect to income Y_a, then the new equilibrium is stable given the following two conditions: (i) the input coefficient matrix is 'productive'[7] and (ii) the average propensity to consume is less than unity. Evidently, this second condition is the stability condition obtained by Keynes.

However, this clear conclusion does not follow from the second system. An increase in the exogenous demand for commodity i, q_i, induces an increase in p_i (as we now have excess demand in the commodity market). This in turn induces an increase in profits of industry i, where the effective demand has been increased, while the profits of other industries which use the output of i as their input will diminish, because of the increase in p_i. Such a change in profits induces a change in outputs; some outputs increase and others decrease. As we now have both a price change and an income change, the net effects on the active demands for commodities are uncertain. This induced change in active demands will, in addition, give rise to changes in prices, outputs and the employment of factors, but the directions of these changes are also uncertain. In some cases the primary and induced changes are cumulative, so that the total effects may be large. If so, there will be a bottleneck in some factor market and the factor prices will then start to change. Taking into account all these changes we cannot say anything about the final net effect on total effective demand. It is not impossible that an increase in autonomous demand will give rise to a new equilibrium in which unemployment is worse than before.

Thus, an increase in Q has completely different consequences in the two economies. Unlike Walras, general equilibrium theorists do not usually discuss how output x is adjusted in the constant returns economy; they therefore do not meet the problem of choosing between the two sets of adjustment assumptions. If we choose one, we shall be led to Keynesian conclusions,

[7] For the definition of productiveness of A, see footnote 4 of Chapter 3.

while the other makes us concentrate on the neoclassical price mechanism. Although various possible adjustment assumptions have been examined in recent developments of the theory of stability of general equilibrium, most are unfortunately of the impaired neo-classical type, which lacks independent adjustment of outputs, although a new generation of mathematical economists have finally become interested in the dynamic formulation of Keynes' theory of involuntary unemployment.[8]

The above formulation of the general equilibrium of production is in contrast with the stylized one which assumes that diminishing returns to scale prevail in every sphere of production. On this point Walras wrote: 'What this fundamental distinction evidently amounts to is a division of products into two categories: one consisting of a small number of products which cannot be increased in quantity, and the other of a large number of products which can be increased without limits. This being granted, the English economists left to one side the first category and confined their attention to the second. . .'[9] This is a passage from a chapter of the *Elements* in which he criticizes the English cost theory of the price of products. We may interpret his second category as referring to the case where we have constant returns to scale. In a later part of the chapter Walras quotes from Mill, in order to allow for a third category, consisting of commodities of which more can be produced at a greater cost, that is the case of diminishing returns to scale.

However, most of the cases belonging to the third category can be reduced to the second. If the total demand for a commodity is very large in comparison with the quantity of the same commodity which a single firm can produce at a minimum cost, the commodity will be produced by a large number of small firms of the optimum size, rather than a small number of large firms. In such a case, therefore, the aggregate production function of

---

[8] As an example of the old tradition we may point to Glustoff's contribution, which dealt with the existence of an equilibrium of the Keynesian type. To find it he used a mapping of prices of the Walrasian *tâtonnement* type and gave no explicit place to the principle of effective demand in his model. He did not discuss stability, but the stability condition which would have followed from his mapping for *tâtonnement* would be more or less of the Walrasian type, rather than Keynes' stability condition (ii) above. E. Glustoff, 'On the Existence of a Keynesian Equilibrium', *Review of Economic Studies* (1968), pp. 327–34.

[9] Walras, *Elements*, p. 399.

the industry is under constant returns to scale, even if the firms in that industry are subject to diminishing returns. Walras ruled out the commodities in the third category, since he paid no attention to monopoly and confined himself to examining how competitive economies work. Also, he considered that the commodities in the first category would form only a small part of the mass of commodities daily exchanged in the market. Thus the second category embraces the majority of things bought and sold. With this conclusion, in the case of variable coefficients of production, he proceeded with his analysis of production on the assumption that production coefficients are related to one another by an implicit production equation (*équation de fabrication*), or, equivalently, that production functions are homogeneous of degree one in the factors of production employed.[10]

Finally let us show that the conditions (i) and (ii) on p. 67 imply the stability of the equilibrium outputs. As $c(p, Y_a)$ is assumed to be linear with respect to Y_a, we may write $c(p, Y_a) = c(p)Y_a + c_0$, where c_0 is a constant vector. Since prices are set in such a way that the actual excess profit Π_a vanishes, we have $Y_a = v'N$ from (17). Moreover, it is assumed that there are no bottlenecks in the factor markets, so that $N = Bx$ from (16). Therefore, (18) is reduced to

$$\dot{x}_i = \gamma_i \{[A + c(p)v'B - I](x - x^0)\}_i \quad (i = 1, ..., n), \quad (19)$$

where x^0 is the equilibrium output vector corresponding to the given final demand vector Q. As A is productive by (i), the p satisfying $p' = p'A + v'B$ is positive. On the other hand, we have $p'c(p) < 1$ by (ii). Hence, in view of $v'B > 0$, we obtain

$$p(A + c(p)v'B) < p \quad \text{for } p > 0,$$

which means the productiveness of the augmented input-coefficient matrix $A + c(p)v'B$ so that x^0 is stable; in other words, $x(t)$ obtained by solving (19) approaches x^0 as t tends to infinity.

[10] *op. cit.*, p. 384.

PART II
Economic Growth

CHAPTER 5

Capital formation and credit

Although Walras is celebrated for his studies in the utility theory of exchange and the general equilibrium theory of production, these are, in the full analysis which he offers, no more than an *hors d'oeuvre* to introduce the main dishes: the theory of capital formation and credit and the theory of circulation and money. Sometimes, *hors d'oeuvres* are more delicious and more substantial than the main dishes. But not in Walras' case; contrary to the vulgar view, I do rate his growth and money theory much more highly than his exchange and production theory. They are incomplete and need corrections and revisions, as we shall see later. Nevertheless they are serious and of a solid nature; there is no doubt that they are a masterpiece.

Unlike exchange and production theory, growth theory can no longer assume that the stocks of goods available for consumption and production are constant. They will change from period to period; capital goods for production, for example, will be worn out in use, but those newly installed by investment may be more or less in quantity than those to be replaced. Positive net investment of accumulation of stocks of goods is impossible if no individual saves, or if all goods produced are either consumed by individuals or used up by firms.

The concepts of savings and investment are utterly foreign to the conventional environment of general equilibrium analysis. They do not refer to demand for or supply of a particular commodity; we may save in the form of money, bonds or physical goods; we may invest in various commodities. Therefore, there is no particular market where aggregate savings are equated with aggregate investment. The traditional market approach in terms of demand and supply of commodities is not directly applicable to the accounting concepts such as savings and investment, unless some appropriate alterations are made to it. Thus Walras was confronted with the same problem as was later discussed by Keynes. Walras' theory of growth is not a mere application or a simple extension of the conventional general equilibrium analysis; it is a consolidation of the supply–demand and savings–investment analysis.

Walras wrote: 'consequently, it is not enough for the landed capital, personal capital and capital proper...to produce new income; our three categories of capital must also produce new capital goods proper to replace the capital goods worn out in use and destroyed by accident, and even to increase, if possible, the existing quantity of capital proper. Here we have one of the indices of economic progress. Imagine that we arrest the process of production again after a certain interval of time...as we did before; and imagine that we find an enlarged quantity of capital goods proper. That would be a sign of a progressive state. One of the characteristic traits of economic progress is an increase in the quantity of capital goods proper.'[1] 'According as the excess of income over consumption in the aggregate is greater or less than the excess of consumption over income in the aggregate, an economy is either progressive or retrogressive...New capital goods are exchanged against the excess of income over consumption; and the condition of equality between the value of the new capital goods and the value of the excess gives us the equation required for the determination of the rate of new income.'[2] These quotations make almost the same point as Harrod's proposition: 'Dynamics will specifically be concerned with the effects of continuing changes and with rates of change in the values that have to be determined ....Positive saving, which plays such a great role in the *General Theory*, is essentially a dynamic concept...In static economics we must assume that saving is zero...the so-called acceleration principle is essentially a dynamic principle.'[3]

Thus aggregate investment and savings play a very important role in Walras' growth theory. He did not encounter any particular difficulty in measuring aggregate investment.

[1] *Elements*, p. 221.
[2] *Elements*, p. 269.
[3] Harrod, R. F., *Towards a Dynamic Economics* (London: Macmillan, 1948), pp. 8–12.

Investment may be made in new capital goods to be used in future production and in consumption and capital goods to be kept either in the homes of consumers or in the bins and store-rooms of producers. Capital goods installed in factories provide productive services, while goods stored provide services of availability. These services must not be confused with the goods rendering them. C denotes the list of consumption goods and C' the list of the services of availability of consumption goods. In the case of capital goods, K denotes the list of goods, K' the list of their services of availability and K'' the list of their productive services. Let H_K be the column vector of investments in capital goods K for production and $H_{C'}$ and $H_{K'}$ be the column vectors of inventory investments in consumption and capital goods, C and K, respectively. Prices of consumption and capital goods, prices of their services of availability, and prices of the productive services of capital goods are denoted by π_C, π_K, $\pi_{C'}$, $\pi_{K'}$ and $\pi_{K''}$, respectively. They are expressed in terms of the *numéraire* (a particular consumption good a) and all row vectors. (Later we shall use p_C, p_K, etc. to express prices in terms of money.) Evidently aggregate investment (in terms of commodity prices) amounts to

$$\pi_C H_{C'} + \pi_K (H_K + H_{K'}), \qquad (1)$$

which brings forth gross income or gross returns, per period, amounting to

$$\pi_{C'} H_{C'} + \pi_{K''} H_K + \pi_{K'} H_{K'}. \qquad (2)$$

On the other hand, in measuring aggregate savings, Walras had to use a somewhat tricky method. As usual, he defined savings as the excess of income over consumption. This gives credits to savers in proportion to the amounts they have saved. However, since Walras developed his general equilibrium theory of capital formation as a real growth theory, assuming a pure credit economy in which money and other monetary goods, except bonds, are all absent, individuals can only save in his model either in the form of bonds or by increasing the quantities of durable goods they hold. The bond (B) in Walras' system consists of one unit of the *numéraire* per annum payable in perpetuity. The savings in various forms are measured in terms of it. Walras referred to the bond, when taken as the unit for measuring savings, as 'commodity E'. The price of this commodity is of course equal to the price of the bond, that is $\pi_B = 1/r$ in terms of the *numéraire*, where r represents the current rate of interest, or the rate of perpetual net income, explained later. In terms of 'commodity E' aggregate real savings are measured as E (or D_e in Walras' own notation), so that the total value of savings is $\pi_B E$ (or his $p_e D_e$).

For investment and savings decisions we may construct two different models. One assumes that investment is decided by the firms or entrepreneurs, and savings by capitalists, land-owners and workers; the former borrow from the latter the amount of savings necessary to finance their investment. The other assumes that capitalists, land-owners and workers save their income in the physical form of capital goods for production or consumption and capital goods for store; and the real capital formed in this way in the past and accumulated in the hands of the savers are lent to entrepreneurs or firms through the capital services markets. The first model is more realistic than the second, but Walras considered that from the theoretical point of view the choice between the two would be immaterial, while the first would be preferable to the second from the point of view of practical convenience. Walras then chose as his model for the theory of capital formation the second model, that is the one which he regarded as practically inconvenient.[4]

Was Walras' choice harmless? My answer to this question is conditional: it is 'Yes' as far as what I call Say's law holds true, but 'No' if not. Therefore, considering that Say's law is hardly satisfied in actual capitalist societies, especially in modern matured ones, I have to recommend the first model, rather than the one which Walras adopted. In this chapter I refrain from explaining how I reached this conclusion; I want to postpone this to a later chapter, where I discuss Say's law. As the law is closely related to the problem of monetary general equilibrium, a full explanation can be given in a more appropriate and convenient way after the introduction of money and monetary goods into the model.[5]

Walras chose the second model and confined himself to a world where Say's law prevails, so that he exhibits no

---

[4] Walras, *Elements*, p. 270.
[5] See Chapter 12 below.

logical inconsistency.[6] In this Part (and also in Part III below), however, I adopt the first model, instead of the unrealistic second one, in spite of Say's law being assumed to hold true in the main model. This departure from Walras is harmless and, in fact, very advantageous; it enables us, on the one hand, to reproduce the essentials of Walras' theory, without any significant revision, in our main model, and on the other, to generalize his theory by negating Say's law, like Keynes, so that we can examine the consequences of inconsistencies between individuals' decisions to save and firms' decisions to invest.

Let $\bar{X}_{K''}$ be the column vector of the existing quantities of capital goods installed for production in the firms, and $\bar{X}_{C'}$ and $\bar{X}_{K'}$ the column vectors of the existing stocks of consumption and capital goods stored for inventory purposes. They are the aggregate results of accumulation or saving in the past. We assume that not only investments in capital goods but also inventory investments in consumption goods are undertaken by firms or entrepreneurs; consumers who want to keep goods in their cellars or cupboards borrow the necessary quantities of the goods from firms and pay them the price of the services of availability for each period until the term of the borrowing expires. Thus, in our model, $\bar{X}_{C'}$, $\bar{X}_{K'}$ and $\bar{X}_{K''}$ are entirely owned by the firms, but they borrowed from individuals in order to invest in the past, so that they now have to pay interest to the individuals. The bond is the only medium of borrowing and lending in the model. Let $-\bar{X}_B$ be the total quantity of bonds issued by firms in the past. The total amount of interest to be paid is $-\bar{X}_B$, which is distributed among the individuals in proportion to the saving they have done in the past. We denote the interest income of individual i by $\bar{q}_{iB}$.

Although, when used for production, capital goods are worn out sooner or later, they are not all subject to the same rate of wear and tear. Let μ be the diagonal matrix having the rate of depreciation of each capital good on the diagonal. Ignoring, for simplicity, wear and tear of those consumption and capital goods which are stored in order to render services of availability, the

[6] Or more properly, we may put it in the following way: Walras adopted the second model, so that he was forced to confine himself to Say's world in order to avoid logical inconsistency.

total depreciation charge is calculated as

$$\pi_K \mu \bar{X}_{K''}, \qquad (3)$$

which is set aside and accumulated within the firms to replace those capital goods which have ceased to serve in production.

In addition to interest income, individual i receives rents if he is a land-owner, wages if he is a worker, or entrepreneurial profit if he is an entrepreneur. Let $\bar{q}_{iL}$ and q_{iL} be the column vectors of the quantities of land and labour held by i before and after trade, respectively; let π_L be the row vector of the rent and wage rates in terms of the *numéraire*. The rents and wages individual i receives will amount to $\pi_L(\bar{q}_{iL} - q_{iL})$. Let p_i be the entrepreneurial profit i earns. On the other hand he will consume consumption goods in the amounts d_{iC}, and keep them in his home in the amounts $q_{iC'}$. (Note that d_{iC} and $q_{iC'}$ are volume vectors of the same dimensionality as the total number of kinds of consumption goods.) He must pay consumption good prices for d_{iC} and the prices of the services of availability of consumption goods for $q_{iC'}$. Therefore, the saving of individual i, that is the excess of his income over the amount he pays for the goods and services he consumes, is given by

$$\pi_B e_i \equiv \pi_L(\bar{q}_{iL} - q_{iL}) + \bar{q}_{iB} + p_i - \pi_C d_{iC} - \pi_{C'} q_{iC'},$$

where e_i represents the individual's real saving in terms of 'commodity E'. As saving is done by increasing the quantity of bonds held,[7] e_i equals $q_{iB} - \bar{q}_{iB}$, where q_{iB} represents the quantity of the bond to be held after saving.

In the aggregate, overall individuals, we have

$$\pi_B E = \pi_L(\bar{Q}_L - Q_L) + \bar{Q}_B + P - \pi_C D_C - \pi_{C'} Q_{C'}, \qquad (4)$$

where capital letters, E, $\bar{Q}_L$, $\bar{Q}_B$, etc. represent the aggregates of the individuals' quantities symbolized by the corresponding lower case letters; for example, $E = \sum_i e_i$, that is the aggregate real savings in terms of 'commodity E'. In view of equation

$$\pi_B E = \pi_B(Q_B - \bar{Q}_B), \qquad (5)$$

[7] Remember that the present model assumes that no individual can save in the form of physical goods.

(4) can be put in the form

$$\pi_C D_C + \pi_{C'} Q_{C'} + \pi_B Q_B = \pi_L(\bar{Q}_L - Q_L) + P + (1 + \pi_B)\bar{Q}_B, \quad (6)$$

which is no more than the sum of the individuals' budget equations.

On the other hand, firms own the stocks of commodities $\bar{X}_{C'}$, $\bar{X}_{K'}$, and $\bar{X}_{K''}$; they used land and labour, productive services of capital goods and services of availability of consumption and capital goods in the amounts Z_L, $Z_{K''}$, $Z_{C'}$, $Z_{K'}$, and produce consumption and capital goods in the amounts X_C and X_K. They also invest in capital goods for production, to the amount H_K and make inventory investments in consumption and capital goods of $H_{C'}$ and $H_{K'}$. Entrepreneurs earn profits of the amount P. The budget equation for all firms, that is the sum of their individual budget equations, is written as

$$\pi_C X_C + \pi_K X_K + \pi_{C'}\bar{X}_{C'} + \pi_{K'}\bar{X}_{K'} + \pi_{K''}\bar{X}_{K''} + (1 + \pi_B)\bar{X}_B$$
$$= \pi_L Z_L + \pi_{C'} Z_{C'} + \pi_{K'} Z_{K'} + \pi_{K''} Z_{K''} + P + \pi_C H_{C'}$$
$$+ \pi_K(H_K + H_{K'}) + \pi_B X_B, \quad (7)$$

where $-X_B$ stands for the total quantity of bonds issued by the firms up to the end of the period; $\pi_{K'}$ and $\pi_{K''}$ are prices of services of availability of capital goods and capital services for production. This equation may be rewritten in the following form of income equation

$$[\pi_C X_C + \pi_K X_K + \bar{X}_B] - P$$
$$= [\pi_L Z_L + \pi_{C'}(Z_{C'} - \bar{X}_{C'}) + \pi_{K'}(Z_{K'} - \bar{X}_{K'}) + \pi_{K''}(Z_{K''} - \bar{X}_{K''})]$$
$$+ [\pi_B(X_B - \bar{X}_B) + \pi_C H_{C'} + \pi_K(H_K + H_{K'})]. \quad (8)$$

The left-hand side represents the aggregate income of the firms (the part in square brackets) minus entrepreneurial profit, while on the right-hand side the parts within the two pairs of square brackets give aggregate expenditure and corporate gross savings, respectively.

Let us now measure aggregate corporate savings in terms of 'commodity E' as F; then

$$\pi_B F = \pi_B(X_B - \bar{X}_B) + \pi_C H_{C'} + \pi_K(H_K + H_{K'}). \quad (9)$$

This shows that firms can save either in the form of bonds or in physical forms. In equilibrium, the total savings of the society, i.e. the sum of the individuals' savings and corporate savings, must be equal to the gross investment

$$\pi_B(E+F) = \pi_C H_{C'} + \pi_K(H_K + H_{K'}), \tag{10}$$

which is seen from (5) and (9) to be equivalent to the equilibrium condition for bonds,

$$Q_B + X_B = 0, \tag{11}$$

because $\bar{Q}_B + \bar{X}_B = 0$. Equation (11) implies that the quantity of bonds held by individuals equals the total quantity issued by firms. Of course, the same equilibrium condition should have been satisfied in the past, so that the sum of $\bar{Q}_B$ and $\bar{X}_B$ should be zero.

Given the prices of commodities, π_C, π_K, and the rate of interest, r, the prices of services of availability of consumption and capital goods, $\pi_{C'}$, $\pi_{K'}$, and the prices of the productive services of capital goods, $\pi_{K''}$, are calculated according to the following formulas:

$$\pi_{C'} = r\pi_C, \quad \pi_{K'} = r\pi_K, \quad \pi_{K''} - \pi_K\mu = r\pi_K. \tag{12}$$

It can be seen that $\pi_{K''}$ includes the depreciation charges $\pi_K\mu$, as well as the net prices of production services of capital goods K, $r\pi_K$. The formulas (12) also show that the rate of net return of each item of investment is equalized with the rate of interest. The costs of reproduction of commodities are determined on the basis of $\pi_{C'}$, $\pi_{K'}$, $\pi_{K''}$ thus calculated. Subtracting the total cost of production including depreciation,

$$\pi_L Z_L + \pi_{C'} Z_{C'} + \pi_{K'} Z_{K'} + \pi_{K''} Z_{K''},$$

from the total value of output, $\pi_C X_C + \pi_K X_K$, let us express the remainder, if there is one, as Π:

$$\Pi = \pi_C X_C + \pi_K X_K - \pi_L Z_L - \pi_{C'} Z_{C'} - \pi_{K'} Z_{K'} - \pi_{K''} Z_{K''}. \tag{13}$$

Π represents the excess profit. We then have from (4), (8) and (13) the equation

$$[\pi_L(\bar{Q}_L - Q_L)] + [\pi_{C'}\bar{X}_{C'} + \pi_{K'}\bar{X}_{K'} + \pi_{K''}\bar{X}_{K''}] + \Pi$$
$$= [\pi_C D_C + \pi_{C'} Q_{C'}] + [\pi_B(E+F)], \tag{14}$$

because $\bar{Q}_B + \bar{X}_B = 0$. This equation states that the aggregate gross income equals consumption and gross savings. On the left-hand side, the part in the first square brackets represents wages and land rents, the part in the second brackets the aggregate gross returns from capitals, C', K' and K'', and Π the excessive profit, while on the right-hand side the first part represents consumption and the second aggregate gross savings. Comparing (14) with (4), we have the equation

$$P + \bar{Q}_B = [\pi_{C'} \bar{X}_{C'} + \pi_{K'} \bar{X}_{K'} + \pi_{K''} \bar{X}_{K''}] + \Pi - \pi_B F, \quad (15)$$

that is to say, retaining the corporate gross savings within firms, the rest of the total gross profit (i.e. the aggregate gross returns from capitals *plus* the excess profit) is distributed among individuals, either as entrepreneurial profits or as interest on bonds.

Equation (15) is somewhat different from the corresponding equation in Walras' own system. First, Walras assumed the identity of the entrepreneurial profit P with the excessive profit Π, so that both P and Π disappear from (15). Furthermore, he assumed $P = 0$. Secondly, in his model stocks of capital goods $\bar{X}_{K''}$ and inventories $\bar{X}_{C'}$ and $\bar{X}_{K'}$ are held by capitalists, rather than firms; therefore, the whole of the returns from capital, including depreciation, is shared among capitalists. The part in square brackets of (15) is transferred from the left-hand side of (7) to the right-hand side of (4), as it now becomes a part of the individuals' income. Thirdly, investment is entirely decided by capitalists; so the investment terms disappear from (9) and we have $\pi_B F = \pi_B(X_B - \bar{X}_B) = \bar{X}_B$ from (7) and (9). Moreover Walras was concerned with the case of corporate savings F being absent; so $\bar{X}_B = 0$. This enables us to eliminate $\bar{Q}_B$ from the individuals' income equation (4), because it is zero by the equilibrium equation for the bond in the previous period, $\bar{Q}_B + \bar{X}_B = 0$. Then (4) can be put in the form

$$\pi_L(\bar{Q}_L - Q_L) + [\pi_{C'} \bar{X}_{C'} + \pi_{K'} \bar{X}_{K'} + \pi_{K''} \bar{X}_{K''}]$$
$$= \pi_C D_C + \pi_{C'} Q_{C'} + \pi_B E,$$

which is Walras' income equation (the last of equations (2) on p. 279 of the *Elements*) in the special case where there is no demand for K' and K'' from individuals.

In his theory of growth Walras was mainly concerned with the temporary equilibrium that will be established in a particular period, provided that prices, outputs and investments are all perfectly flexible. He wrote: '[E]quilibrium...will be established *effectively* by the reciprocal exchange between savings to be accumulated and new capital goods to be supplied *within a given period of time*, during which *no change in the data is allowed*.'[8] If all inventory investments and all net investments of new capital goods for production are positive in a state of equilibrium during a period, then an economy with a growing labour force will be expanding or progressive in that period.[9] 'Although the economy is becoming *progressive*, it remains [for the time being – W. Jaffé] *static* because of the fact that the new capital goods play no part in the economy until later in a period subsequent to the one under consideration.'[10] We may take the length of the period arbitrarily; so 'imagine...a determinate period of, let us say a day, or better a year, in order to allow for seasonal fluctuations'.[11]

In a particular period, the prices of goods and services, the rate of interest, and the quantity of consumption and capital goods produced are determined by the whole set of temporary equilibrium conditions, which will be elaborated in the next chapter, corresponding to the given initial endowments of primary factors and capital goods of the period. When the economy enters the second period, the situation will be different from that in the first. The quantities of some primary factors available at the beginning of the second period will be larger (or smaller) than those of the first, but those of other primary factors, say, land, will remain unchanged. The new Walrasian equilibrium which will be established in the second period by the same principle as that which ruled in the first will be different from the temporary equilibrium established in the first period, because of changes in the initial endowments; it will result in further changes in initial endowments in the third period. Continuing in such a manner, we have a dynamic movement through periods. In fact, Walras wrote: 'Our economy will then

---

[8] *Elements*, pp. 282–3. Walras' italics.

[9] If they are all zero or negative, the economy is stationary or retrogressive. In the case of net investment in one capital good being positive and that in another being negative, it is progressive in one direction and retrogressive in another direction.

[10] *op. cit.* Walras' italics.   [11] *Elements*, p. 378.

be ready to function, and we shall be in a position, if we so desire, to pass from the static to the *dynamic* point of view. In order to make this transition we need only suppose the data of the problem, viz. the quantities possessed, the utility or want curves, etc., to vary as a function of *time*. The *fixed* equilibrium will then be transformed into a *variable* or *moving* equilibrium, which re-establishes itself automatically, as soon as it is disturbed.'[12]

This analysis of economic growth by Walras is very similar to Hicks' approach in *Value and Capital*. It is interesting to note that Hicks took over his temporary equilibrium analysis, not from Walras, but from Marshall and Lindahl. Hicks assumed that there was an easy passage to temporary equilibrium in each period, his 'week', so that he could conceive of the economic system as following the path of moving temporary equilibria. Walras also had to make an assumption to a similar effect. He wrote: 'We shall suppose the basic data of the economic problem (viz. the quantities possessed of capital goods, the utilities of consumers' goods and services, and the utility of additions to net income) to remain fixed, so as to give us something in economics analogous to what is called a *stable system* in mechanics. Moreover, we shall assume not only that the preliminary phase of groping has been completed with equilibrium established *in principle*, but also that the phase of static equilibrium has actually commenced, so that equilibrium is established *in fact*.'[13]

But this is a very unrealistic assumption, because in the real world there are many obstacles and frictions which, in any period, prevent temporary equilibrium from being established. Also, all things are in flux. Therefore, Walras wrote: '[I]n order to come still more closely to reality, we must drop the hypothesis of an annual market period and adopt in its place the hypothesis of a continuous market. Thus, we pass from the static to the dynamic state. For this purpose, we shall now suppose that the annual production and consumption, which we had hitherto represented as a constant magnitude for every moment of the year under consideration, change from instant to instant along with the basic data of the problem... Every hour, nay, every minute, portions of these different classes of circulating capital are disappearing and reappearing. Personal capital, capital goods

---

[12] *Elements*, p. 318. Walras' italics. [13] *op. cit.* p. 378. Walras' italics.

proper and money also disappear and reappear, in a similar manner, but much more slowly. Only land capital escapes this process of renewal. Such is the continuous market, which is perpetually tending towards equilibrium without ever actually attaining it, because the market has no other way of approaching equilibrium except by groping, and, before the goal is reached, it has to renew its efforts and start over again, all the basic data of the problem, e.g. the initial quantities possessed, the utilities of goods and services, the technical coefficients, the excess of income over consumption, the working capital requirements, etc., having changed in the meantime.'[14] Thus the actual path determined in the 'continuous market' will differ from the moving equilibrium one, which the sequence of temporary equilibria trace out. Though Walras clearly and distinctly proposed a truly dynamic analysis, he could not develop it in a proper mathematical way himself.

A final remark many be helpful for understanding the model. General equilibrium theory assumes that prices are determined in markets, the prices of consumption and capital goods, π_C and π_K, in the product market, rents and wages, π_L, in the factor market, the price of the bond, π_B, or the rate of interest, r, in the bond market, and the prices of services of availability of consumption goods, $\pi_{C'}$, in the markets where consumers borrow the amounts of goods which they want to store for emergency purposes, etc., from firms, which have the stocks of these goods and lend them at the supply prices $\pi_{C'}$ determined as (12). In the case of the prices of services of availability and productive services of capital goods, $\pi_{K'}$ and $\pi_{K''}$, however, our model has no market for them, because capital goods are owned by the firms which used them, so that no capital services are traded. Therefore, $\pi_{K'}$ and $\pi_{K''}$ are not market prices but should be interpreted as imputed prices calculated by firms, according to the formula (12), in order to determine the production prices of their products.

[14] *op. cit.*, p. 380.

CHAPTER 6

A neoclassical theory of growth

Although Walras anticipated Keynes, as we shall see in the next chapter, he was a neoclassical economist. His departure from the classical school was not complete; his theory retained classical elements, such as the production–price equation with the equal rate of profit. Indeed, in the *Elements* he devoted one chapter to the Physiocrats and three chapters to the English classical school. From the neoclassical point of view, we would find in Walras many inheritances from the classical school, while from the point of view of classical economists there would be many neoclassical heterogeneities. Moreover, we find seeds which could have grown into the Keynesian principle of effective demand.

Since Walras was at a unique point of contact between three schools of economic thought, it is very important to reformulate his theory precisely and to know what he really concluded. A mere reproduction of Walras' mathematical model of capital formation is meaningless and probably misleading, because, as we saw in the last chapter, it assumes that capitalists save their income in the physical form of capital goods for production or consumption and capital goods for store, whereas in the real world investments in physical goods are decided not by capitalists but by entrepreneurs. In this chapter we give the complete set of conditions for a temporary equilibrium of capital formation and credit for the economy discussed in the last chapter, i.e. Walras' literary model, in which entrepreneurs finance their investment by the saving which capitalists have made. We derive from these conditions three rules, the rule of free goods, the rule of investment, and the rule of profitability, all of which a competitive economy must obey to be in equilibrium at some time. We also try to sketch Walras' view of how such an economy will work through time.

There are a finite number of individuals in the economy, some of whom are workers, while the remainder may be land-owners, capitalists or entrepreneurs. In addition to making the production plan of the firm, an entrepreneur decides the investment of his company; he borrows money from the capitalist for a given period and 'converts this money into capital proper [i.e. capital goods] and at the expiration of the contract he returns the money to the capitalist'.[1] In what follows we assume that he receives positive or negative entrepreneurial profit out of the excess profit of the firm as the reward for his work; he will, however, do his work even when no payment can be made for it because excess profit is zero. Therefore, in a state of equilibrium where excess profits vanish entirely, entrepreneurs have no income and, hence, cannot buy anything in the consumption goods markets. Obviously, entrepreneurs are not interested in such a state; in fact, if an equilibrium of this kind is established at every point of time, then they will lose interest in the economy, so that it cannot be maintained. They can live only in a turbulent world; we have, therefore, a paradox, that the competitive system can be reproduced and maintained only if competitive equilibrium is not realized.

For this reason a satisfactory treatment of entrepreneurs is impossible as far as we adopt the conventional approach, analysing a process of change into a series of temporary equilibria, on the assumption that no unforeseeable events happen and consequently no risks are taken. We do not propose to deal with this problem in the present chapter. We prefer to follow Walras in accepting the paradoxical hypothesis: entrepreneurs work without payment; then only workers, land-owners and capitalists remain in the markets for consumption goods as demanders at the point of time when equilibrium is established and entrepreneurs' income P vanishes. Entrepreneurs will join the game of *tâtonnement* and appear in these markets when they have non-zero incomes during the process of groping for equilibrium prices, though they have no role to play when their incomes eventually become zero. Workers' and land-owners' full employment income amounts to $\pi_L \bar{Q}_L$, capitalists receive interest $\bar{Q}_B$ from their holding of the bonds and entrepreneurs earn

[1] Walras, *Elements*, p. 228. We assume this type of financial structure. But since no money is circulated in the economy, borrowing and lending are made by issuing (selling) or buying bonds.

profit P, where we use the same notation as in the last chapter; as before, we take a particular consumption good a as the *numéraire*. The aggregate full employment income Y is the total sum of these individual incomes; thus we have

$$Y = \pi_L \bar{Q}_L + \bar{Q}_B + P. \tag{1}$$

This definition of income is different from the one used elsewhere in this book, that is $\pi_L(\bar{Q}_L - Q_L) + \bar{Q}_B + P$. But this does not cause any substantial change in the theory or the conclusions to be derived.

Throughout the following we assume, for convenience, that the aggregate demand for each consumption good is independent of the distribution of income among individuals. Such aggregate demand functions are obtained when all individuals have identical tastes. It must be noted, however, that this assumption is made only for the sake of simplicity of expression; the following discussion and conclusions are completely independent of the particular form of the demand functions.

We may then express the market demand for consumption goods D_C as a function of the price of consumption goods π_C, the prices of services of availability of consumption goods $\pi_{C'}$, wage rates and rents from various kinds of land π_L, the price of the bond π_B, and aggregate income Y:

$$D_C = D_C(\pi_C, \pi_{C'}, \pi_L, \pi_B, Y). \tag{2}$$

Similarly, the individuals' demand for services of availability of consumption goods and their demand for land and labour may be written as

$$\begin{aligned} Q_{C'} &= Q_{C'}(\pi_C, \pi_{C'}, \pi_L, \pi_B, Y), \\ Q_L &= Q_L(\pi_C, \pi_{C'}, \pi_L, \pi_B, Y), \end{aligned} \tag{3}$$

respectively, so that the excess of the existing quantity of land and labour, $\bar{Q}_L$, over the individuals' demand, Q_L, i.e. $\bar{Q}_L - Q_L$, gives the supply of land and labour to firms.

In our model capitalists do not directly own capital goods. They save a part of their income and lend it to firms, so as to enable the latter to buy new capital goods. Aggregate savings are measured as E in terms of the bond B (i.e. the perpetuity paying one unit of the *numéraire* per period). Evidently, the price of the bond π_B is the reciprocal of the interest rate r; E is obtained as savings, S (i.e. the excess of income over consumption) divided by π_B. Taking the demand functions (2) and (3) into account, we see that savings are a function of prices, $\pi_C, \pi_{C'}, \pi_L, \pi_B$ and income Y, so that E depends on the same variables. Thus we have the savings function

$$E = E(\pi_C, \pi_{C'}, \pi_L, \pi_B, Y),\qquad(4)$$

and the definitional identity

$$Y = \pi_L Q_L + \pi_C D_C + \pi_{C'} Q_{C'} + \pi_B E.\qquad(5)$$

Finally savings are made in the form of acquisition of the bond; so we have

$$\pi_B E = \pi_B(Q_B - \bar{Q}_B).\qquad(6)$$

Let us now turn to the analysis of the input–output relations. The economy consists of the consumption goods and capital goods industries. Let A_{LC} be the matrix of production coefficients of the consumption goods industries, a column of which lists the quantities of land and labour required to produce one unit of a consumption good, and $A_{K''C}$ the matrix of capital coefficients of the same industries, defined and arranged in a similar way. For the capital goods industries we have the production coefficient matrix A_{LK} and the capital coefficient matrix $A_{K''K}$. Let X_C and X_K be the column vectors of the total outputs of the consumption goods industries and of the capital goods industries. Then the aggregate demands for land and labour Z_L, and those for productive services of capital goods, $Z_{K''}$, are given by

$$\left.\begin{array}{l} A_{LC}X_C + A_{LK}X_K = Z_L, \\ A_{K''C}X_C + A_{K''K}X_K = Z_{K''} \end{array}\right\}\qquad(7)$$

respectively.

As consumers have to keep bread, meat, vegetables, oils, firewood, etc. in their homes to guard against contingent events, so producers are required to store those raw materials which they use and those final products which they sell in appropriate amounts in their storerooms or shops, in order to carry on production and trade smoothly. Throughout what follows we pay no attention to stocks of raw materials. We denote the matrices of inventory coefficients of consumption goods industries concerning consumption goods and capital goods by $J_{C'C}$ and $J_{K'C}$, respectively; a column of either lists the quantities of consumption goods or capital goods which have to be held in the store-rooms of the firm, as a precaution, per unit output of the corresponding consumption good. The inventory coefficient matrices of capital goods industries are defined in the same way and represented by $J_{C'K}$ and $J_{K'K}$. Then the total inventory demands for the stocks of consumption goods, $Z_{C'}$, and those for the stocks of capital goods, $Z_{K'}$, are determined as

$$
\begin{aligned}
J_{C'C} X_C + J_{C'K} X_K &= Z_{C'}, \\
J_{K'C} X_C + J_{K'K} X_K &= Z_{K'}.
\end{aligned}
\quad (8)
$$

Needless to say, the excess of the price of a product over its unit cost gives the profit per unit of that product. Unit costs of consumption goods include wages and rents, $\pi_L A_{LC}$, and depreciation, $\pi_K \mu A_{K''C}$, where μ is the diagonal matrix with the rates of depreciation on the diagonal, so that unit profits of consumption goods industries are given by the row vector,

$$
\pi_C - \pi_L A_{LC} - \pi_K \mu A_{K''C}.
$$

On the other hand, the production of consumption goods requires productive services of capital goods and services of availability of consumption and capital goods. As depreciation allowances have already been included in unit costs, the productive capital services required to produce consumption goods are evaluated, after deducting depreciation charges, at $(\pi_{K''} - \pi_K \mu) A_{K''C}$, the capitalized equivalent being $(\pi_{K''} - \pi_K \mu) A_{K''C}/r$. The services of availability of consumption and capital goods amount to $\pi_{C'} J_{C'C} + \pi_{K'} J_{K'C}$ or, after capitalization, $(\pi_{C'} J_{C'C} + \pi_{K'} J_{K'C})/r$. These two capitalized vectors are then summed to obtain a third vector, which lists the total capital needed for producing one unit of each consumption good.

Dividing the elements of the profit vector by the corresponding ones of the capital vector, we obtain the rates of profit of consumption goods industries. They may be different from each other; in equilibrium, however, they cannot exceed the rate of interest r, because we ignore risks entirely. This is because in the absence of risks capitalists would not lend money to entrepreneurs; instead they would themselves start a business if they found that its rate of profit would exceed the rate of interest. We thus obtain an inequality: the profit vector $\leqq r \times$ the capital vector. It is evident that a similar inequality must hold for capital goods. After rearranging terms, these inequalities may be written as:

$$\left.\begin{array}{l} \pi_C \leqq \pi_L A_{LC} + \pi_{K''} A_{K''C} + \pi_{C'} J_{C'C} + \pi_{K'} J_{K'C}, \\ \pi_K \leqq \pi_L A_{LK} + \pi_{K''} A_{K''K} + \pi_{C'} J_{C'K} + \pi_{K'} J_{K'K}. \end{array}\right\} \quad (9)$$

If (9) holds with strict inequality for some commodity, the entrepreneur producing that commodity earns negative entrepreneurial profits.

Walras himself did not put any equilibrium condition in inequality form and hence (9) appears in his system as equations. He referred to the right-hand side of (9) as the 'costs of production' of consumption or capital goods, which include unit profits at the normal rate, r. The Walrasian equations between the selling prices of commodities and their 'costs of production' imply that a uniform rate of profit has to prevail throughout all spheres of production. Clearly that set of equations can be considered as the Walrasian counterpart of Ricardo's or Marx's production price equations, from which the wage–profit frontier (or the factor–price frontier) is derived.

If the selling price of a commodity is greater than its 'cost of production', the quantity produced will increase and its selling price will fall. Conversely, if its selling price is lower than its 'cost of production', the quantity produced will diminish and its selling price will rise. This is Walras' mechanism, whereby the selling prices and the 'cost of production' are equated in equilibrium.[2] In the case of inequalities (9), however, the discrepancies between the left-hand and the right-hand sides give excessive industrial profits per unit of production; so their sum multiplied by the outputs of the respective commodities provides the aggregate excessive profits Π:

$$\Pi = \pi_C X_C + \pi_K X_K - C_C X_C - C_K X_K \quad (10)$$

where C_C and C_K represent the 'unit costs of production' of consumption goods and of capital goods, given on the right-hand sides of inequalities (9). We impose the condition that in equilibrium the total amount of profit which entrepreneurs obtain

[2] *Elements*, p. 271.

should be non-negative and should not exceed the excessive profit Π; thus

$$\Pi \geqq P \geqq 0. \tag{11}$$

It goes without saying that P is determined so as to satisfy the budget equation of the firms, i.e. equation (7) of the last chapter, which is reproduced in the form (12) below. As Zs depend on Xs by (7) and (8), this defines the firms' demand for (or supply of) the bond as a function of Xs, Hs, πs and P:

$$\pi_C X_C + \pi_K X_K + \pi_{C'} \bar{X}_{C'} + \pi_{K'} \bar{X}_{K'} + \pi_{K''} \bar{X}_{K''} + (1 + \pi_B) \bar{X}_B$$
$$= \pi_L Z_L + \pi_{C'} Z_{C'} + \pi_{K'} Z_{K'} + \pi_{K''} Z_{K''} + P + \pi_C H_{C'}$$
$$+ \pi_K (H_K + H_{K'}) + \pi_B X_B \tag{12}$$

In the last chapter, the relationships between the prices of services from commodities and their commodity prices were given, as they were by Walras, in the form of an equality, like equations (12) in that chapter. More generally, however, we may replace the equations by inequality relationships. The net rate of return from holding a unit of commodity and lending it to another person (either an individual or a firm), so as to enable him to enjoy services of availability from it, is obtained by dividing an appropriate element of $\pi_{C'}$ or $\pi_{K'}$ by the corresponding one of π_C or π_K, for a consumption good or a capital good, respectively.[3] Similarly the ratios of the elements of $\pi_{K''} - \pi_K \mu$ to the corresponding elements of π_K give the rates of net return of the respective capital goods obtained when they are employed by themselves, to produce commodities. In a state of equilibrium no firm can charge higher than normal prices for services C', K', K'', so that none of the above rates of net return exceeds the rate of interest; therefore, we have

$$\pi_{C'} \leqq r\pi_C, \quad \pi_{K'} \leqq r\pi_K, \quad \pi_{K''} - \pi_K \mu \leqq r\pi_K. \tag{13}$$

In equilibrium, equality between demand and supply is established for each good. First, the supplies of land and labour are $\bar{Q}_L$, while the demands for them are Q_L from individuals and Z_L from firms. Secondly, the quantities of capital goods already installed in the firms are $\bar{X}_{K''}$; they provide the same quantities of productive capital services, because these are

---

[3] Note that we assume that commodities do not depreciate at all when they are held as an inventory.

measured so that each unit of capital goods offers one unit of capital services. Quantities $\bar{X}_{K''}$ are confronted with the demands for capital services, $Z_{K''}$. Thirdly, inventories of consumption goods and of capital goods are available in the amounts $\bar{X}_{C'}$ and $\bar{X}_{K'}$, respectively. As for consumption goods, the services of availability are demanded by the consumers in the amounts $Q_{C'}$ and by the firms in the amounts $Z_{C'}$, while those of capital goods have no demand from individuals and go entirely to the firms, which demand them in the amounts $Z_{K'}$. Finally, in the commodity markets, consumption goods are produced by firms in the amounts X_C and are demanded by individuals in the amounts D_C or accumulated by firms in the amounts $H_{C'}$ as inventories. Capital goods are produced in the amounts X_K; they are either installed in the firms for production in the future or stored as inventories, in the amounts H_K and $H_{K'}$, respectively. In equilibrium supplies cannot fall short of the corresponding demands; thus we have the equilibrium inequality conditions:

$$X_C \geq D_C + H_{C'}, \quad X_K \geq H_K + H_{K'}, \quad \bar{Q}_L \geq Q_L + Z_L, \Big\}$$
$$\bar{X}_{K''} \geq Z_{K''}, \quad \bar{X}_{C'} \geq Q_{C'} + Z_{C'}, \quad \bar{X}_{K'} \geq Z_{K'}. \Big\} \quad (14)$$

A similar condition for the bond is written as

$$Q_B + X_B \leq 0. \quad (15)$$

The final equilibrium condition is the equality between gross savings and gross investment. Gross savings are the sum of the savings made by individuals, $\pi_B E$, and the savings of firms, $\pi_B F$. As was explained in the last chapter,[4] firms can save in a physical form as well as in the form of the bond; so we have

$$\pi_B F = \pi_B(X_B - \bar{X}_B) + \pi_C H_{C'} + \pi_K(H_K + H_{K'}). \quad (16)$$

The total saving of the amount $\pi_B(E + F)$ is equivalent with holding $E + F$ units of bonds.

On the other hand, aggregate gross investment includes investment in productive capital goods and inventory investment. They are measured, in this context, in terms of the capitalized values of the returns from investments in various goods, as $\pi_{K''}(rI + \mu)^{-1} H_K$ and $r^{-1}(\pi_{C'} H_{C'} + \pi_{K'} H_{K'})$, where I refers to the identity matrix. These amounts are equivalent to holding $\pi_{K''}(I + \pi_B \mu)^{-1} H_K$ units and $(\pi_{C'} H_{C'} + \pi_{K'} H_{K'})$ units of the

[4] See equation (9) in Chapter 5 above, p. 76.

bond, respectively, We impose a condition to the effect that in equilibrium the gross investment thus measured must be at least as large as the gross savings in terms of the Walrasian 'commodity E' (or the bond)

$$E + F \leqq \pi_{K''}(I + \pi_B \mu)^{-1} H_K + (\pi_{C'} H_{C'} + \pi_{K'} H_{K'}). \quad (17)$$

This condition is *prima facie* different from the corresponding one, i.e. condition (10) in the last chapter, in two respects. First, the present condition is an inequality and is expressed in terms of the 'commodity E', while the previous one is an equation and is in terms of total value. Secondly, in aggregating investments in individual commodities the capitalized service prices are here used as weights of aggregation, while the commodity prices were used there; so that different concepts of gross investment are used in the two places. We refer to the one in this chapter as investment at service prices and to that in the last chapter as investment at commodity prices.

These differences, however, do not have any significant effect on the conclusions. In fact, as will be seen below, they disappear when an equilibrium is established. In equilibrium the savings–investment condition (17) is satisfied with equality and gross investment at service prices becomes equal to that at commodity prices; so condition (17) is shown to be equivalent to condition (10) in the last chapter.

Now, let there be l kinds of land and labour, m kinds of consumption goods and n kinds of capital goods. The system includes $l + 2m + 3n - 1$ prices $\pi_L, \pi_C, \pi_{C'}, \pi_K, \pi_{K'}, \pi_{K''}$;[5] 1 rate of interest r, or its reciprocal π_B; $m + n$ outputs X_C, X_K; $m + 2n$ investments $H_{C'}, H_K, H_{K'}$; $2l + 3m + 2n$ demands $Q_L, D_C, Q_{C'}, Z_L, Z_{K''}, Z_{C'}, Z_{K'}$; the aggregate income Y; the aggregate entrepreneurial profit P; the excessive profit Π; the aggregate savings E and F; and the demands for the bond, Q_B and X_B. We have

$$3l + 7m + 8n + 7$$

variables. On the other hand, the system (1)–(17) consists of $2l + 3m + 2n$ demand functions (2), (3), (7), (8); $2m + 3n$ price inequalities (9), (13); $l + 2m + 3n + 1$ supply–demand conditions (14), (15); 1 income equation (1); 2 savings functions (4), (16);

[5] One of the consumption goods, say the ath one, is taken as the *numéraire*; so that the ath element of π_C always takes on the value 1.

2 demand equations for the bond (6), (12); 1 excessive profit equation (10); 2 conditions on the entrepreneurial and the excessive profit (11); 1 savings–investment condition (17); and 1 budget identity (5). We thus have $3l + 7m + 8n + 10$ conditions plus one identity.

In the original formulation of Walras all the equilibrium conditions were given in the form of equations; so he would have $3l + 7m + 8n + 10$ equations, plus one budget identity which contains $3l + 7m + 8n + 7$ unknowns.[6] He showed that, by virtue of the budget identity, one of the equations, say the savings–investment equation, can be eliminated from the system. Secondly, it is obvious that entrepreneurial profit is zero, i.e. (11) is satisfied, if the price–cost equations (9) hold. Thirdly, bearing in mind that (13) holds with equality rather than inequality and considering (6), (16) and $\bar{Q}_B + \bar{X}_B = 0$, we can see that the demand for the bond is equated with its supply, i.e. (15) holds with equality, provided that the savings–investment equation is satisfied, i.e. (17) holds with equality. Thus three equations are eliminated; there remain as many independent equations as unknowns. These elimination procedures hold *mutatis mutandis* for our revised inequality system as well.

To show this let us begin by verifying that the system satisfies Walras' law. In the context of the general equilibrium of capital formation and credit, Walras' law means that the total sum of the values of the excess demands for consumption and capital goods, land and labour, capital services for production, services of availability of consumption and capital goods, and the bond is identically zero, irrespective of whether equilibrium prices prevail or not; i.e.[7]

$$\pi_C(D_C + H_{C'} - X_C) + \pi_K(H_K + H_{K'} - X_K) + \pi_L(Q_L + Z_L - \bar{Q}_L)$$
$$+ \pi_{K''}(Z_{K''} - \bar{X}_{K''}) + \pi_{C'}(Q_{C'} + Z_{C'} - \bar{X}_{C'})$$
$$+ \pi_{K'}(Z_{K'} - \bar{X}_{K'}) + \pi_B(Q_B + X_B) \equiv 0. \tag{18}$$

[6] Strictly speaking, the number of equations in Walras' own system is different from this, because he did not allow for inventories C' and K' in his model of capital formation and credit. But the number of unknowns is also correspondingly different. Our formulation contains a few other modifications, so that the number of equations exceeds the number of unknowns by 3, rather than 1 as Walras saw from his model.

[7] Note that Walras' own model does not satisfy Walras' law.

This identity can be verified in the following way: First, taking the income equation (1), the households' saving equation (6) and the firms' budget equation (12) into account, we may write the left-hand side of (18) as

$$\pi_L Q_L + \pi_C D_C + \pi_{C'} Q_{C'} + \pi_B E - Y + (1 + \pi_B)(\bar{Q}_B + \bar{X}_B).$$

Therefore, considering $\bar{Q}_B + \bar{X}_B = 0$, we find that the value of this expression is identically zero because of the budget identity (5). We call (18) Walras' Law Form 1.

Again, in view of $\bar{Q}_B + \bar{X}_B = 0$, we find from savings equations (6) and (16) that the value of the excess demand for the bond is always equal to the excess of gross savings over gross investment in terms of *commodity* prices, so that we may put (18) in the following alternative form, which we call Walras' Law Form 2:

$$\begin{aligned}
&\pi_C(D_C + H_{C'} - X_C) + \pi_K(H_K + H_{K'} - X_K) + \pi_L(Q_L + Z_L - \bar{Q}_L) \\
&+ \pi_{K''}(Z_{K''} - \bar{X}_{K''}) + \pi_{C'}(Q_{C'} + Z_{C'} - \bar{X}_{C'}) + \pi_{K'}(Z_{K'} - \bar{X}_{K'}) \\
&+ [\pi_B(E + F) - \pi_C H_{C'} - \pi_K(H_K + H_{K'})] \equiv 0. \tag{19}
\end{aligned}$$

In (19) the aggregate investment in terms of commodity prices may further be replaced by that in terms of *service* prices. Then (19) must be revised so as to contain a residual term, representing the difference between the two values of aggregate investment. This may be split into three elementary terms, each representing the difference between the two evaluations of H_K, $H_{K'}$, or $H_{C'}$, at service prices and commodity prices. Walras' law (19) is then put in the following Form 3:

$$\begin{aligned}
&\pi_C[D_C + H_{C'} - X_C] + \pi_K[H_K + H_{K'} - X_K] + \pi_L[Q_L + Z_L - \bar{Q}_L] \\
&+ \pi_{K''}[Z_{K''} - \bar{X}_{K''}] + \pi_{C'}[Q_{C'} + Z_{C'} - \bar{X}_{C'}] + \pi_{K'}[Z_{K'} - \bar{X}_{K'}] \\
&+ \pi_B[E + F - \pi_{K''}(I + \pi_B \mu)^{-1} H_K - \pi_{C'} H_{C'} - \pi_{K'} H_{K'}] \\
&+ [\pi_{K''}(rI + \mu)^{-1} - \pi_K] H_K + [r^{-1}\pi_{C'} - \pi_C] H_{C'} \\
&+ [r^{-1}\pi_{K'} - \pi_K] H_{K'} \equiv 0. \tag{20}
\end{aligned}$$

In (20) the parts in square brackets all take on non-positive values in the state of equilibrium, whereby demand does not exceed supply for each good and for each service, as (14) requires; gross savings do not exceed gross investment in terms of the service prices as (17) requires; and none of the net rates of return from holding C', K', or K'' exceeds the rate of interest,

as (13) requires. On the other hand, prices πs and gross investments Hs are all non-negative; therefore, each term of (20) is
either zero or negative. But it is impossible for some terms to
take on a negative value, because the sum of all terms must be
zero by the Walras Law Form 3, i.e. (20). This means (i) that
the equilibrium price should be set at zero for a good, or a service,
for which demand falls short of its supply;[8] (ii) that the rate of
interest is infinity (i.e. $\pi_B = 0$) if, in terms of 'commodity E',
savings fall short of investment at the service prices; and (iii) no
investment should be made in stocks of goods which yield returns
at a rate less than the rate of interest. Proposition (i) states the
rule of pricing which is sometimes referred to as the 'rule of free
goods'; proposition (ii) is an alternative version of the rule of
free goods concerning the bond (but as will soon be seen, the
bond never becomes free); proposition (iii) gives the rule of
investment which resembles Keynes' law of the marginal
efficiency of capital.[9] From (iii) it follows that aggregate gross
investment in terms of commodity prices equals that in terms of
service prices. This, together with (ii), establishes the equality
between aggregate savings and aggregate investment at commodity prices, that is, equilibrium condition (10) in the last
chapter.

Aggregate excessive profit is defined by formula (10), which is
rewritten as

$$\Pi = [\pi_C - \pi_L A_{LC} - \pi_{K''} A_{K''C} - \pi_{C'} J_{C'C} - \pi_{K'} J_{K'C}] X_C$$
$$+ [\pi_K - \pi_L A_{LK} - \pi_{K''} A_{K''K} - \pi_{C'} J_{C'K} - \pi_{K'} J_{K'K}] X_K.$$
$$(21)$$

In equilibrium the parts in square brackets are non-positive by

[8] This further implies that the *numéraire* should not be a free good, because its
price is 1.

[9] It is seen from Walras' Law Form 1, i.e. (18), that the rule of free goods holds
for the bond as well; that is, the rate of interest is infinitely large if there is an
excess supply of the bond, or an excess of borrowing over lending, in equilibrium.
Dividing the elements of $\pi_{K'} - \pi_K \mu$ by the corresponding elements of π_K, let us
call the resulting ratios the marginal efficiencies of commodities K. Similarly, we
define the marginal efficiencies of K' and C' as the ratios of the elements of π_K and
$\pi_{C'}$ to the respective elements of π_K and π_C. Then rule (iii) in the text may
alternatively be stated in the following Keynesian way: in equilibrium, the interest
rate is not exceeded by the marginal efficiency of any good, and investment is
concentrated on those goods whose marginal efficiencies equal the interest rate.

(9); so Π too is non-positive, because outputs X_C and X_K are non-negative. On the other hand, (11) requires that Π be non-negative; hence Π, as well as the entrepreneurial profit P, cannot but be zero in equilibrium. It then follows (iv) that if excessive profit per unit of output is negative for a good, it will never be produced. Production is confined to those goods whose excessive profits are zero. By this rule of production, which is often referred to as the 'rule of profitability', the rate of return from capital is maximized in equilibrium.

When they are supplemented with the rules (i)–(iv), we can now see that three equilibrium conditions may be derived from the rest. First, if condition (13) holds with rule (iii) and condition (14) with rule (i), it follows from Walras' Law Form 3, (20), that gross savings equals gross investment at service prices, in terms of 'commodity E', that is, condition (17) is satisfied since π_B does not vanish.[10] Secondly, because of (13) with rule (iii), investment at service prices equals investment at commodity prices. Considering this, together with equations (6) and (16), we find that (15) is satisfied, as (17) holds with $\pi_B \neq 0$. Thirdly, if condition (9) holds with rule (iv), it then follows from (21) that Π is zero; that is, condition (11) is satisfied with equality. Thus we can derive three equilibrium conditions from other equilibrium conditions, in the same way as Walras did for his equation system. However it is evident that our system, where equilibrium is defined by inequalities, is less restrictive than Walras' in terms of equations; consequently, it has to be made more restrictive by supplementing it by rules (i)–(iv), in order to be able to eliminate three equilibrium conditions from the others.

We can show that there exists a temporary equilibrium; that is, the system (1)–(17) has a non-negative solution under some reasonable assumptions.[11] In the state of equilibrium the existing

[10] It is evident that no one refuses to accept the perpetuity yielding one unit of the *numéraire* per annum if it is free. Therefore, the demand for the bond exceeds its supply when $\pi_B = 0$, so that it cannot be free.

[11] I have shown that there exist general equilibrium solutions to a system that is very close to Walras' original model of capital formation and credit. See my *Equilibrium, Stability and Growth* (Oxford, 1964), pp. 83–92. That model is different, in mathematical structure as well as economic aspects, from the present one. The latter *inter alia* assumes that capitalists save and lend the amounts saved to entrepreneurs who decide investment, while in the former capitalists make both decisions, to save and to invest. Mathematically, the present model satisfies the

amounts of land and labour, the stocks of capital goods for production $\bar{X}_{K''}$ and the stocks of consumption and capital goods for inventory purposes, $\bar{X}_{C'}$, $\bar{X}_{K'}$, are fully employed, except those which are free; the full employment income Y is realized.

It must be remembered, however, that this neoclassical 'full employment' conclusion is obtained because we have assumed that not only prices πs and the interest rate r, but also outputs Xs and investments Hs, are flexibly adjusted so as to satisfy equilibrium conditions, (1)–(17). Therefore, aggregate investment,

$$\pi_{K''}(I+\pi_B\mu)^{-1}H_K+\pi_{C'}H_{C'}+\pi_{K'}H_{K'}$$

is perfectly flexible; that is to say, the system lacks a non-trivial investment function, whereas it has a well defined savings function (4). It is really because of this lack of an investment function that investment can smoothly and quickly be adjusted to savings in our model and *not* vice versa. Such an economy, with perfectly flexible investment, is said to satisfy Say's law.[12] With this law, there is no obstacle to full employment equilibrium. It is indeed because of the premise of Say's law that neoclassical economists could be confident of full employment equilibrium; therefore, it was a prime target of Keynes' attack. In fact, he rejected the perfect flexibility of investment by introducing an investment function; then he found that the system was over-determined and full employment was not attainable.

Throughout the rest of this chapter let us assume that temporary equilibrium is strongly stable in each period, so that movements of economic variables through time may satisfactorily be described by sequences of their temporary equi-

Walras law, while the previous one statisfies, instead of Walras' law, an identity to the effect that the sum of the values of excess demand over all goods and services *plus* the excess of savings over investment, *plus* the sum of the excessive profits of all industries, vanishes identically.

In spite of these apparent differences between the two models, however, the present one can be transformed into a model with the same mathematical structure as the previous one. We can, therefore, *mutatis mutandis* apply essentially the same method of proof as the one which I used in *Equilibrium, Stability and Growth*, to the system obtained by the transformation.

[12] This definition of Say's law is entirely different from the now popular definition due to Lange. See Lange, O., 'Say's Law: A Restatement and Criticism', *Studies in Mathematical Economics and Econometrics*, ed. O. Lange *et al.* (Chicago, 1942). A more comprehensive discussion of Say's law will be presented in Chapter 12 below.

librium values, entirely neglecting fluctuations in these variables during the process of equilibration in each period. For a given period let $\bar{\pi}$s, $\bar{r}$, $\bar{X}$s and $\bar{H}$s represent the temporary equilibrium values of prices, the rate of interest, outputs and investments, respectively.[13] Then, in the next period the firms are provided with initial stocks, of C', K' and K'' in the amounts

$$\bar{\bar{X}}_{C'} = \bar{X}_{C'} + \bar{H}_{C'}, \quad \bar{\bar{X}}_{K'} = \bar{X}_{K'} + \bar{H}_{K'},$$
$$\bar{\bar{X}}_{K''} = \bar{X}_{K''} - \mu \bar{X}_{K''} + \bar{H}_K,$$

respectively. On the other hand, individuals are given endowments of land and labour of the amounts $\bar{\bar{Q}}_L$. For land, the elements of the new endowment vector $\bar{\bar{Q}}_L$ will take on the same values as those of the old vector, $\bar{Q}_L$, unless land was created or destroyed during the past period, but the labour elements of $\bar{\bar{Q}}_L$ will probably be larger than the corresponding ones of $\bar{Q}_L$, because of the natural growth of the labour force. With $\bar{\bar{Q}}_L$, $\bar{\bar{X}}_{C'}$ $\bar{\bar{X}}_{K'}$ and $\bar{\bar{X}}_{K''}$ a new temporary equilibrium is established; in this second period, equilibrium prices, $\bar{\bar{\pi}}$s, and the equilibrium rate of interest, $\bar{\bar{r}}$, prevail in the market; commodities are produced in the amounts $\bar{\bar{X}}_C$, $\bar{\bar{X}}_K$, and investments in C', K' and K'' are made in the amounts $\bar{\bar{H}}_{C'}$, $\bar{\bar{H}}_{K'}$ and $\bar{\bar{H}}_K$.

The temporary equilibrium established in the second period is different from that in the first, unless we have $\bar{Q}_L = \bar{\bar{Q}}_L$, $\bar{X}_{C'} = \bar{\bar{X}}_{C'}$, $\bar{X}_{K'} = \bar{\bar{X}}_{K'}$ and $\bar{X}_{K''} = \bar{\bar{X}}_{K''}$. The last three of these conditions require that $\bar{X}_{C'}$, $\bar{X}_{K'}$ and $\bar{X}_{K''}$ be the particular amounts of stocks that would generate a temporary equilibrium with $\bar{H}_{C'} = 0$, $\bar{H}_{K'} = 0$ and $\bar{H}_K = \mu \bar{X}_{K''}$. Thus, except in some very special cases, temporary equilibria are not permanent or stationary, but moving; endowments of land and labour will change and stocks of goods will be accumulated from period to period. If the economy was moving in the second period, it carries out *tâtonnement* in the third period with new endowments and accumulated stocks, and the temporary equilibrium established in the third period is different from that in the second. Walras took a sequence of moving equilibria obtained in this

---

[13] Note that the bar which we now apply to an output variable X_C or X_K and the bar which we have applied to a stock variable have completely different implications. $\bar{X}_C$, $\bar{X}_K$ stand for *equilibrium* outputs of C and K, while $\bar{X}_{C'}, \bar{X}_{K'}, \bar{X}_{K''}$ represent the _initial_ stock of C', K' and K''.

manner as simulating, in some tolerable degree, the process of change that happens in the actual economy through time.

We have so far assumed that the production coefficients and inventory coefficients are given and do not figure as unknowns of the problem. However, except in the extreme case of one and only one method of production being available to each industry, they are not determined *a priori*; rather, entrepreneurs can choose methods of production from the list of alternatives. Walras explained the problem of choice of techniques by marginal productivity theory and considered production coefficients as depending on relative factor prices.[14] On the basis of the variable production coefficients thus determined he derived the laws which he called 'the laws of variation of prices in a progressive economy'.[15] They are, I believe, of far-reaching importance and may be considered as the Walrasian version of Marx's 'general law of capitalist accumulation'.

Unfortunately Walras did not give a rigorous proof of the laws; it would be more appropriate to call them conjectures. In fact, in order to establish them exactly, some additional, restrictive conditions have to be imposed. We need, for this purpose, a number of comparative statics laws, but generally we have only a meagre collection which is not enough to verify Walras' conjectures. Nevertheless, we must say that the conjectures would be true *de facto*, though not on an *a priori* basis, and are in accord with neoclassical economists' standard view of economic growth. While not intending to spell out in detail the list of the conditions for his conclusions, we are content here to summarize his reasoning and conclusions.

Walras discussed the matter in the following way. First, if the respective quantities of a given type of land-service required for the production of single units of consumption and capital goods remained unchanged, then it would be impossible to produce more than certain quantities of commodities determined by the existing quantity of that type of land. However, in the case of many alternative methods of production being available to the firms, it is possible to save quantities of land-services per unit of output of consumption and capital goods, by increasing the

---

[14] However, he was never concerned with variableness of inventory coefficients. He had no theory of portfolio selection and no theory of inventory investment.

[15] *Elements*, p. 382.

quantities of the services of capital goods employed. 'The indefinite multiplication of products can only take place to the extent that capital-services can be substituted more and more for land-services though never wholly replacing them. We have to distinguish between two cases...*economic* progress [and]... *technical* progress.'[16] We can then easily understand the following proposition of Walras: 'Progress, which consists in [an increase in consumption per man] along with an increase in population, is possible, in spite of the failure of the quantity of land to increase, thanks to the increase in the quantity of capital goods proper, provided, however, that this increase in the quantity of capital goods proper precedes and is proportionately greater than the increase in population.'[17]

However, entrepreneurs will substitute capital for land only when rents rise and the interest rate falls. 'In production entrepreneurs will pay higher rent, but they will employ less land-services in the manufacture of their products. They will pay lower interest charges, but they will employ more capital-services. Thus costs of production will remain approximately the same as they were before and will be equal, or very nearly equal, to selling prices. The land-owners, workers and capitalists, in their role as consumers, will sell less land-services, but they will sell them more dearly. They will sell more capital-services, but they will sell them less dearly. Thus they will have nearly the same income as before, and they will, on the whole, be able to buy at least the same quantity of the same products at approximately the same selling prices which will continue to be equal, more or less, to the costs of production.'[18]

After these arguments Walras proposed the following two laws. First: '*In a progressive economy, the price of labour (wages) remaining substantially unchanged, the price of land-services (rent) will rise appreciably and the price of capital-services (the interest charge) will fall*

---

[16] *Elements*, p. 383. Walras' italics. He distinguished 'economic progress', whereby some scarce factors of production are substituted by other less scarce factors, from 'technical progress', whereby the production function itself shifts as a result of an invention. In deriving 'the laws of the variation of prices in a progressive economy' Walras disregarded technical progress and considered only economic progress, though he recognized that both kinds would take place simultaneously in the actual world.

[17] *Elements*, p. 387. (Italicized in the original text.)

[18] *Elements*, p. 390.

appreciably.'[19] Secondly: Because the prices of capital services fall while the prices of capital goods, equal to their cost of production, remain almost constant, '*in a progressive economy the rate of net income* [hence, the rate of profit] *will fall appreciably*'.[20]

The second law is comparable with Marx's 'law of the tendency of the rate of profit to fall',[21] from which he concluded that capitalism should sooner or later reach deadlock. But, in contrast, Walras emphasized the first law and wrote: 'The truth is that a progressive rise in the values of land and its services, which may take place without necessarily bringing about an increase in the value of its products, is, along with the expansion of capital and population, the essential characteristic of economic progress.'[22] Walras' view of social reform, that the state should take over private properties such as land, natural monopolies, etc., is perfectly consistent with this analytical conclusion. He concludes: 'By clearly demonstrating this truth, pure economics sheds as much light on social economics, as in other respects, it sheds on applied economics.'[23]

[19] *Elements*, pp. 390–1. Walras' italics.

[20] *Elements*, p. 391. Walras' italics.

[21] This states: 'the gradual growth of constant capital in relation to variable capital must necessarily lead to a gradual fall of the general rate of profit, so long as the rate of surplus-value, or the intensity of exploitation of labour by capital, remain the same'. K. Marx, *Capital*, Vol. III, Progress Publishers, Moscow, 1966, p. 212.   [22] *Elements*, pp. 391–2.   [23] *ibid.*

CHAPTER 7

Towards Keynes

In the Tokugawa period, when Christianity was prohibited in Japan, a picture of Christ or Mary was used as a test of faith. If a suspected Christian would desecrate the picture by treading on it, this proved his innocence. Is there such a powerful test for finding Keynesians or anti-neoclassicists? Some might think that the type of production function assumed would serve as the litmus paper. In fact, Solow argued that, in the Harrod–Domar model, with no substitution between capital and labour, equilibrium growth would be stable, while the neoclassical growth path of full employment of labour and full utilization of capital would converge to the steady equilibrium-growth path if substitutions between capital and labour were possible. Others, perhaps students of Nicholas Kaldor and Joan Robinson, might think that the marginal productivity or 'double switching' thesis would serve the purpose, although the latter has finally recognized the unimportance of the latter proposition.[1]

We are interested here in the problem of identifying the two schools of economists in the long-run context, as was done in the 1930s and 1940s, just after the publication of Keynes' *General Theory*, for the short-run context. However, the criteria proposed above were not used as a test in the 1930s and 1940s. Keynes' theory of the short-run underemployment equilibrium is perfectly consistent with the marginal productivity theory, as well as substitutions between capital and labour. In this chapter, comparing the Walrasian neoclassical general equilibrium model with the Keynesian, we shall show that in the long-run context, too, the production function is irrelevant for distinguishing between the two theories and that the tests for short-run identification, such as the negation of Say's law, the downwards rigidity of the wage rate, and the savings–investment theory of income determination,

[1] Robinson, J., 'The Unimportance of Reswitching', *Quarterly Journal of Economics*, Vol. 89, No. 1 (February 1975), pp. 32–9.

can serve the purpose in the long-run context as well, if they are carried out in an appropriate way. We shall derive Keynes' theory from Walras' model by removing Say's law from the latter, which was constructed under the obvious influence of Ricardo and, therefore, assumed Say's law. Indeed, it is the main purpose of this book to show how close Walras was to Keynes. Walras could easily have found a microeconomic version of Keynes' theory, if he had been more deeply involved in the analysis of investment; in this sense he could be considered as an anticipator of Keynes.

The Keynesian model to be developed in this chapter shares the following features with the neoclassical model in the last chapter: there is no government expenditure and there are no exports; the monetary aspects of the economy are all disregarded;[2] it consists of two groups of industries producing consumption goods and capital goods, respectively. We assume that each industry is not provided with a smooth production function but has a finite number of discrete production processes, instead of a single one as it had in the last chapter, from which it chooses the one which maximizes the rate of profit. Thus the smoothness (or differentiability) of the production functions is not assumed, because it is one of our purposes to show that this has nothing to do with the division of economists into the two schools. The choice of techniques is made according to marginal productivity theory in the broad sense, and as we assume there are many kinds of capital goods, there are 'double switching' possibilities.

The models differ mainly in the following points: the Walrasian neoclassical model assumes the household's demand and supply functions, which are derived by maximizing utility subject to the budget constraint. The budget constraint restricts the household's demand for goods, demand for land, leisure and savings, so that their total value does not exceed the total value of the household's income. When there is no satiation point, utility is maximized at a point where the constraint is fulfilled with equality; that is to say, consumption plus savings plus demand for (or retention of) land and labour equals the total value of land and labour which the household could offer, plus the total

---

[2] Except in a few paragraphs at the end of the chapter. Taking account of the monetary aspects, the problem will be revisited in Chapter 12 below.

interest income from the bonds it owns, plus the entrepreneurial profit it receives from the firms (if the head of the household is an entrepreneur). Using the notation of the previous chapter, we may write the sum of the budget equation over all households as

$$\pi_L Q_L + \pi_C D_C + \pi_{C'} Q_{C'} + \pi_B E = \pi_L \bar{Q}_L + \bar{Q}_B + P, \qquad (1)$$

where, on the left-hand side, the first term represents the total value of the demands for land and labour, the sum of the second and third terms consumption and the fourth savings, while, on the right-hand side, the first term represents the households' full employment income from land and labour, the second their interest income, and the third entrepreneurial profit. On the other hand, the firms' demands and supplies satisfy the corporate budget equation[3]

$$\pi_C X_C + \pi_K X_K + \pi_{C'} \bar{X}_{C'} + \pi_{K'} \bar{X}_{K'} + \pi_{K''} \bar{X}_{K''} + \bar{X}_B$$
$$= \pi_L Z_L + \pi_{C'} Z_{C'} + \pi_{K'} Z_{K'} + \pi_{K''} Z_{K''} + P + \pi_C H_{C'}$$
$$+ \pi_K (H_K + H_{K'}) + \pi_B (X_B - \bar{X}_B), \quad (2)$$

where the difference between the sum of the first two terms on the left-hand side (i.e. the value of outputs) and the sum of the first four terms on the right (i.e. the value of inputs) gives the excessive profit of the firms, Π, while the sum of the last three terms on the right-hand side gives corporate savings, $\pi_B F$.

Equation (2) says that total gross profit (i.e. the normal gross profit from goods C', K', K'' plus the excessive profit) is distributed among entrepreneurs after deducting gross savings and paying interest on the bond. Adding (1) and (2) and considering $\bar{Q}_B + \bar{X}_B = 0$,

$$\pi_L Q_L + \pi_C D_C + \pi_{C'} Q_{C'} + \pi_B (E + F)$$
$$= \pi_L \bar{Q}_L + \pi_{C'} \bar{X}_{C'} + \pi_{K'} \bar{X}_{K'} + \pi_{K''} \bar{X}_{K''} + \Pi. \qquad (3)$$

As excessive profit vanishes in equilibrium, it is seen from (3) that consumption (including the individuals' demands for land and labour) plus savings (including the corporate savings) equal the full-employment, full-capacity income, that is the sum of the first four terms on the right-hand side of (3). Thus consumption

[3] Equation (2) is no more than a reproduction of equation (12) in Chapter 6. Reference has also to be made to (16) there.

and savings are determined so as to add to the full-employment, full-capacity income.

However, these neoclassical consumption and savings functions are not appropriate to explain the consumption and savings behaviour of the household in modern society, especially that of the working class. As has been recognized by Keynesians, the wage rate is hardly ever lowered, even when there are workers who cannot find an employer in the market; a strong downwards rigidity of the wage rate prevails. Because of the involuntary unemployment which may be caused in this way, actual income may differ from full-employment, full-capacity income. The disappointed household has to revise its consumption and savings schedules so that they are consistent with its actual income. The consumption function which is active and effective in the market is the one which is obtained after this re-examination; similarly for actual savings; therefore, the actual consumption and savings are different from the neoclassical, notional ones, which could be effective only if the household were actually fully employed. In the Keynesian model, this two-stage decision-making is explicitly taken into account.[4] Thus, one of the distinguishing characteristics between the two models is the one- versus two-stage decision-making process.

Secondly, a device which is complementary to two-stage decision-making is the downwards rigidity of factor prices. In the general equilibrium model of the traditional Walrasian type, it is assumed that all prices are perfectly flexible, so that in equilibrium, demand is equated to supply, unless the good is free. This consequence of the postulate of perfectly flexible prices contradicts what actually happened in the UK in the 1920s: a large amount of unemployment persisted, while the wage rate did not fall significantly. Keynes, in looking at this, modified the wage adjustment hypothesis so that the wage rate would be raised if there was excess demand for labour, but remained unchanged if there was excess supply. In our Keynesian model, we enforce this downwards rigidity hypothesis so that it holds not only in the labour market, but also in the land and capital

[4] Clower, R. W., 'The Keynesian Counterrevolution: A Theoretical Appraisal', in F. H. Hahn and F. P. R. Brechling (eds.), *The Theory of Interest Rates* (London, Macmillan; New York, St Martin's Press). Also, see Morishima, *The Economic Theory of Modern Society* (Cambridge University Press, 1976), pp. 335–6.

markets. In fact, as we have often observed, land rents and the prices of capital services (and hence profits) do not fall to zero even though existing land and capital are not fully utilized. In our Keynesian model, the price mechanism works very differently in the factor markets from the way it works in the commodity markets, where prices are flexible in both directions, upwards and downwards. In the neoclassical model, in contrast, there is no such distinction between factor and commodity markets.

Thirdly, neoclassical growth theorists, like Walras in his general equilibrium model of capital formation and credit, assume that investment is completely adjusted to savings. There is no specific non-trivial investment function. This assumption of the perfect adaptability of investment to savings was rejected by Keynes. Saving is decided by capitalists and investment by entrepreneurs, so that they are independent of each other; the former is in accord with the individuals' propensity to consume, while the latter with the firms' investment function. As will be seen later, an independent investment function is an obstacle to the realization of the neoclassical full-employment, full-capacity equilibrium. The aggregate demand which corresponds to the full supply of labour, land and capital stocks is not necessarily created. Say's law, asserting that supply creates its own demand, does not work. It is negated and replaced by the Keynesian principle of effective demand, to the effect that aggregate effective demand determines the actual level of aggregate income.

As a plausible investment function we may assume one of the adaptable acceleration principle types proposed by Harrod, according to which the ratio of investment to the existing stock of capital depends on the degree of excess capacity of the capital stock.[5] When only part of existing capital is used for production, the current rate of investment is judged as being more than required, so that the rate of investment will be decreased and even the present level of utilization of capital will hardly be maintained. More excess capacity will follow and the rate of investment will decrease further. In this way, an adverse divergence process from the full-employment, full-capacity equi-

[5] Morishima, M., *Theory of Economic Growth* (Oxford University Press, 1969), pp. 61-3.

librium will start. This is an instability process, known as the Harrodian process. On the other hand, in the neoclassical model, where investment and prices adjust perfectly, full employment of capital, land and labour is established without any difficulty, so that there is no problem of Harrodian instability.

These three differences between the Keynesian and neoclassical economies were discussed in the short-run context before the Second World War. In this chapter it is pointed out that the same differences are important in distinguishing Keynesian from neoclassicists in the long-run context. To show this I do not pay particular attention to post-war elements such as double switching, the Pasinetti long-run distribution equilibrium and so on, with the intention of showing their irrelevance.[6] In the following we shall be concerned with an economy where some industries may have diminishing returns to scale. The extension of the case of all industries having constant returns to scale to the more general case of diminishing returns being possible will affect the laws of working of the economy that result. If the economy is of the neoclassical type (i.e. if Say's law prevails), there is no substantial change in the conclusions, but in the case of the Keynesian economy clear-cut policy recommendations such as Keynes proposed cannot be made if industries with diminishing returns to scale play a considerable part in the economy. Consequently, the dominance of constant-returns-to-scale industries must be considered as one of the premises for Keynes' principle of effective demand.

Our Keynesian model works in the following way. As the assumption of perfect flexibility of factor prices in both directions is replaced by that of one-directional flexibility, an excess supply of labour, land or capital services gives rise to no change in their prices, while an excess demand raises the prices in the same way as in the neoclassical model. Beginning with prices of land and labour arbitrarily given, the prices of consumption and capital goods and the prices of capital services will be determined so that the price–cost inequalities and the marginal-efficiency-of-capital inequalities, i.e. (9) and (13) in Chapter 6, are satisfied.

---

[6] We can show that double switching may occur in the neoclassical model as well and that the Pasinetti long-run equilibrium is consistent with the neoclassical hypothesis. See for the first, my *Equilibrium, Stability and Growth*, pp. 122–30, and for the latter my *Theory of Economic Growth*, pp. 34–43.

For the sake of simplicity, we assume that there is only one set of techniques which is superior to all others. If at these prices, there prevails an excess supply in factor markets, there will be no change in the factor prices and hence in the product prices, so that our economy is now reduced to that which Hicks called 'the fixprice economy'.[7]

In what circumstances do we have an excess supply in the factor markets? In the neoclassical economy, there is no independent investment function; investment is adjusted to saving. But in the Keynesian economy, causality is reversed. Investment is independently determined, either autonomously or according to an investment function. Then saving is adjusted to investment, and the demands for consumption goods are determined so as to be consistent with the amount of saving thus determined. For example, in a special case where the propensity to save and the propensity to consume each commodity depend only on prices and the rate of interest and are independent of the level of income, the demands for consumption goods and aggregate savings are determined so as to be proportional to these propensities. If the aggregate gross investment is given at a low level, then saving is low, so that the demands for consumption goods are also small; needless to say, the total value of capital goods produced to meet the gross investment is scanty. Thus a sufficiently low investment produces a state where capital goods and consumption goods are all produced in small quantities, so that the demands for factors of production are also small. There must be unemployment in the land and labour markets; the existing capital is underutilized and the existing inventories are sufficient. On the other hand, if investment is not set at a low level, we have a bottleneck in some or all factor markets and the factor prices will be revised. This has repercussions on commodity prices via the price–cost inequalities.

We have now determined the outputs of consumption and capital goods. Therefore, we now have the total national product. When investment is given as small, this total national product is produced with unemployment of some labour and some capital stock, so that it is less than the full-employment, full-capacity output. The actual national income is then lower than the full-employment, full-capacity income; the neoclassical premise that

[7] See Hicks, J. R., *Capital and Growth* (Oxford University Press, 1965), p. 28.

all factors are fully employed is no longer true. There must be some disappointed workers and capitalists. They are unsuccessful in achieving the potential or target income which they planned originally, and therefore they cannot enjoy the level of consumption for which they hoped when they maximized their utility subject to the budget equation. These people are forced to be satisfied with a lower income and their consumption plan is revised to be consistent with their actual income.

Thus, equilibrium with unemployment occurs if the aggregate gross investment is sufficiently small. It must be emphasized, however, that the degree of smallness required depends on the prevailing factor prices. Suppose we have an under-employment equilibrium when the prices of land and labour are set at π_L^0 and investment is at I^0. The price-cost inequalities and the marginal-efficiency-of-capital inequalities determine the prices of consumption goods, capital goods, capital services and services of availability of consumption and capital goods, corresponding to the given prices of the primary factors of production. (The price of the representative consumption good is fixed at one because it is taken as the *numéraire*.) Let us assume for the sake of simplicity that an increase in the prices of the factors of production from π_L^0 to π_L^1 does not give rise to any change in the techniques adopted; even in this case it has effects, positive or negative, on the other prices and the rate of interest. That is to say, the new prices and the new interest rate corresponding to π_L^1 are higher or lower than the old. Since the propensities to consume commodities depend on prices and the interest rate, the demands for consumption goods will change. Also, if aggregate gross investment remains at I^0 in spite of these changes, the demands for capital goods will change, because if they were unchanged, their total value evaluated at their new prices would not equal I^0. After the change in outputs of consumption and capital goods to meet the new demands for them, the demands for labour and capital services may have been increased or decreased. Therefore, the given amount of I^0 may be too big to produce no excess demand for factors (or may still be insufficient to generate full-employment equilibrium).

In fact, in the case of the two-sector economy with one consumption good, one capital good and no land, it can be shown that an increase in the real wage rate, w, gives rise to an increase in the price p of the capital good, provided that the consumption good industry is more capital-intensive than the capital good industry, so that, with aggregate gross real investment ph being fixed, the demand h for the capital good is decreased, while the demand d for the consumption good remains unchanged, as the inter-sectoral multiplier $d = (c/s)\,ph$ shows, where c is the average propensity to consume and s the average propensity to save.[8] Thus the output of one industry decreases while that of the other does not increase, so that the total demands for labour and capital services must decline. Therefore, at a higher (or lower) level of real wages, a bigger (or smaller) amount of real investment is necessary to establish a state of full-employment equilibrium.[9]

On the other hand, let us consider a case where investment is increased, keeping the factor prices unchanged. As this induces no change in product prices, the same techniques are adopted by the industries. An increase in investment certainly has repercussions on the outputs of consumption and capital goods industries; that will all be increased according to the Leontief inter-industrial multiplier formula. Therefore we expect, from an increase in investment, certain decreases in unemployment, until investment reaches a critical value where one of the factor markets meets a bottleneck.

We have so far tacitly assumed that all industries have constant returns to scale, but this is an unrealistic assumption, at least for the short-run analysis, and Keynes' model does not exclude industries with diminishing returns. In the following we consider, for the sake of simplicity, a four-good, three-factor economy: commodities 1 and 2 are consumption goods and 3 and 4 are capital goods. The industries producing the odd-numbered commodities have diminishing returns to scale, while those producing even-numbered commodities have constant returns to scale. Labour is the sole primary factor of production, and there is no inventory investment. Finally we neglect depre-

---

[8] We assume that c and s are constant. The multiplier directly follows from $d = cY$ and $ph = sY$, where Y is the aggregate real income.

[9] When the real wage rate is fixed at zero, the price p of the capital good will be $p = a/\alpha$, where a is the capital coefficient of the capital good industry and α that of the consumption good industry. If such a p is not sufficiently low, a given real investment I^0 does not produce a large investment demand for capital goods; so we may have unemployment. Thus, if I^0 is set at a sufficiently low level, a wage cut, even to zero wages, does not bring forth full employment.

ciation. These assumptions for simplicity are harmless; we would obtain the same conclusions without them.

Let X_i be the output of industry i. Outputs of the odd-numbered industries X_1 and X_3 depend on prices, because of diminishing returns to scale, while outputs of the even-numbered industries X_2 and X_4 can vary independently, because of constant returns to scale. There are three factors of production: labour and the two services from capital goods 3 and 4. Let N_{ji} be the demand for factor j of industries $i = 1, 3$. They are given as functions of prices. The demand for the factors of industries $i = 2, 4$ are given as $a_{ji} X_i$, where a_{ji} is the production coefficient which depends on prices.

The households' demands for the consumption goods 1 and 2 depend on prices and, in view of the two-stage decision rule, on actual income. As demands for labour and capital services do not exceed their supplies in the state of equilibrium, as will be seen later, actual income will be

$$
\begin{aligned}
Y = {}& w(N_{01}+N_{03}+a_{02}X_2+a_{04}X_4) \\
& + q_3(N_{31}+N_{33}+a_{32}X_2+a_{34}X_4) \\
& + q_4(N_{41}+N_{43}+a_{42}X_2+a_{44}X_4) + \Pi_1 + \Pi_3
\end{aligned} \qquad (4)
$$

where w is the wage rate and q_3 and q_4 the prices of the capital services from capital goods 3 and 4, and where subscript o stands for labour and 3 and 4 for the capital services from capital goods 3 and 4. Π_1 and Π_3 are the excessive profits of the industries 1 and 3 with diminishing returns to scale. (The excessive profits are zero for the industries with constant returns to scale.) Denoting the prices of goods by p_i, $i = 1, 2, 3, 4$, Π_i is written as

$$
\Pi_i = p_i X_i - wN_{0i} - q_3 N_{3i} - q_4 N_{4i} \quad (i = 1, 3), \qquad (5)
$$

which is, in view of (6) and (7) below, a function of prices only.

We denote investments in capital goods 3 and 4 by H_3 and H_4, total savings by S, the existing stocks of capital goods by K_3 and K_4, and the labour force by L. We now have the following functions:

the supply functions of output:

$$
X_i = X_i(p_i, w, q_3, q_4) \quad (i = 1, 3); \qquad (6)
$$

the demand functions of factors:

$$N_{ji} = N_{ji}(p_i, w, q_3, q_4) \quad (i = 1, 3; j = 0, 3, 4); \qquad (7)$$

the production coefficients:

$$a_{ji} = a_{ji}(p_i, w, q_3, q_4) \quad (i = 2, 4; j = 0, 3, 4). \qquad (8)$$

Functions (6) and (7) are obtained by maximizing profit Π_1 or Π_3 subject to the production function of industry 1 or 3, which has diminishing returns to scale, while functions (8) are obtained by minimizing the unit cost of production[10] subject to the production function of industry 2 or 4, which has constant returns to scale.

The equilibrium conditions are:

the price–cost equation for the industries with constant returns to scale:

$$p_i = wa_{0i} + q_3 a_{3i} + q_4 a_{4i} \quad (i = 2, 4); \qquad (9)$$

the equal rates of return of capital goods:

$$q_3/p_3 = q_4/p_4; \qquad (10)$$

the demand–supply conditions for the consumption goods industries:

$$\left.\begin{aligned} D_1(p_1, p_2, Y) &= X_1(p_1, w, q_3, q_4), \\ D_2(p_1, p_2, Y) &= X_2; \end{aligned}\right\} \qquad (11)$$

the demand–supply conditions for the capital goods industries:

$$\left.\begin{aligned} H_3 &= X_3(p_3, w, q_3, q_4) \\ H_4 &= X_4; \end{aligned}\right\} \qquad (12)$$

the demand–supply conditions for factors:

$$\left.\begin{aligned} N_{01} + N_{03} + a_{02}X_2 + a_{04}X_4 &= L, \\ N_{31} + N_{33} + a_{32}X_2 + a_{34}X_4 &= K_3, \\ N_{41} + N_{43} + a_{42}X_2 + a_{44}X_4 &= K_4; \end{aligned}\right\} \qquad (13)$$

[10] i.e. wage cost plus capital cost per unit of output.

the aggregate investment equation:

$$p_3 H_3 + p_4 H_4 = I; \tag{14}$$

the investment–savings equation:

$$I = S(p_1, p_2, Y). \tag{15}$$

In this system, equation (10) is considered as an equation for determining the prices of productive services of capital goods. The ratio of q_i to p_i equals the normal rate of return; so that the q_3 and q_4 calculated according to (10) represent the normal prices of capital services. Substituting them into (9) we obtain the normal production price of commodities 2 and 4. It should be noted that the rates of profits derived from (9) and (10) give the (normal) rates to the capital stock used, but not the actual rates to the stock of capital which the respective industries actually have. As far as capital goods are fully utilized, the actual rates of profit of industries 2 and 4 are equalized to the normal rate. But, as will be seen below, if (13) is violated and there is an idle capacity in either capital good, the actual rates may differ between industries 2 and 4, depending on their degrees of utilization of capital stocks.

Next, the aggregate investment I is regarded as given. The variables are four commodity prices p_i, two prices of capital services q_i, the real wage rate w, two outputs of the industries with constant returns to scale X_i, two investments H_i, two excessive profits Π_i, and income Y. One of the prices, say p_2, is fixed at one by taking consumption good 2 as the *numéraire,* so that the system consisting of (4), (5) and (9)–(15) contains thirteen unknowns, while it has fifteen equations. As we have the identity (Walras' law)

$$Y = p_1 D_1 + p_2 D_2 + S, \tag{16}$$

one of the equations, say the first equation of (11), can be derived from the others. But, after the elimination, the system is still overdeterminate.[11]

This problem can be solved in two ways. The first solution, which was adopted by Walras, assumes that investment is not determined independently but is adjusted to saving. In our

[11] The problem of overdeterminacy will be discussed again in Chapter 12 below.

present case, this means that $p_3 H_3 + p_4 H_4$ need not be equated with a given value of I. Equations (14) and (15) are reduced to a single equation,

$$p_3 H_3 + p_4 H_4 = S(p_1, p_2, Y).$$

The number of independent equations becomes equal to the number of unknowns.

However, Keynes did not adopt this way of solving the problem because he did not accept Say's law, which is equivalent to assuming that investment is perfectly flexible and adjusts to saving without any obstacle. He took aggregate investment as given (or determined by an independent function) and the real wage rate as a parameter. A subsystem consisting of twelve equations, say (4), (5), (9)–(12), the second equation of (13) and (14), will then determine the values of the remaining twelve unknowns.[12] He then replaced the first and third equations of (13) by inequalities

$$\left. \begin{array}{l} N_{01} + N_{03} + a_{02} X_2 + a_{04} X_4 \leqq L, \\ N_{41} + N_{43} + a_{42} X_2 + a_{44} X_4 \leqq K_4, \end{array} \right\} \quad (17)$$

and found the values of w which establish both of the above inequalities. If one of them is not fulfilled, the wage rate changes, while if both are fulfilled, even though either holds with strict inequality, there is no further change in w. This asymmetric behaviour of w is due to the assumed upwards flexibility and downwards rigidity of the wage rate.

In more detail, the system may be solved in the following way. We take w as a parameter and normalize prices so that $p_2 = 1$. Then the three equations (9) and (10) include unknowns p_3, q_3, p_4 and q_4; so given p_3, the other three are determined. Next we can eliminate Y from (11) by using (4). Taking (5)–(8) into account, we find that the demand–supply equation for goods (11) and (12), the demand–supply equation for capital services 3 (i.e. the second equation of (13)) and the investment equation (14) include six variables, p_1, p_3, X_2, X_4, H_3 and H_4. In the markets for goods produced by the industries with diminishing returns to scale, demand and supply are adjusted by changing

[12] If these equations are satisfied, (15) too is satisfied, because the identity (16) holds.

prices, while in the markets for goods from industries with constant returns to scale, demand and supply are adjusted by changing their outputs. The neoclassical price mechanism will work in the former markets while the Keynesian principle of effective demand works in the latter. Investments H_3 and H_4 may be considered as being determined by the remaining equations, i.e. the equation for capital services 3 and the investment equation. If aggregate investment I is given small enough , then the factor markets will satisfy conditions (17). However, if they are not small, then one or both conditions of (17) will be violated. In this case, the wage rate w will change and finally settle at the value at which both conditions of (17) are fulfilled.

In the special case of the absence of the industries 1 and 3 with diminishing returns to scale, the above system is reduced to the simple two-sector Keynesian model where constant returns to scale prevail. The first equation of (11) and the first of (12), as well as equations (5) and (10), do not hold. The second terms on the right-hand side of (9) and the first two terms on the left-hand side of (17) disappear. Also, H_3 disappears from (14). When investment I is set at a low value we have an under-employment equilibrium, and employment increases without any effect on prices when I is increased, up to a critical value at which full employment is established.

Our general system has another special case, i.e. the case of no industries having constant returns to scale. In this case, (9) and the second equations of both (11) and (12) disappear. (14) is reduced to $p_3 H_3 = I$, and (17) to

$$\left.\begin{array}{l} N_{01} + N_{03} \leqq L, \\ N_{31} + N_{33} \leqq K_3. \end{array}\right\} \tag{17'}$$

We can show that one of the three equations (the revised versions (11), (12) and (14)) can be eliminated by virtue of the Walras law, even though I is determined independently; the remaining equations determine two of the three unknowns, say p_3 and q_3, as functions of the third, w. (p_1 is taken as 1.) The value of w is adjusted so that (17') is fulfilled. As factor prices are assumed to be rigid downwards, there is no change in factor prices under (17'), so that we have an under-employment equilibrium.

It seems worth mentioning that the under-employment

equilibrium thus obtained in a system where no industries have constant returns to scale works differently from the Keynesian system with constant returns to scale. In the latter, as can easily be seen, an increase in investment does not disturb the price system, but in the former, an increase in investment H_3 will give rise to an increase in the price of commodity 3. As output X_3 is increased and the price p_3 rises, income Y will increase. Therefore, demand and supply for the consumption good will be disturbed so that a further change in price is induced to restore (11). In the case of one consumption good and one capital good, it is not difficult to find the directions of price changes, but in the general, more realistic models with many commodities, some prices will rise and others will fall, due to the substitution-complementary relationships among commodities, and therefore the resultant effect upon employment is difficult to predict.

Let e_{oi} be the elasticity of output of commodity i with respect to an increase in the expenditure, Y_i, on commodity i. e_{pi} is the corresponding elasticity of the price p_i.[13] Then for some commodity i, e_{pi} may be negative or zero so that e_{oi} is greater than or near one, while for some other commodity i, e_{pi} may exceed one and hence e_{oi} may be negative. To make a definite policy recommendation, Keynes assumed that all the e_{pi}s are negligible and all the e_{oi}s are nearly equal to one. This Keynesian hypothesis will be acceptable when we have unemployment of labour and capital services, but it implies that the degree of diminishing returns to scale is negligible in every industry. When supplemented with this hypothesis, the second special case is not significantly different from the first.

Similarly, we can construct a neoclassical model containing industries with diminishing returns to scale and industries with constant returns. Assuming that investment I is perfectly flexible (Say's law), the system (4)–(15) determines the neoclassical full-employment, full-capacity equilibrium. This system also has two special cases, one consisting of industries with diminishing returns to scale only, and the other of those with constant returns to scale only. However, when we have some autonomous change in the demand functions or supply functions in either of the special cases, prices are always affected according to the neoclassical law of demand and supply.

[13] Evidently, $e_{oi} + e_{pi} = 1$.

We have used all the four tools which Keynes used for establishing the existence of an unemployment equilibrium: (1) the
two-stage decision rule, (2) the downwards rigidity, (3) the
negation of Say's law, and (4) the negligible importance of
industries with diminishing returns to scale. Among these, the first
two are sometimes emphasized more than the others. Suppose
now that Say's law is true. Then there exists a neoclassical full-
employment, full-capacity equilibrium. Even in this case, if
the wage rate is set at a level such that the inequalities (17) are
satisfied, then no forces work to move the economy towards the
equilibrium, because of the downwards rigidity of the wage rate.
That is to say, the neoclassical equilibrium is prevented from
prevailing in spite of its existence. If this were the case, we might
ascribe the causes of unemployment to the downwards rigidity
of wages and hence to the trade unions. Keynes, however,
opposed this view; he believed that the neoclassical full-employment, full-capacity equilibrium does not exist, because investment is determined independently of savings and, therefore,
even if the wage is perfectly flexible, the economy cannot settle
at any point because of the overdeterminacy. Only the downwards rigidity stops this endless fluctuation, but it is not the
cause of under-employment because the removal of it will not
lead to full employment.

The four devices are all necessary parts of Keynesian economics. Among them, I believe Keynes took the third, the
negation of Say's law, as the most important. This is supported
by a sociological and historical fact: that is, the rise of the entrepreneur–executive class which decides production and investment, independently of the capitalist-shareholder class. The
fourth, the hypothesis that e_{oi} is nearly equal to one and e_{pi} is
nearly equal to zero for all industries i, is the basis of Keynes'
clear-cut policy recommentation and may be accepted as
reasonable in circumstances where all firms are carrying on
their business with excess capacity. By virtue of this last hypothesis the Keynesian economy works in the same way as Hicks'
'fixprice economy' does.

Finally, I want to point out that if we have only the first two
devices, they will lead to a view of unemployment which is
different from Keynes'. Suppose there are n workers. Divide
them into two groups. The workers in the first group are free

while those in the second are thrown into jail. The free workers form a neoclassical economy with capitalists whose investment decisions are perfectly flexible. An equilibrium will be established and the free workers are fully employed. The workers in jail are then freed and decide their supply of labour and demand for commodities in view of the prevailing neoclassical equilibrium prices. They appear as excess suppliers of labour, but cannot lower the wage rate because of the assumption of downward rigidity of wages; therefore they will not be able to find employers. They will adjust their demand for commodities to their jobless position, and because of this dual decision-making their original demand becomes ineffective. It is important to realize that the unemployment equilibrium resulting from the downward-rigidity hypothesis and the dual-decision hypothesis in this way does not necessarily give Keynesian unemployment. We may throw an arbitrary number of workers into jail so that the level of involuntary unemployment and of savings are left undetermined. Keynesian unemployment is the particular unemployment which corresponds to that level of savings which equals the level of investment independently determined. Thus the negation of Say's law is crucial for Keynes' theory.

We have so far been concerned with a temporary equilibrium with given capital stocks and labour; we have followed Keynes in regarding investment as given. The dynamic investment function which explains how investment changes through time has not yet been incorporated; obviously the dynamic movement of the economy depends on which type of investment function is assumed. In what follows we assume the flexible acceleration principle of investment decisions which, as we shall see, leads to an unstable movement as Harrod suggested. This conclusion is consistent with the view that a different investment function will generate a different dynamic movement.

We assume a simple Keynesian economy consisting of one consumption good industry and one capital good industry only, in each of which constant returns to scale prevail. Ignoring land and inventories, let us suppose that at the real wage rate w there prevails an under-employment, under-capacity temporary equilibrium. We assume that each industry chooses a single technique at w; we have $$a_C X_C + a_K X_K \leqq K, \tag{18}$$

where a_C and a_K are the capital coefficients of the consumption good and the capital good industry and X_c and X_K their outputs. Writing the left-hand side of (18) as K_D and dividing it by K, we obtain

$$\frac{K_D}{K} = \left[a_C \frac{X_C}{X_K} + a_K \right] \frac{X_K}{K}. \tag{19}$$

We also assume that consumption and savings are proportional to income. Then we have, from temporary equilibrium conditions,

$$\frac{X_C}{X_K} = \frac{c}{s} \frac{p_K}{p_C} \quad \text{(the inter-sectoral multiplier)} \tag{20}$$

where the average propensity to consume c and the average propensity to save s are assumed to be constant, and p_K and p_C are determined by the price–cost equations, as w is given. Thus (20) and hence the part in brackets of (19) are constant, as long as there is no change in w. Equation (18) implies that K_D/K does not exceed 1.

The flexible acceleration principle may be formulated as

$$\text{sign} \frac{d(X_K/K)}{dt} = \text{sign} \left(\frac{K_D}{K} - 1 \right); \tag{21}$$

in other words, the capitalist increases or decreases the rate of investment in capital, X_K/K, when the demand for capital services K_D is greater or less than the existing stock of capital K. Then, if K_D/K is set at less than one at the beginning, X_K/K decreases by (21) and hence K_D/K also decreases by (19). The rate of utilization of capital becomes worse and worse; the temporary equilibrium diverges further and further from the full-employment, full-capacity equilibrium.

This instability has been discussed by Harrod.[14] Harrodian instability is clearly seen in the one-capital-good world where the flexible acceleration principle prevails and production lags are assumed to be nil. This kind of instability should not be confused with other types which occur in different circumstances. We can mention the dual stability–instability discussed notably

[14] Harrod, R.F. *Towards a Dynamic Economics*, pp. 59–66.

by Jorgenson[15] and the Marxian instability which I have discussed elsewhere.[16] The former occurs in a many-capital-goods economy where prices can change in a flexible way. Jorgenson's theorem states that if prices are stable, outputs are unstable and vice versa, but it must be remembered that this movement was obtained, *inter alia*, under the assumption that all capital goods are always fully utilized. Jorgenson's theorem fits the neoclassical world better than the Keynesian world. We may take it as an illustration that even the neoclassical economy will suffer from instability as soon as heterogeneous capital goods are explicitly taken into account.[17]

My Marxian instability may be considered as a special case of dual stability–instability, but the following differences should be noted. In my Marxian dynamic process prices are kept throughout at the production prices corresponding to the given real wage rate; this is caused not by the existence of heterogeneous capital goods, but by the fact that both the consumption and capital goods industries take time to produce their outputs. Throughout the process, as in the dual stability–instability process, capital goods are fully utilized, but this is a phenomenon in the fixprice economy. Therefore, we may conclude that the Keynesian economy may suffer from at least three kinds of instability; one due to the maladjustment of investment, say by the flexible acceleration principle, the second due to production lags and the third due to intercommodity relationships among heterogeneous capital goods. The price flexibility emphasized by neoclassical economists may mitigate the instability, but we do not know how effective it will be, except for simulations by use of simple models in a test-tube experiment.

One might think that the interpretation of Keynes' economics which we have so far developed, confining ourselves within the framework of the real economy, is not entirely Keynesian, because Keynes raised a strong objection against abstracting

[15] Jorgenson, D. W., 'A Dual Stability Theorem', *Econometrica*, vol. 28 (October, 1960), pp. 892–9.

[16] Morishima, M., *Marx's Economics: A Dual Theory of Value and Growth* (Cambridge University Press, 1973), pp. 117–28.

[17] Also, see Hahn, F. H., 'On the Disequilibrium Behaviour of a Multi-sectoral Growth Model', *Economic Journal*, Vol. 73 (1963), pp. 442–57; 'Equilibrium Dynamics with Heterogeneous Capital Goods', *Quarterly Journal of Economics*, Vol. 80 (1966), pp. 633–46.

money from the economy. I do not want to consider this problem in detail here; my monetary view will be presented in greater detail in the next part of the book, where I examine Walras' theory of general equilibrium of money and circulation. In the rest of this chapter I simply assume the conventional demand–supply equation for money and see how it can be synthesized with the real economic theories, Keynesian or neoclassical, which we discussed above.

Let M be the existing quantity of money and $L(r, pY)$ the demand function of money, where Y, p and r stand for the aggregate real income, the absolute level of prices and the rate of interest, respectively. Let us begin by examining the Keynesian case. In the Keynesian monetary economy, what is determined independently of aggregate savings is not real investment, but the money value of aggregate investment. Let it be fixed at J; then

$$pI = J, \qquad (22)$$

where I is the aggregate real investment and p the absolute level of prices. In addition to this, we have the demand–supply equation for money

$$M = L(r, pY). \qquad (23)$$

Consider a monetary economy which consists of equations for the real sectors (4)–(16), the investment equation (22) and the money equation (23). In this economy, real investment I is flexible, so that equations (4)–(16) can determine the equilibrium values of all real economic variables, e.g. outputs, inputs, real investment, relative prices, the rate of interest[18] and so on, except the absolute level of prices. Hence, (22) and (23) include only one variable p, as r, Y, I are determined by (4)–(16) and J and M are given. In the neoclassical economy, where Say's law prevails, aggregate investment J is not fixed and is adjusted to pI, where I is determined so as to be equal to real savings $S(p_1, p_2, Y)$ (see (15)); the price level p is determined by the money equation; and we have no problem of overdeterminacy. However, in Keynes' case, with J being determined exogenously or according to some independent investment function, there is in general no price level which satisfies both (22) and (23) simultaneously. The overdeterminacy thus caused will produce

[18] The rate of interest should equal the rate of return on capital goods determined by (10).

ceaseless fluctuations unless some variables lose their flexibility.

The downward rigidity of the money wage rate is thus introduced; that is, the money wage rate remains unchanged even if the demand for labour falls short of its supply. In addition to this, it is hypothesized that the price of capital services is determined at some positive value even if capital stocks are not fully utilized. We may then consider a system consisting of equations (4)–(12), the second equation of (13), (14)–(16), (22), (23), and the new money-wage equation

$$pw = v, \qquad (24)$$

where v represents the given money wage rate insisted on by workers. This new system, having no new variable, contains as many unknowns as equations, because its equations are less by one than those of the previous system which has one degree of overdeterminacy; so the new system is neither over- nor under-determinant. Regarding the money value of the aggregate investment J, and the money wage rate v, as well as the existing quantity of money M, as given, this new system can be solved; and then it may be seen whether the solutions thus obtained satisfy the Keynesian unemployment conditions, i.e. inequalities (17) above. If they are satisfied, the solutions give a Keynesian equilibrium, because the economy will settle at that point by virtue of the assumed downwards rigidity of the money wage rate and the price of the capital service. It can be seen that the Keynesian equilibrium to be established depends on the level of the money wage rate v which is taken as given. If it is set at a very low level, there will perhaps be no Keynesian equilibrium, because either inequality of (17) is not satisfied; that is, either the demand for labour exceeds its supply, or there may be a deficiency of capital stocks. On the other hand, if it is high enough, relative to the level of aggregate investment J, we have a Keynesian equilibrium; and the equilibrium values of the variables depend on the money wage rate v, the aggregate investment J and the quantity of money M, which are more or less controlled mainly by the trade unions, the entrepreneurs and the banks, respectively.

In the case of the neoclassical economy where Say's law prevails, there is no constraint on aggregate real investment; it is smoothly adjusted to aggregate real savings. The relative prices, the interest rate, outputs, employment and so on are determined so as to establish a full-employment, full-capacity equilibrium in the real sectors (4)–(16). Let Y^0 and r^0 be the level of aggregate real income and the rate of interest which are realized at the neoclassical equilibrium. Substituting these values into the money equation, we have $M = L(r^0, pY^0)$, which determines the absolute level of prices p. When M increases, only p will be increased, all other variables being kept unchanged. Because of Say's law, J is flexible, so that it must not be taken as given in (22) but is adjusted so as to establish (22). No consideration is given to the pressure on the wage rate exerted by the trade unions; so the money wage rate v is flexible and determined by (24).

Our view that the Keynesian system produces underemployment because of its overdeterminacy may claim a unique place among interpretations of Keynes' theory. According to a conventional interpretation, equation (10) of the equal rates of capital goods is replaced by

$$f_3\left(\frac{q_3}{p_3}, H_3\right) = f_4\left(\frac{q_4}{p_4}, H_4\right), \tag{10'}$$

where f_3 and f_4 stand for the expected marginal efficiency schedules of capital goods 3 and 4 respectively. It is assumed that the expected marginal efficiency of capital good i depends on its current efficiency, q_i/p_i, and the amount of investment in it, H_i. Equation (10') implicitly defines the aggregate investment function.[19] After this replacement, the system has as many unknowns as independent equations, so that a full employment equilibrium exists. One might think that this provides a counter-example, showing that full-employment equilibrium is compatible with the investment function (10') of the Keynesian type and, hence, does not require Say's law.

Generally speaking, however, the full-employment equilibrium obtained in this way does not realize the equality between the current rates of return of capital goods; that is to say, $q_3/p_3 \neq q_4/p_4$

---

[19] Evidently, (10') is nearer than (10) to Keynes' law that investments in various capital goods are determined so that their marginal efficiencies are equal. Also, from the expected marginal efficiency schedules, $f_i = f_i(q_i/p_i, H_i)$, $i = 3, 4$, we have investment functions, $H_i = H_i(q_i/p_i, f_i)$, $i = 3, 4$, which, in turn, are put in the form, $H_i = H_i(q_i/p_i, r)$, where $f_3 = f_4 = r$ (the rate of interest).

in most cases. Such a state of affairs can hardly be regarded as an equilibrium state because, where (10) is not fulfilled, the prices, p_2 and p_4, determined by (9) do not necessarily yield the uniform, normal mark-up rate, so that the constant-returns-to-scale industries, 2 and 4, violate the mark-up principle of pricing which is seen to prevail in such industries of the modern capitalist economy. The mark-up pricing uses (10) as the formula of calculating capital costs. Moreover, the right of having a capital good which yields returns at a higher (or lower) rate will be bought (or sold) at a higher (or lower) price until the rates of return of capital goods are finally equated. Thus equation (10) must be restored; then (10') becomes redundant, so that the entire system having (10) and (10') as its constituents is obviously overdeterminate.

PART III

Money and Interest

CHAPTER 8

The Walrasian prototype

Walras' final, fourth model of general equilibrium deals with an economy where goods and services are evaluated in terms of money, trades are made in exchange for money, and consumers and producers may hold money for the future. Obviously only models which explicitly take these functions of money into account can give a comprehensive, analytical picture of the real world. We may regard the three preceding models of exchange, of production and of capital accumulation, throughout which money is completely ignored, as moneyless facets of Walras' monetary model, or as intermediate products obtained in the preliminary process of groping towards it. Walras in fact wrote: 'The time has now come to introduce these elements [money and its substitutes] in order to complete our general problem of economic equilibrium.'[1]

In spite of its importance to his theory as a whole, Walras' theory of money, like his theory of growth, has been neglected or misunderstood for a remarkably long time. Even in recent times the participants in the so-called Patinkin controversy have concerned themselves with the classical dichotomy between the real and the monetary sector, without examining Walras' theory in depth. It is true that Patinkin himself devoted thirty pages of his book to summarizing Walras' theory of money.[2] In doing so, however, he was concerned with an economy with no firms and ignored the individual's demand for goods for inventory purposes so that he obtained a simplified Walrasian model, a pure exchange economy with money. In my opinion, this produces only a superficial imitation of Walras, according to whom, the theory of money can be developed only after the real theory of growth, as he in fact developed it in a part following the growth

---

[1] Walras, *Elements*, p. 315.

[2] Patinkin, D., *Money, Interest and Prices*, 2nd edition (Evanston: Row, Peterson, 1965), pp. 451–72.

part in his *Elements*. He believed that no money problem can be thoroughly discussed with a model where investment and saving are not made, so that a pure exchange economy with money was inconceivable to him.[3]

As I have just mentioned, money has three functions, as a standard of value, as a generally accepted means of exchange, and as a store of value. The first two aspects can be discussed in a timeless model of exchange with or without production, while the third can be elucidated only in a model with a time dimension, in which individuals' and firms' current decisions are not separable from what they want to do in the future. Money is a link connecting the present and the future, but it is only one such link, though it is the most convenient one. We may consider, at least as an abstract model for theoretical speculation, a moneyless economy working through time, in which value is stored in kind in the form of productive physical capital stocks or inventories, that is to say, a real growth model. Walras was rightly of the opinion that the function of money as a store of value can be explained, not by introducing it into the exchange (or production) model, but by monetarizing real growth theory. In Walras' model the demand for cash balances is a way of saving and is very much related to investment in commodity inventories; there is no demand for money in the Walrasian sense in the system of pure exchange and that of simple reproduction, since there is no place for savings and investment in these systems. This is an important characteristic of Walras' view of money: there may be a *numéraire* in a static timeless system of exchange and production, while 'money' can appear only in dynamic systems in which individuals and firms are allowed to save and invest.

Thus Walras' money theory is related, in an intrinsic way, to the theory of saving, the theory of inventory investment, the theory of portfolio selection, and so on. Without proper recognition of these relations, participants in the Patinkin controversy have often modified and distorted Walras' monetary equilibrium model into a timeless general equilibrium model of production (or exchange) *with money and without capital accumulation* and discussed this vulgarized counterfeit at great length. However, it would be somewhat one-sided to blame only the monetary economists for this, because when the controversy was in progress,

---

[3] For more detail, see Chapter 9, footnote 25 below.

Walras' growth theory had not been completely clarified, even to those specialists who were taking part in the work of establishing the neo-classical theory of growth; they, too, misunderstood, misrepresented and distorted his growth theory.

The main purpose of this Part is to expound Walras' theory of circulation and money, in the spirit of his theory of *encaisse désirée*. At first I naturally wanted to reproduce it in its original form. I tried my best and nevertheless had finally to conclude that it was either impossible or absurd to do so, because I realized that alterations, some of which would change important characteristics of the model, were inevitable. I am now concerned to obtain a general and more acceptable Walrasian model, with minimum corrections and alterations to the original.

Two reasons which led to this decision may be worth mentioning. First, Walras' theory of money should be regarded as an unfinished work, because it is incomplete and obscure in various points and even inconsistent, in that it contains a careless technical slip which has of course to be removed.[4] Secondly, Walras' economy consists of four classes of people: land-owners, workers, capitalists and entrepreneurs. Unlike Marx, who identified the entrepreneur with the capitalist, Walras distinguished the two roles; on the other hand, he rejected the view that regards the entrepreneur as 'a worker charged with the special task of managing a firm'.[5] According to him, the entrepreneur is a distinct fourth person, 'whose role it is to lease land from the land-owner, hire personal faculties from the labourer, and borrow capital from the capitalist, in order to combine the three productive services in agriculture, industry or trade'.[6] In spite of this clear statement, however, Walras' model was incomplete; he was concerned with an economy where capital goods and inventories directly owned by capitalists are rented to firms or entrepreneurs, and decisions concerning investment are, therefore, made by capitalists (i.e. savers) themselves, so that there is no inconsistency between investment and saving such as Keynes emphasized.[7]

---

[4] This was pointed out by T. Yasui, *Kinko Bunseki no Kihon Mondai* (Tokyo: Iwanami, 1955). His point is summarized in Chapter 9, footnote 16 below.

[5] *Elements*, p. 222.   [6] *op. cit.*

[7] This model of Walras, as I have pointed out in Chapter 5 and will explain more fully below, can be in accord with his other view of the four-class society

It is clear that such a model is not suitable for examining the working of the modern, developed capitalist economy. In such an economy investment decisions are made by entrepreneurs or executives of firms and, hence, are separated from saving decisions made by capitalists, so that investment will be inconsistent with saving. We therefore revise Walras' model so that capitalists decide only saving and do not own capital goods and inventories, decisions concerning capital accumulation and inventory investment being left entirely to entrepreneurs. We may distinguish two cases: (i) the case in which, although investment is decided by entrepreneurs, their schedules are so flexible that investment is smoothly and quickly adjusted to saving decided by capitalists, and (ii) the case where entrepreneurs' investment schedules are not perfectly flexible, so that equality is not necessarily established between investment and savings unless some equilibrium condition, say the condition of full employment of labour, is violated. The former, which is referred to as the case satisfying Say's law, has been discussed by neoclassical economists. It is virtually identical with Walras' model in which decisions concerning investment are made by capitalists who own capital goods and inventories, so that the neoclassical propositions can be examined in Walras' model. However, it is clear that assuming such a model, we cannot discuss the second case, the case where Say's law does not hold; therefore, if, like Keynes, we decide to deny Say's law, we must admit that Walras' model should be revised.

One of Walras' deficiencies must be ascribed to the fact that he did not know Walras' law. The law states that in the monetary economy the only way people can acquire (or dispose of) money is by supplying (or demanding) commodities. It implies that each individual's and each firm's demands and supplies of goods, services and money satisfy the respective budget equations. It is of course true that Walras has some form of budget equation for individuals, though it would have to be rewritten to be a perfect one; but, on the other hand, for firms we can find no budget

distinguishing entrepreneurs from capitalists, only in the neoclassical case of Say's law prevailing; otherwise the view underlying the model must be reduced to that of the three-class society where capitalists themselves decide investment. Thus some revision of the model is inevitable in order for us to be able to discuss Keynesian problems in its framework.

equation in his system of general equilibrium of circulation and money.[8] To obtain a complete valid monetary model it is necessary to reconstruct his model in such a way that the budget equations of firms have an explicit place in it.

In developing his 'cash-balance' theory of money, Walras used a number of novel concepts. As the first general equilibrium growth theorist, the problem he had to solve was how to reconcile the aggregate accounting equilibrium between savings and investment with the multi-sectoral supply–demand equilibrium concerning goods and services. For him it was very difficult to conceive of an equilibrium between savings and investment without imagining a corresponding market where it is established by changing the price of saving up and down; therefore, he assumed existence of a commodity E, a perpetuity yielding a unit of the *numéraire* commodity per period, and measured savings in terms of E. In his real economic model, saving may be made either by buying E, or by directly accumulating physical stocks of capital goods and durable consumption goods; it can be shown that the supply–demand equilibrium of commodity E is equivalent with the equalization of savings and investment. In Walras' monetary economy, however, saving may alternatively be made in the additional form of increasing the amount of money held.

Concepts which play important roles in Walras' theory are thus d_e, the individuals' savings measured in terms of E, and p_e, the price of E. There are other concepts, peculiar to Walras, which are also important. These are the individuals' demands for the services of availability of goods A', B', ... and the perpetual net income E', not in kind, but in money, denoted by d_α, d_β, ..., d_ε;[9] the price for the service of availability of money, $p_{u'}$; and so on. All these remain not entirely clear, in spite of Jaffé's painstaking, useful 'Note',[10] and have obstructed the understanding of Walras' theory of money by economics students. Moreover, his theory is unfortunately incomplete in a number of points, as I have mentioned; we shall not be able to

[8] To my knowledge, Hicks was the first economist to formulate a monetary general equilibrium system in full recognition of Walras' law. See his *Value and Capital*, pp. 153–62.

[9] In Walras' notation, the prime applied to the symbol representing a commodity denotes the service of availability rendered by that commodity.

[10] *Elements*, pp. 497–558.

derive the coherent Walrasian theory from Walras' teachings, unless we decide to be flexible in our interpretation of his key concepts and make corrections or alterations in the parts of his model where we find them desirable. We leave this task of revision to the following chapter and explain, in the rest of this chapter, what Walras wanted to show by the use of his model.

His model of general equilibrium of money and circulation may be outlined as follows. It consists of the three subgroups of equations:

(I)   (1) The individuals' supply functions of primary factors of production;
     (2) the individuals' demand functions for consumption goods;
     (3) the capitalists' supply functions of productive services of capital goods;
     (4) the firms' demand functions for primary factors of production and productive services of capital goods;
     (5) the supply–demand equations for primary factors, productive services of capital goods, and consumption goods;
     (6) the price–cost equations for consumption goods.

(II) (7) The individuals' demand functions for the services of availability of goods in kind;
     (8) the firms' demand functions for the services of availability of goods in kind;
     (9) the individuals' savings functions;
    (10) the price–cost equations for capital goods;
    (11) the supply–demand equations for capital goods, and services of availability of goods in kind;
    (12) the savings–investment equation;
    (13) the equations for the equal rate of net income from holding goods in kind as inventories and from using capital goods in production.

(III) (14) the equation of the individuals' demand for money;
    (15) the firms' demand functions for the services of availability of goods in money;
    (16) the firms' demand function for money;
    (17) the supply–demand equation for money.

The equations in group (I) have appeared in the general equilibrium model of production; those in (II) are new in the real growth model; and those in (III) are first introduced in the money model for monetization.

These three groups are not isolated but interrelated to each other. For example, equations in (I), say the firms' demand functions (4), depend on those variables which appear in the growth model for the first time, say outputs of capital goods, and *vice versa*. Also it would be wrong to carelessly accept the divisibility of the whole system into the real sectors (I) and (II) and the monetary sector (III) without a rigorous proof, because they are geared with each other. Nevertheless, as Walras in fact did, we may consider, as a first approximation, that the variables of the production model are determined mainly by equations in group (I), the variables peculiar to the growth model mainly by those in (II) and finally the price of money mainly by those in (III).

The determination of the prices of the primary factors of production, the prices of productive capital services, the prices of consumption goods and the outputs of consumption goods in subsystem (I) has been discussed in Part I; moreover, it is familiar to all economics students from any standard textbook on general equilibrium analysis, so that we need not explain it again here. Also, the determination of the rate of interest (or the rate of income from capital goods), the prices of the services of availability of goods and the prices and outputs of capital goods has been studied in detail in Part II; but a brief summary of it may be helpful, because subsector (II) is particularly and peculiarly Walrasian.

Fortunately a very neat summary is available in Walras' own words: 'Given...a certain sum of savings on the one hand, and certain quantities of newly manufactured capital goods on the other hand, these savings and these new capital goods are exchanged against each other on the *capital goods market*, in a ratio which depends, in conformity with the mechanism of competition, on the prices of the consumers' and productive services yielded by the capital goods, these prices being determined by virtue of the theories of exchange and of production. Hence we have a certain rate of income, and for each capital good a certain selling price, which is equal to the ratio of the price of its service to the rate of income. The manufacturers of new capital goods, like those of consumers' goods, expand or contract their output according as the selling price exceeds the cost of production or the cost of production exceeds the selling price.'[11] In short, Walras persisted in deriving the rate of interest from the savings–investment equation.[12]

Once the prices of all goods and services are determined in terms of the *numéraire a*, say wheat, it remains only to determine the price of money in terms of the *numéraire*, or equivalently the price of the *numéraire* in terms of money. This is the problem of monetary equilibrium. In a money economy, individuals and firms may hold the circulating capital rendering services of availability, either in kind or in money. Walras' *encaisse désirée*, or desired cash balance, is no more than the total value of the services of availability of goods which are kept in money; it is determined by equations (14)–(16) in group (III). Let N be the real value of the total desired cash balance in terms of the *numéraire* and M the existing total quantity of money; then the supply–demand equation for money (17) may be written as

$$M = N/\pi_m \quad \text{or} \quad M = p_a N$$

where π_m is the *numéraire* price of money and p_a the money price of the *numéraire a*, that is the reciprocal of π_m. Provided that N is independent of π_m or p_a, i.e. N depends on the rate of interest, the relative prices and the outputs of commodities only, all of which have been determined in the real sectors (I) and (II), the above money equation implies the following proposition of the quantity theory of money: the *numéraire* price of money (or the money price of the *numéraire* commodity) is inversely (or directly) proportional to the quantity of money.[13]

As he obtained this conclusion, Walras wrote in defence of the quantity theory of money: 'In reply [to the opponents of the theory] it can be easily shown: (1) that the quantity theory relates only to the quantity of money; (2) that the theory affirms a direct proportionality to utility at the same time as an inverse proportionality to quantity; and (3) that it assumes *all other things to remain constant*, a condition which is never satisfied in reality because of the length of time required for the phenomena in question to develop. In the case of an increase in the quantity

[11] *Elements*, pp. 42. Walras' italics.   [12] See also *Elements*, p. 46.
[13] *op. cit.*, p. 329.

of money resulting from the issue of paper money or other paper currency, the reactions take place more rapidly and the proportionality of the inverse movements becomes much more apparent. For example, the issue of 30 to 40 milliards in assignats in France from 1789 to 1796 lowered the value of the medium of exchange in the proportion of 100 to 2.5 or 3. This grandiose experiment cannot be repeated as often as would be necessary to convince the opponents of the quantity theory; and that is why it is particularly fortunate that economics is a science in which the process of reasoning makes up for the ambiguities and the deficiencies in our experience.'[14]

It is thus clear that Walras asserted the determination of the rate of interest by the savings–investment equation (the classical theory of interest in Keynes' sense) and the determination of the absolute level of prices by the money equation (the quantity theory of money). But we must also admit, on the other hand, that he asserted these only on the first approximation assumption that cross effects between subsectors (I), (II), (III) are not significant. As a general equilibrium theorist, indeed, the originator of the theory, he of course maintained the general conclusion that the rate of interest and the price level are determined, simultaneously with the other variables, relative prices, outputs of goods and so on, by the whole system of equations of general equilibrium.

As I have said, Walras' theory should be revised and generalized. We shall be concerned with this work in the next chapter. From the point of view of the corrected theory, not only the classical theory but also other theories of interest are then reviewed and compared in Chapter 10, while problems concerning the quantity theory of money are dealt with separately in Chapter 11.

At this point we must consider the fact that Walras' equations for the general equilibrium of money, (1)–(17), do not include any significant investment function. It is true that they have the savings–investment equation (12), which requires that investment be equated with saving, which is determined by the individuals' savings function (9). But there is no independent investment function in the proper sense; outputs of capital goods and outputs of consumption goods for inventory purposes, as well

---

[14] *op. cit.*, p. 367. Walras' italics.

as their prices, are perfectly flexible, so that the aggregate investment, which is the sum of the value of capital goods produced
and the value of consumption goods produced in order to be
stocked, is smoothly and quickly adjusted to aggregate saving.
This is the case where Say's law prevails and there is no obstacle
to realizing full-employment equilibrium. Where Say's law
prevails, investment decisions made by entrepreneurs are always
consistent with saving decisions by capitalists, so that in such an
economy, entrepreneurs merely play a superficial and nominal
role and cannot form an independent fourth group confronting
workers, land-owners and capitalists.

Thus the negation of Say's law is essential for Walras' four-
class view of capitalist society, as well as Keynes' theory of
involuntary unemployment. Walras' theory was related to and
anticipated Keynes in this respect. In the following chapters we
shall not reproduce Walras' mathematical model of general
equilibrium in its original form, but reformulate it in line with
his vision of the four-class society. Our model introduces money
into the real-growth model which has been discussed in Part II,
an adaptation or reformulation of Walras' theory of capital
accumulation in such a way that it fits four-class societies. As
long as Say's law is assumed, it does not significantly differ from
Walras' own mathematical model. However, it is so generalized
as to be able to accommodate Keynes within it; as will in fact be
seen in Chapter 12, it can produce an equilibrium accompanied
by involuntary unemployment.

Finally, in our formulation of the Walrasian theory of growth
in Chapters 5 and 6 the bond has played two roles, one as a means
of storing purchasing power and the other as the standard for
measuring savings. Walras himself disregarded the first role; the
bond appeared, in his growth theory, simply as commodity E
used to measure savings. He eliminated the demand–supply
equation for the bond and retained the savings–investment
equation. In the money theory, Walras adopted the same procedure, but there is no reason why only the bond equation, and
nothing else, should be eliminated. In the general formulation
of the general equilibrium of money, the bond and other means
of storing value, money, durable commodities, etc., should be
treated symmetrically, which means that they each have to be
given full membership of the model.

CHAPTER 9

General equilibrium with encaisse désirée

This chapter aims at presenting a monetary general equilibrium model which provides the most general framework for discussing monetary problems. Our model is constructed in parallel with Walras' own model, on the assumption that no time is needed for production. But it revises and generalizes the prototype in a number of other important respects. Nevertheless, I regard the two as being of the same sort, and call ours the generalized Walrasian model.

Let us first explain the notation we use in this chapter. Consumption goods may be consumed by consumers or may be stored either in the larders and cupboards of consumers or in the storerooms and salesrooms of producers. When they are consumed they are denoted by C; when they are stored, their services of availability are referred to as C'. Capital goods may be held for sale in the storerooms of producers, or may be used for production of commodities in the factories of users; we denote capital goods themselves by K and their services of availability and productive services by K' and K'', respectively. A unit of a capital good is assumed to offer a unit of its availability service, or a unit of its productive service, per period; similarly for a consumption good and its availability service. We assume, for the sake of simplicity, that consumption goods and capital goods are undamaged if they are kept in consumers' cupboards or producers' storerooms, so that we may ignore the depreciation and insurance cost of circulating capital. On the other hand, capital goods suffer from wear and tear if they are used for production. Primary factors of production, labour and land, are denoted by L. As far as monetary equilibrium is concerned, the distinction between labourers and land-owners is inessential, though it is of a crucial importance in the growth theory as well as the theory of income distribution.

[133]

The quantities of these goods and services are represented by q (or x), and their prices by p, with subscripts, C, C', K, K', K'' and L. The q, x, and p thus obtained are all vectors. Those who do not like vectors and matrices may regard each as a number, as if the economy produces only a single consumption good and a single capital good by using a single primary factor of production and a single capital good. In this case each production coefficient matrix defined later is also reduced to a number.

There is only one kind of bond, denoted by B, in the economy; it is a perpetuity yielding one unit of the *numéraire* (denoted by a) per period. p_B stands for the price of the bond; it equals the price of the *numéraire* in terms of money divided by the interest rate, $p_B = p_a/r$, where p_a is the money price of the *numéraire* and r the money rate of interest. Finally, money M is a fiat paper money.

Let us first consider an individual who has at his disposal $\bar{q}_L$ of land and labour at the beginning of the present period. He wants to hold the amount q_L for his own use or leisure. $\bar{q}_L$ and q_L are column vectors. If a component of q_L falls short of (or exceeds) the corresponding component of $\bar{q}_L$, the rest is offered to (or obtained from) other persons or firms at prices p_L. The individual buys d_C of consumption goods at prices p_C and keeps $q_{C'}$ of the same kinds of goods in his cupboards by borrowing them from firms, for which he pays $p_{C'}$ per period. Note again that d_C and $q_{C'}$ are column vectors. The individual's budget constraint may be written as:

$$p_L \bar{q}_L + \bar{q}_M + (p_a + p_B)\,\bar{q}_B + p$$
$$= p_L q_L + p_C d_C + p_{C'} q_{C'} + q_M + p_B q_B, \quad (1)$$

where $\bar{q}_M$ and $\bar{q}_B$ are the amounts of money and bonds he holds at the beginning of the period; q_M and q_B the amounts which he wants to hold at the end of the period; and p the entrepreneurial profit he receives if he is an entrepreneur. $\bar{q}_M$ and q_M are non-negative, while $\bar{q}_B$ and q_B may be positive or negative according as the individual is a lender or a borrower in the previous and the current period, respectively. On the left-hand side of (1) the term $p_a \bar{q}_B$ appears as interest accruing from the holding of bonds $\bar{q}_B$, since a unit of the bond yields a unit of commodity a (say, gold) in each period; in fact p_B grows at r because

$$p_a + p_B = p_B(1 + r).$$

Needless to say, in the present Part prices, which are denoted by ps, are prices in terms of money. They are distinguished from the prices, πs, in terms of the *numéraire* in the previous Part. A similar distinction applies to entrepreneurial profits in the two Parts, though the same symbol p is used for each, because no confusion is expected.

Let us now convert the budget equation into the income–consumption–savings accounting. An acquisition of cash of $q_M - \bar{q}_M$ implies loss of an opportunity to obtain income amounting to $r(q_M - \bar{q}_M)$ as the interest which would accrue to the individual at the beginning of the next period if the same amount were invested in the bond. The *present value* of the loss (or the forgone income) is $p_M(q_M - \bar{q}_M)$, where $p_M = r/(1+r)$;[1] so the opportunity income y of the individual is defined, by deducting it from his actual income, as

$$y = p_L(\bar{q}_L - q_L) + p_M(\bar{q}_M - q_M) + p + p_a \bar{q}_B, \qquad (2)$$

where the last term represents his interest income. Defining savings s as the excess of income over consumption, we have the income identity:

$$y = p_C d_C + p_{C'} q_{C'} + s. \qquad (3)$$

Comparing this with the budget equation (1), we obtain

$$s = \frac{1}{1+r}(q_M - \bar{q}_M) + p_B(q_B - \bar{q}_B), \qquad (4)$$

which states that the savings were held partly in cash and partly in the form of bonds. In the savings equation (4) it is noted that the savings in cash are discounted at the rate $1 + r$, while that in bonds appears at its full value. This asymmetric treatment of bonds and money corresponds to the fact that the individual will receive interest payments of $p_a(q_B - \bar{q}_B)$ for a new investment in bonds of $p_B(q_B - \bar{q}_B)$, while no interest accrues from his saving

---

[1] Walras does not discount the loss $r(q_M - \bar{q}_M)$, so that p_M (or $p_{u'}$ in his notation) equals r in his model. A reduction in an individual's cash account by the amount $(\bar{q}_M - q_M)$ is divided into two parts, $(\bar{q}_M - q_M)/(1+r)$ and $p_M(\bar{q}_M - q_M)$. If the former is converted into the bond, it will have grown to the original amount $(\bar{q}_M - q_M)$ at the beginning of the next period. Returning the $(\bar{q}_M - q_M)$ obtained in this way to the cash account, it is kept intact between the two periods. Then the remaining part $p_M(\bar{q}_M - q_M)$ may be regarded as a gain by the individual from this operation, so that it becomes part of his income.

in cash. Therefore, at the beginning of the next period, the savings s gives him the sum of money amounting to

$$(q_M - \bar{q}_M) + (p_a + p_B)\,(q_B - \bar{q}_B).$$

As $p_a + p_B = (1 + r)\,p_B$ (because $p_B = p_a/r$), this sum equals $(1 + r)\,s$, which implies that savings of £1 grow to £$(1 + r)$ in one period. We may thus say that interest is the reward for 'saving'.[2]

At this point we may conveniently compare Walras and Keynes in their definitions of income and savings. Keynes does not reckon the loss of interest accruing when one holds money in cash as a foregone income, while Walras does allow for it. Income in the sense used by Keynes amounts to

$$y = p_L(\bar{q}_L - q_L) + p_a\bar{q}_B + p,\qquad(2')$$

from which savings in Keynes' sense follows, in view of (1) and (3), as

$$s = (q_M - \bar{q}_M) + p_B(q_B - \bar{q}_B).\qquad(4')$$

It is seen that there is no discounting for savings in the form of cash, as we have in the Walrasian case. Therefore, from Keynes' definition it follows, as he stated clearly, that the rate of interest cannot be a return to savings, but is the reward for parting with liquidity for a specified period. In fact Keynes wrote: 'It should be obvious that the rate of interest cannot be a return to saving or waiting as such. For if a man hoards his savings in cash, he earns no interest, though he saves just as much

---

[2] In Walras' own system the individual can directly invest in capital goods, so that his total income includes the income from selling the productive services of the capital goods he owns, while his total saving includes saving in the form of investment in capital goods. We have

$$s = \frac{1}{1+r}(q_M - \bar{q}_M) + p_B(q_B - \bar{q}_B) + p_K d_K,$$

where d_K represents the quantities of new capital goods the individual buys during the period. From the capital goods d_K he may expect to receive, in the next period, an income of $p_{K''} d_K$ by selling their services to firms, although their value will be reduced to $(p_K - p_K\mu)\,d_K$ due to wear and tear, where μ is the diagonal matrix having the rates of depreciation of capital goods on the diagonal. Therefore, the net yield from holding d_K is $rp_K d_K$ (because $p_{K''} = p_K r + p_K\mu$ in equilibrium), so that the rate of return to saving equals the rate of interest, in Walras' system, where individuals can save in the form of physical goods, as well.

as before. On the contrary, the mere definition of the rate of interest tells us in so many words that the rate of interest is the reward for parting with liquidity for a specified period.'[3] He also wrote: 'Walras...argues expressly that, corresponding to each possible rate of interest, there is a sum which individuals will save and also a sum which they will invest in new capital assets, that these two aggregates tend to equality with one another, and that the rate of interest is the variable which brings them to equality ...Thus he is strictly in the classical tradition.'[4]

Once we realize that Walras' definition of income is not the same as Keynes', it is evident that these statements of Keynes, based on his definition of income, cannot be applied to Walras. Thus it seems that Keynes was not aware that Walras' definition of income differed from his own. It should be noted, however, that in equilibrium the difference vanishes for the aggregate income, because the sum of the terms $q_M - \bar{q}_M$ over all individuals and firms is nil when the money market is in equilibrium.

Walras measures savings in terms of the bond. Dividing s by the price of the bond p_B, we obtain $e = s/p_B$; savings s is equivalent, in its rate of return as well as its worth, with holding e units of the bond. The bond B, as far as it is taken as the unit for measuring saving, was referred to by Walras as commodity E. Therefore, E consists of one unit of commodity a per annum payable in perpetuity.[5] Thus the perpetuity has two names; we call it B as far as it is traded as a commodity and E as far as we use it to measure savings.

Let us now write the individual's utility function as

$$u = U(q_L, d_C, q_{C'}, q_B, q_M/\rho),$$

where ρ is the usual price index and therefore linear-homogeneous in all prices except p_M and p_B. At first sight, this specification of the utility function seems to differ from Walras', because he recognized that money has no utility of its own.[6] But we may derive the utility function of the above form as the 'semi-indirect'

[3] Keynes, J. M., *The General Theory of Employment, Interest and Money* (London: Macmillan, 1936), pp. 166–7.

[4] *op. cit.*, pp. 176–7.

[5] See Walras, *Elements*, pp. 274–5.

[6] Walras, *op. cit.*, p. 320.

utility function from a multi-period model of consumer behaviour.[7] Eliminating q_B from the utility function by the use of the savings equation (4) and expressing savings in terms of E, we obtain

$$u = U\left[q_L, d_C, q_{C'}, e + \bar{q}_B + \frac{1}{p_B(1+r)}(\bar{q}_M - q_M), \frac{q_M}{\rho}\right].$$

We now classify goods and services into two groups. The first group includes primary factors of production L, consumption good C and the service of availability a' that the holding of a particular consumption good a (say, gold) gives the individual. The second group includes the other services of availability $\bar{C}'$ (where $\bar{C}'$ stands for the complement of a' in the set C'), the bond B and money M. The first group consists of perishable goods and services and the second of storable goods, with the exception of a', which is storable but belongs to the first.

In addition to the conventional assumptions about the utility function (e.g. continuity, twice differentiability, diminishing marginal rates of substitution, etc.) let us postulate the following: first, all first-class commodities are 'separable' from each of the second-class commodities. This weakens the additivity of utilities which Walras assumed and is identical with the assumption that the marginal rate of substitution between any two first-class commodities is independent of the quantity to be held of any second-class commodity. Secondly, the marginal utility of a' is 'constant' in the Hicks–Marshall sense that a change in the stock of gold (i.e. a change in $q_{a'}$) has no effect on the marginal utility of the gold stock (though it may affect the marginal utility from the consumption of gold) in terms of any commodity of the first class; that is, the marginal rate of substitution between the gold stock and any first-class commodity is independent of the stock of gold.[8] It can be shown that these two assumptions

[7] See for example, Lluch, C. and M. Morishima, 'Demand for Commodities under Uncertain Expectation,' in M. Morishima and others, *Theory of Demand: Real and Monetary* (Oxford: Clarendon Press, 1973), p. 178. Of course, we may put Walras' theory in a more elaborate and sophisticated form by taking uncertain expectations into account.

[8] This is Hicks' interpretation of Marshall's assumption of the constant marginal utility of money, provided that gold plays the role of money as well. Hicks, *Value and Capital*, p. 26.

together imply a utility function of the following form:[9]

$$u = U\left[\phi(q_L, d_C) + q_{a'}, q_{\overline{C'}}, e + \bar{q}_B + \frac{1}{p_B(1 + r)}(\bar{q}_M - q_M), \frac{q_M}{\rho}\right].$$

$$(5)$$

Substituting for y from (2), the income equation can be written

$$p_L \bar{q}_L + p_M \bar{q}_M + p_a \bar{q}_B + p$$
$$= p_L q_L + p_C d_C + p_{C'} q_{C'} + p_B e + p_M q_M. \quad (6)$$

As has been pointed out by R. W. Clower,[10] this equation considers money as a mere store of value and does not take into account the function of money as the medium of exchange. To deal with this criticism, a further constraint, to the effect that the total expenditure on goods and services must not exceed the initial amount of money held (i.e., $p_M \bar{q}_M + p_a \bar{q}_B \geqq p_C d_C + p_{C'} q_{C'}$), should be imposed in the maximization. Now, maximizing (5) subject to (6) only, we obtain the subjective equilibrium conditions for the individual: (i) The marginal rate of substitution between a' and any other first-class commodity equals their price ratio. (ii) The marginal rate of substitution between a' and any second-class commodity equals their price ratio. These two sets of conditions, jointly with the income equation (6), determine the subjective equilibrium values, q_L^1, d_C^1, $q_{C'}^1$, e^1, q_M^1. However, in more detail, it is seen that equations (i) alone determine q_L^1 and d_C^1 independently of the other equations (ii) and (6); this is because equations (i), whose number is the same as the number of commodities L and C, contain only q_L and d_C as unknowns, as a result of the assumed separability and 'constant marginal utility' of a'. Equations (i) involve only $p_L/p_{a'}$ and $p_C/p_{a'}$ as parameters, so that we have

$$q_L^1 = g_L(p_L, p_C, p_{a'}), \atop d_C^1 = g_C(p_L, p_C, p_{a'}),} \quad (7)$$

which are homogeneous of degree zero in prices. On the other

[9] See, for example, Geary, P. T. and M. Morishima, 'Demand and Supply under Separability', in M. Morishima and others, *Theory of Demand: Real and Monetary*.

[10] Clower, R. W., 'A Reconsideration of the Microfoundation of Monetary Theory', *Western Economic Journal*, 6 (1967).

hand, $q_{C'}^1, e^1, q_M^1$ are determined by the whole system, consisting of the budget equation (6) and the equilibrium conditions (i) and (ii). Therefore they depend not only on the prices and the rate of interest but also on the initial purchasing power of the individual. We have

$$\left. \begin{aligned} q_{C'}^1 &= g_{C'}(p_L, p_C, p_{C'}, p_B, \rho, r, w), \\ e^1 &= g_e(p_L, p_C, p_{C'}, p_B, \rho, r, w), \\ q_M^1 &= g_M(p_L, p_C, p_{C'}, p_B, \rho, r, w), \end{aligned} \right\} \tag{8}$$

where w stands for $p_L \bar{q}_L + p_a \bar{q}_B + p_M \bar{q}_M + p$, the initial purchasing power of the individual. We can show that $q_{C'}^1$ and e^1 of (8) are homogeneous of degree zero in all the variables except the rate of interest, while q_M^1 is homogeneous of degree one in the same variables.

Furthermore, the assumption of the separability and the assumption of the constant marginal utility of a' jointly enable us to put the demand function of money in an alternative form, as Walras did. Let us fix q_M at o and maximize (5) subject to (6). We then obtain the same conditions as (i) and (ii) except the one for q_M which was included in (ii). (As q_M is fixed, there is no condition for it.) They, together with (6), provide the quasi-equilibrium values, $q_L^0, d_C^0, q_{C'}^0, e^0$ (the prefix 'quasi' being used because it is not the full equilibrium that is obtained with q_M being adjusted). It is then seen that because of the two assumptions, q_L^0 and d_C^0 thus determined are identical with the true equilibrium values q_L^1 and d_C^1, respectively. Therefore, equation (6) is satisfied at both $(q_L^1, d_C^1, q_{C'}^1, e^1, q_M^1)$ and $(q_L^1, d_C^1, q_{C'}^0, e^0, o)$ so that we obtain[11]

$$p_M q_M^1 = p_{C'}(q_{C'}^0 - q_{C'}^1) + p_a(e^0 - e^1)/r, \tag{9}$$

because $p_B = p_a/r$. It is clear that $q_{C'}^0 - q_{C'}^1$ represents those amounts of C' kept in the form of money which would be held in kind if the individual were debarred from holding them in cash. On the other hand, e/r represents the bonds that would yield the same amount of income per year as savings $p_a e/r$. In the

---

[11] Obviously our two assumptions are restrictive. If they are not satisfied, we have, instead of (9),

$$p_M q_M^1 = p_L(q_L^0 - q_L^1) + p_C(d_C^0 - d_C^1) + p_{C'}(q_{C'}^0 - q_{C'}^1) + p_a(e^0 - e^1)/r.$$

absence of money, the individual's savings would be $p_B e^0$, while it is $p_B e^1$ in the actual monetary economy; he would keep the difference between them in the form of money, which is equivalent with the interest income from the bond amounting to $(e^0 - e^1)/r$.

Now put $n_{C'} = q_{C'}^0 - q_{C'}^1$ and $n_{e'} = (e^0 - e^1)/r$. Subtracting $p_M \bar{q}_M$ from both sides of (9) and rearranging, we finally get

$$\bar{q}_M - q_M^1 = \bar{q}_M - \frac{p_{C'} n_{C'} + p_a n_{e'}}{p_M} \tag{10}$$

which may be considered as a version of Walras' equation for *'encaisse désirée'*.[12]

We now proceed to look at the demand for money of the firm. First of all it is clear that the demand and supply schedules of any firm must satisfy the budget equation (or Walras' law for the firm), though Walras himself does not provide an explicit position for the budget equations of the firms in his model of general monetary equilibrium. For a particular firm $\bar{x}_M$ and x_M represent the amounts of money held in the previous and the current period, respectively; similarly, $\bar{x}_B$ and x_B for the bond. These two may be positive or negative, according as the firm is a lender or a borrower, while $\bar{x}_M$ and x_M are non-negative. Next let x_C and x_K be the outputs of consumption goods and capital goods, respectively, which the firm wants to produce in the present period; let z_L be the demands for primary factors of production. $z_{K''}$ represents the amounts of services of capital goods which the firm uses for production, while $z_{C'}$ and $z_{K'}$ are the amounts of the services of availability of consumption goods C and capital goods K which it requires for trade. $\bar{x}_{C'}$ and $\bar{x}_{K'}$ are the firm's initial inventories of C and K, while $\bar{x}_{K''}$ is the stocks of fixed capital goods which the firm has for production at the beginning of the period. Finally, let h_K, h_C and $h_{K'}$ be investment in capital goods K for production, and inventory investment in products C and K, respectively. All these xs, zs, hs, with or without bar, with subscripts C, K, C', K'', are column vectors. Since in any

---

[12] This identification is subject to the following qualifications. Our equation is different from his in using p_M instead of his p_u'. Although his definition of ϵ is obscure, it seems that our $n_{e'}$ is somewhat different, provided there is no slip on his side; he has $p_{a'}$ in place of our p_a. See Walras, *Elements*, p. 321.

trading money values are exchanged for equal money values, we have the Walras law for the firm:[13]

$$p_C x_C + p_K x_K + p_{C'} \bar{x}_{C'} + p_{K'} \bar{x}_{K'} + p_{K''} \bar{x}_{K''} + \bar{x}_M + (p_a + p_B)\,\bar{x}_B$$
$$= p_L z_L + p_{C'} z_{C'} + p_{K'} z_{K'} + p_{K''} z_{K''} + p_C h_{C'} + p_K(h_K + h_{K'})$$
$$+ x_M + p_B x_B + p. \tag{11}$$

On the right-hand side of this equation, the last term p stands for the entrepreneurial profit which accrues from the activity of the firm; this p should not be confused with the previous p for the individual. However, the sum of the present ps over all firms, of course, equals the sum of the previous ps over all individuals. As I have said, there is no equation to the effect of Walras' law for the firm in Walras' own model. But this plays a crucial role in establishing the same law for the entire economy.

In order for the production schedule transforming z_L, $z_{K''}$ into x_C, x_K to be workable, the firm must have not only stocks $z_{C'}$, $z_{K'}$ but also cash balances x_M. The cost of holding cash, $r x_M$, is incurred at the beginning of the next period; and its discounted value $p_M x_M$ should be reckoned as a part of the cost of production. The excessive profit of the firm equals the excess of the value of output over total cost; so we have

$$\pi = p_C x_C + p_K x_K - (p_L z_L + p_{C'} z_{C'} + p_{K'} z_{K'} + p_{K''} z_{K''} + p_M x_M). \tag{12}$$

The opportunity income of the firm, η, defined as

$$\eta = p_C x_C + p_K x_K + p_M(\bar{x}_M - x_M) + p_a \bar{x}_B, \tag{13}$$

is analogous to the individual's opportunity income y. The excess of it over the actual expenditure of the firm,

$$p_L z_L + p_{C'}(z_{C'} - \bar{x}_{C'}) + p_{K'}(z_{K'} - \bar{x}_{K'}) + p_{K''}(z_{K''} - \bar{x}_{K''}) + p,$$

gives its savings σ, which, in view of (11), can be put in the form:

$$\sigma = \frac{1}{1+r}(x_M - \bar{x}_M) + p_B(x_B - \bar{x}_B) + p_C h_{C'} + p_K(h_K + h_{K'}). \tag{14}$$

σ is measured as $f = \sigma/p_B$ in terms of the bond. No concept

---

[13] Presuming the perfect mobility of stocks of capital goods, equation (11) assumes that if $\bar{x}_i$ exceeds (or falls short of) z_i for some $i \in K''$, then the excess (or the deficit) is sold to (or bought from) other firms; similarly for K' and C'.

corresponding to σ or f (i.e. corporate savings or the firm's demand for commodity E) is found in Walras' own model, but, as will be seen below, it is of crucial importance in eliminating one dependent condition from the system of conditions for monetary equilibrium.

The coefficients of production and the coefficients of inventory are designated as follows. A_{LC} (or $A_{K''C}$) is the matrix of production coefficients, a column of which gives the quantities of land and labour (or the quantities of productive capital services) which are used for the production of one unit of a consumption good. Similarly, A_{LK} and $A_{K''K}$ are the matrices of the production coefficients for the production of capital goods.

$B_{C'C}$ (or $B_{K'C}$) is the matrix of inventory coefficients, a column of which represents the quantities of consumption goods (or capital goods) which are required to be held *in kind* in the store-rooms of the firm, in order to sell one unit of a consumption good. Similarly $B_{C'K}$ and $B_{K'K}$ are the matrices of inventory coefficients for the sale of capital goods. If no inventory of consumption goods is needed for the sale of capital goods, the elements of $B_{C'K}$ are all zero; similarly for $B_{K'C}$.

Finally, $M_{C'C}$ (or $M_{K'C}$) denotes the matrix of coefficients of cash holding, a column of which represents the quantities of consumption goods (or capital goods) which need to be kept *in money* to sell one unit of a consumption good easily and smoothly; $M_{C'K}$ and $M_{K'K}$ are similarly defined for capital goods. These coefficients, which Walras called the coefficients of production made up of the services C' and K' required in money and not in kind for the production of C and K,[14] may more simply and appropriately be called the coefficients of inventory in money.

He assumed that these, as well as the elements of the matrices of coefficients of inventory in kind $B_{C'C}$, etc., are all constant. But, as is easily seen, there is a high degree of substitutability between $B_{C'C}$ and $M_{C'C}$; $B_{K'C}$ and $M_{K'C}$; $B_{C'K}$ and $M_{C'K}$; or $B_{K'K}$ and $M_{K'K}$. In fact, the absolute and relative magnitudes of these matrices depend on prices, expectations, risks, etc., as well as socioeconomic variables which are more stable in the short run, e.g. how markets are organized, how efficient transportation is, and so on. Walras did not provide any theory that could

[14] Walras, *op. cit.*, p. 322.

explain these coefficients; in this chapter we also assume that the elements of the matrices As, Bs and Ms are constants.[15]

It is then clear that we have the following input–output equations:

For L and K_L,

$$A_{LC}x_C + A_{LK}x_K = z_L, \atop A_{K''C}x_C + A_{K''K}x_K = z_{K''}; \Bigg\} \tag{15}$$

for C' and K' in kind,

$$B_{C'C}x_C + B_{C'K}x_K = z_{C'}, \atop B_{K'C}x_C + B_{K'K}x_K = z_{K'}; \Bigg\} \tag{16}$$

and for C' and K' in money,

$$M_{C'C}x_C + M_{C'K}x_K = \delta_{C'}, \atop M_{K'C}x_C + M_{K'K}x_K = \delta_{K'}, \Bigg\} \tag{17}$$

where $\delta_{C'}$ and $\delta_{K'}$ denote the firm's total demands for the services C' and K' in the form of money.

In equilibrium the selling prices of the consumption goods C equal their costs, consisting of the values of L and K'' used for production and the values paid for C' and K' held (in kind or in money) for sale of the outputs; similar equations hold for the newly produced capital goods K. We then have[16]

$$p_L A_{LC} + p_{K''} A_{K''C} + p_{C'}(B_{C'C} + M_{C'C}) \atop + p_{K'}(B_{K'C} + M_{K'C}) = p_C, \atop p_L A_{LK} + p_{K''} A_{K''K} + p_{C'}(B_{C'K} + M_{C'K}) \atop + p_{K'}(B_{K'K} + M_{K'K}) = p_K. \Bigg\} \tag{18}$$

[15] This implies that constant returns to scale prevail in the production of each of the commodities C and K. We can generalize the model so as to allow for flexibility of the elements of the matrices, as the theory of choice of techniques is available to explain As and the theory of portfolio selection to explain Bs and Ms.

[16] Walras defined a_u, b_u, ... (in his notation) as

$$a_u = p_{C'}M_{C'a} + p_{K'} M_{K'a},$$
$$b_u = p_{C'}M_{C'b} + p_{K'}M_{K'b}, \text{ etc.}$$

(see his *Elements*, p. 322) and wrote

$$p_a = p_L A_{La} + p_{K''}A_{K''a} + p_{C'}B_{C'a} + p_{K'}B_{K'a} + p_{u'}a_u;$$

similarly for commodities b, c, ... But $a_u p_{u'}$, $b_u p_{u'}$, ... in these equations should be replaced by a_u, b_u, ... as we have done in (18); otherwise his system would not be consistent, as one can easily see. This was pointed out by Yasui.

In equilibrium excessive profit π vanishes in (12). Then we have from (15)–(18)

$$x_M = \frac{p_{C'}\delta_{C'}+p_{K'}\delta_{K'}}{p_M},\qquad(19)$$

which gives the desired cash-balances of the firm.

We have so far examined the subjective equilibrium of the individual and of the firm. We are now concerned with the objective equilibrium to be established in the market. We denote the market aggregates of stocks of commodities, demands, outputs, inputs and entrepreneurial profit over all individuals or all firms by capital letters corresponding to the symbols we have used for the individual's or the firm's stocks, demands, outputs, inputs and entrepreneurial profit. For example, $\bar{Q}_L$ stands for the total quantities of primary factors of production held by all individuals before trade; D_C for the individuals' total demands for consumption goods; X_K for the firms' total outputs of capital goods, $Z_{C'}$ for the total quantities of consumption goods which the firms want to keep in their storerooms as inventory; E and F for the individuals' and the firms' savings measured in terms of the bond, respectively; P for the total entrepreneurial profit over all individuals, which is necessarily equal to the corresponding sum over all firms; and so on. We have then the budget equation for the individuals,

$$p_L\bar{Q}_L+\bar{Q}_M+(p_a+p_B)\,\bar{Q}_B+P$$
$$=p_LQ_L+p_CD_C+p_{C'}Q_{C'}+Q_M+p_BQ_B,\quad(20)$$

and the budget equation for the firms,

$$p_CX_C+p_KX_K+p_{C'}\bar{X}_{C'}+p_{K'}\bar{X}_{K'}+p_{K''}\bar{X}_{K''}+\bar{X}_M+(p_a+p_B)\,\bar{X}_B$$
$$=p_LZ_L+p_{C'}Z_{C'}+p_{K'}Z_{K'}+p_{K''}Z_{K''}+p_CH_{C'}$$
$$+p_K(H_K+H_{K'})+X_M+p_BX_B+P,\quad(21)$$

from (1) and (11), respectively. Also, the individuals' savings equation,

$$p_BE=[p_L(\bar{Q}_L-Q_L)+p_M(\bar{Q}_M-Q_M)+p_a\bar{Q}_B+P]$$
$$-[p_CD_C+p_{C'}Q_{C'}],\quad(22)$$

and the firms' savings equation,

$$p_B F = [p_C X_C + p_K X_K + p_M(\bar{X}_M - X_M) + p_a \bar{X}_B]$$
$$- [p_L Z_L + p_{C'}(Z_{C'} - \bar{X}_{C'}) + p_{K'}(Z_{K'} - \bar{X}_{K'})$$
$$+ p_{K''}(Z_{K''} - \bar{X}_{K''}) + P], \tag{23}$$

are obtained from the definition of the individuals' and the firm's savings as the excess of their income over their consumption.

By summing the supply functions of primary factors of production and demand functions of consumption goods over all individuals, we have from (7) the individuals' aggregate supply functions of primary factors of production and aggregate demand functions of the consumption goods:

$$\left.\begin{array}{l} \bar{Q}_L - Q_L = \bar{Q}_L - G_L(p_L, p_C, p_{a'}), \\ D_C = G_C(p_L, p_C, p_{a'}). \end{array}\right\} \tag{24}$$

In the same way, by aggregating the individuals' demand functions of the services of availability of consumption goods and savings functions, (8), we have the individuals' total demand functions of the same services and the aggregate personal savings function written as

$$\left.\begin{array}{l} Q_{C'} = G_{C'}(p_L, p_C, p_{C'}, p_B, \rho, r, W), \\ E = G_E(p_L, p_C, p_{C'}, p_B, \rho, r, W) \end{array}\right\} \tag{25}$$

respectively, where W denotes the array of the individuals' initial purchasing powers, $w_1, w_2, ..., w_i, ...$[17] Finally, we have from (10) the equation of the individuals' total demand for money:

$$Q_M = \frac{p_{C'} N_{C'} + p_a N_{E'}}{p_M} \tag{26}$$

where $N_{E'}$ and $N_{C'}$ are function of $p_L, p_C, p_{C'}, p_B, \rho, r, W$.

Let us now assume that firms which produce the same kind of commodity have the same production coefficients and inventory coefficients in kind and in money; we can then simply aggregate the input–output equations for individual firms, (15)–(17), into

---

[17] The initial purchasing power of individual i, w_i, is defined as:

$$w_i = p_L \bar{q}_{iL} + p_M \bar{q}_{iM} + p_a \bar{q}_{iB} + p_i.$$

the firms' total demand equations for primary factors of production and productive services of capital goods,

$$A_{LC}X_C + A_{LK}X_K = Z_L, \atop A_{K''C}X_C + A_{K''K}X_K = Z_{K''};\Bigg\} \qquad (27)$$

the firms' total demand equations for the services of availability of consumption and capital goods in kind,

$$B_{C'C}X_C + B_{C'K}X_K = Z_{C'}, \atop B_{K'C}X_C + B_{K'K}X_K = Z_{K'};\Bigg\} \qquad (28)$$

and the firms' demand equations for the same services in money,

$$M_{C'C}X_C + M_{C'K}X_K = \Delta_{C'}, \atop M_{K'C}X_C + M_{K'K}X_K = \Delta_{K'}.\Bigg\} \qquad (29)$$

From (29), or by aggregating the demands for money of the individual firms, we have the equation of the firms' total demand for money, that is

$$X_M = \frac{p_{C'}\Delta_{C'} + p_{K'}\Delta_{K'}}{p_M}. \qquad (30)$$

The price–cost equations (18) are reproduced and referred to as (31):

the price–cost equations for
$\qquad\qquad$ consumption and capital goods, $\quad$ (31)

which, together with (27)–(30), imply that in equilibrium the total value of outputs equals the total cost of production, i.e.

$$p_C X_C + p_K X_K = p_L Z_L + p_{C'} Z_{C'} + p_{K'} Z_{K'} + p_{K''} Z_{K''} + p_M X_M.$$

Of course this last equation should not be included in the list of independent equations determining the equilibrium.

Now, in equilibrium, equality between demand and supply is established in each market, so that for the primary factors of production, the productive services of capital goods, the services of availability of consumption goods in kind, the services of availability of capital goods in kind, consumption goods and capital goods, we have[18]

$$\bar{Q}_L = Q_L + Z_L, \quad \bar{X}_{K''} = Z_{K''}, \quad \bar{X}_{C'} = Q_{C'} + Z_{C'}, \atop \bar{X}_{K'} = Z_{K'}, \quad X_C = D_C + H_{C'}, \quad X_K = H_K + H_{K'}} \Bigg\} \quad (32)$$

respectively. It is noted that the supply of consumption goods must equal the individuals' demand *plus* the firms' inventory demand for them; also, the supply of capital goods must equal the firms' investment for future production *plus* inventory demand for capital goods.

The supply–demand equation for the bond is written as[19]

$$Q_B + X_B = 0, \quad (33)$$

which means that there is no excess demand (positive or negative) for the bond in the market. Finally, the supply–demand equation for money requires that the sum of the individuals' demand for money, (26), and the firms' demand for money, (30), equals the total supply of money; it may be put in the form,

$$M = \frac{p_{C'}N_{C'} + p_a N_{E'} + p_{C'}\Delta_{C'} + p_{K'}\Delta_{K'}}{p_M}, \quad (34)$$

where M represents $\bar{Q}_M + \bar{X}_M$, the total amount of money that exists in the economy.

In equilibrium, equality must also be established between investment and saving, so that

$$p_B(E+F) = p_C H_{C'} + p_K(H_K + H_{K'}). \quad (35)$$

From the individuals' budget equation (20) and savings equation (22) we have

$$p_B E = \frac{1}{1+r}(Q_M - \bar{Q}_M) + p_B(Q_B - \bar{Q}_B). \quad (36)$$

This equation implies that the individuals' savings are made by

---

[18] Strictly speaking, equilibrium conditions should be given in terms of inequalities rather than equations. However, throughout the following, we ignore this complication, since the inequality approach has been sufficiently explained in previous chapters.

[19] Note that $\bar{Q}_B + \bar{X}_B = 0$ by the equilibrium conditions for the bond in the previous period.

increasing either the cash holding or the quantity of the bond held. It defines the individuals' demand function for the bond implicitly, so that it is referred to as the individuals' demand equation for the bond or lending equation. Similarly for the firms we have, from the firms' budget equation (21) and savings equation (23),

$$p_B F = \frac{1}{1+r}(X_M - \bar{X}_M) + p_B(X_B - \bar{X}_B) + p_C H_{C'} + p_K(H_K + H_{K'}),$$
$$(37)$$

which implies that firms can save either in the form of money or the bond, or in the form of physical goods, by investing in them. It may be referred to as the firms' supply equation of the bond or borrowing equation.

Furthermore, in the state of equilibrium, the rates of net incomes from holding consumption and capital goods in kind as inventories and those from using capital goods in production processes must each be equated with the rate of net income from holding the bond. This law of the equal rate of net income constitutes a part of the Walrasian general equilibrium and is stated as

$$\left.\begin{array}{l} p_{C'} = p_C r, \quad p_{K'} = p_K r, \quad p_{K''} = p_K r + p_K \mu, \\ p_B = p_a/r, \quad p_M = r/(1+r), \end{array}\right\} \quad (38)$$

where μ represents the diagonal matrix having the rates of depreciation of capital goods on the diagonal. In the price–cost equations (18), the capital costs and the costs of holding inventories are determined on the basis of the service prices evaluated according to (38); thus equations (38) are indispensable constituents of the full-cost principle of pricing. Apparently, (38) assumes that consumption and capital goods do not suffer from wear and tear if they are kept in consumers' cupboards or producers' storerooms, while capital goods do if they are used for production. We may of course weaken this assumption.

Finally, the excess profit is defined as the excess of the total value of outputs over the total cost of production. We assume that in equilibrium entrepreneurial profit should be non-negative and should not exceed the excess profit. As there is no positive excess profit in equilibrium, this implies a restrictive equilibrium condition to the effect that entrepreneurial profit should vanish

$$P = 0. \tag{39}$$

However, when the economy is in disequilibrium, P may take on a positive or negative value.

It can easily be seen that the number of conditions for the general equilibrium of circulation and money, (20)–(39), exceeds the number of unknowns by *five*, provided that $\bar{Q}_L$, $\bar{Q}_M$, $\bar{Q}_B$, $\bar{X}_{C'}$, $\bar{X}_{K'}$, $\bar{X}_{K''}$, $\bar{X}_M$, $\bar{X}_B$ and the coefficients of production are all given.[20] But the system contains five equations which are dependent. First, in view of the demand functions for money, (26) and (30), one of the supply–demand equations (32), (33) and (34), say that for money (34), can be shown, as is usual, to follow from (32), (33), and the following Walras law for the entire economy[21]

$$\begin{aligned}
p_L(\bar{Q}_L - Q_L - Z_L) &+ p_{K''}(\bar{X}_{K''} - Z_{K''}) + p_{C'}(\bar{X}_{C'} - Q_{C'} - Z_{C'}) \\
&+ p_{K'}(\bar{X}_{K'} - Z_{K'}) + p_C(X_C - D_C - H_{C'}) \\
&+ p_K(X_K - H_K - H_{K'}) + (M - Q_M - X_M) \\
&+ p_B(- Q_B - X_B) = 0, \tag{40}
\end{aligned}$$

which is obtained by adding the budget equations (20) and (21), because $M = \bar{Q}_M + \bar{X}_M$ and $\bar{Q}_B + \bar{X}_B = 0$. Secondly, there is another dependence among the supply–demand equation for the bond (33), the money equation (34) and the savings–investment equation (35); in fact, adding the lending equation (36) to the borrowing equation (37) and considering (33) and (34), we obtain (35). Thirdly, the lending equation (36) is obtained from the individuals' budget equation and savings equation, (20) and (22); fourthly, the borrowing equation (37) from the firms' budget equation and savings equation, (21) and (23); and fifthly, the equation of the individuals' savings function, the second expression of (25), from their savings equation, (22), and their supply and demand functions, (24), the first expression of (25), and (26). After eliminating these five equations, the system

[20] Note that ρ is a function of other prices.

[21] It implies that the total money value of excess demands for all commodities, the bond and money is identically zero. This holds regardless of whether the economy is in equilibrium or not.

has as many independent conditions as the variables to be determined.

It must be emphasized at this point that the above system is a correction of Walras' own system. In eliminating the five equations, the Walras law for the individuals (20), the Walras law for the firms (21), the savings equation for the individuals (22) and the savings equation for the firms (23) are all absolutely necessary. However, in Walras' own system we cannot find these accounting identities, except (22). Moreover, even (22) does not appear in its exact form, because he assumed that capitalists, rather than firms, own consumption goods and capital goods for sale as well as capital goods for production, so that they themselves decide investment. Instead of (22), Walras obtained the savings equation,[22]

$$p_B E = p_L(\bar{Q}_L - Q_L) + p_{K'} \bar{X}_{K'} + p_{K''} \bar{X}_{K''} + p_{C'}(\bar{X}_{C'} - Q_{C'})$$
$$+ p_M(\bar{Q}_M - Q_M) - p_C D_C \qquad (22')$$

and, instead of (35) the savings–investment equation,

$$p_B E = p_{C'} H_{C'} + p_K(H_K + H_{K'}), \qquad (35')$$

assuming that the firms' savings F are identically zero. This last equation is then eliminated by the use of (22'), (32), (34), and the total output–total cost equation. His procedure of elimination, however, assumes not only $F = 0$ but also $\bar{X}_M = 0$.[23] That is to say, Walras' solutions are valid only under the restrictive assumption that corporate savings and corporate initial cash balances are both zero in the period concerned.

Walras assumed this and was concerned with a monetary economy in which firms were allowed to hold cash balances at

[22] Also note that Walras defines income so as to exclude interest on bonds $p_a \bar{Q}_B$. In his notation (22') is written as

$$p_e D_e = p_t O_t + p_p O_p + p_{k'} O_{k'} + \ldots + p_{a'} O_{a'} + p_{b'} O_{b'} + \ldots$$
$$+ p_{u'} O_u - (p_a D_a + p_b D_b + \ldots).$$

[23] Considering (32), (34) and the total output–total cost equation, equation (22') can be written as

$$p_B E = p_{C'} H_{C'} + p_K(H_K + H_{K'}) - p_M \bar{X}_M.$$

Therefore, Walras' equation (35') holds if and only if $\bar{X}_M = 0$. This provides a eason why his system should be substantially revised.

the end of the period. But it is clear that if firms have cash balances and bonds at the close of period t, then their cash balances at the beginning of the next period $t+1$ will not be zero. Then Walras' assumption does not hold for period $t+1$.

In addition to this defect, Walras' own system has another peculiar property: it does not satisfy Walras' law. To show this, add the definitional equation of excess profit, Π:

$$\Pi \equiv p_C X_C + p_K X_K - p_L Z_L - p_{C'} Z_{C'}$$
$$- p_{K'} Z_{K'} - p_{K''} Z_{K''} - p_M X_M,$$

to the sole identity $(22')$ in Walras' own system, and then subtract from both sides another definitional equation,

$$p_B G \equiv p_{C'} H_{C'} + p_K (H_K + H_{K'}),$$

where G represents total investment measured in terms of commodity E. Rearranging the terms we get:

$$\Pi \equiv p_L(\bar{Q}_L - Q_L - Z_L) + p_{K''}(\bar{X}_{K''} - Z_{K''})$$
$$+ p_{C'}(\bar{X}_{C'} - Q_{C'} - Z_{C'}) + p_{K'}(\bar{X}_{K'} - Z_{K'})$$
$$+ p_C(X_C - D_C - H_{C'}) + p_K(X_K - H_K - H_{K'})$$
$$+ p_M(\bar{Q}_M - Q_M - X_M) + p_B(G - E). \qquad (40')$$

Walras did not distinguish commodity E and the bond B and considered G and E, respectively, as the supply and demand of commodity E. Then the right-hand side of $(40')$ represents the total sum of excess supplies of all commodities, money and commodity E. Walras' law for the entire economy requires that the right-hand side of $(40')$ identically vanish, but excess profit is zero only in the state of equilibrium, where the total value of outputs equals the total cost of production. Hence the above identity does not imply the Walras law and this conclusion for Walras' monetary model is consistent with what we have obtained from his production and growth models.

Finally it should be added that it was impossible for Walras to discuss monetary problems in his system of pure exchange or his system of simple reproduction, because the services C' and K' and commodity E had no place in these systems.[24] In fact, equations (25), (28), (29) and, hence, the demand functions of money (26) and (30) are difficult to obtain in a purely static

[24] See Walras, *op. cit.*, pp. 153–263.

system without growth. Thus any adaptation of Walras' money theory to an exchange or production system violates his view of money.[25] Furthermore, a simple *literatim* reproduction of his money theory is meaningless, because, as we have pointed out, it contains a number of imperfections, confusions and even obvious slips. However, if it is revised and generalized in the way we have done in this chapter, it can be regarded as a synthesis of all the representative money theories so far presented, enabling us to derive each of them as a special case as we shall in fact see in the next chapter.

[25] Such an adaptation was made by Patinkin. He considered an exchange economy with no firms and no services of availability C'. Individuals in his economy do not store commodities C in order to get the services of availability C' but, instead, hold amounts of money which are enough to buy certain amounts of C. However, if no individual holds inventories of consumption goods, it is senseless (and even impossible) to reserve C in the money form, because no one has stocks of consumption goods to sell to the person who wants to convert his money holding into holding C in kind.

Patinkin stated: 'For Walras...the individual holds money, not out of choice, but out of necessity: he plans to buy a given quantity of goods; for some reason, he cannot buy it now but only at a fixed date in the future; consequently, he is compelled by the force of circumstances to hold his money in 'storage' until then.' However, if we allow for C', as Walras did, the problem of demand for money is seen to be nothing else than the problem of choice between the services of availability in kind and in money. Walras was concerned with this problem, though his solution was not entirely satisfactory.

Also, in an economy where C' exists, stocks of C' will be increased or decreased. This is the problem of inventory investment. In any case the money problem is closely related with investment and savings. This explains why Walras discussed the problem of monetary equilibrium only after he had been concerned with the growth problem. We must conclude that Patinkin's alteration deforms Walras' model. See Patinkin, *op. cit.*, pp. 546–58.

CHAPTER 10

Alternative theories of interest

It has been pointed out by Modigliani and others that Keynes' economic model is a model from which supply and demand for bonds have already been eliminated. In Walras' own model too, no explicit attention is given to the bond market. They are contrasted, in this respect, with Hicks' *Value and Capital* model, where equilibrium between supply and demand is established in the bond market and the money market, in addition to the ordinary commodity markets, whereas the equation expressing equality between savings and investment has no visible place there. Furthermore, Wicksell was concerned with a pure credit economy where money obviously plays no role. The present chapter discusses whether these models can be coordinated in the general framework of the general equilibrium model of interest and money depicted in the last chapter, that is a correction and an extension of Walras' original model.

With this intention, we begin our investigation by summarizing the findings of the last chapter. The system consists of the following 20 sets of equations:

(i) the budget equation for the individuals – equation (20) of the previous chapter;

(ii) the budget equation for the firms – equation (21);

(iii) the individuals' savings equation – equation (22);

(iv) the firms' savings equation – equation (23);

(v) the individuals' supply functions of primary factors of production and demand functions for consumption goods – equations (24);

(vi) the individuals' demand functions for the services of availability of consumption goods and their savings function – equations (25);

(vii) the equation of the individuals' demand for money – equation (26);

(viii) the firms' demand functions for primary factors of

production and productive services of capital goods – equation (27);

(ix) the firms' demand functions for the services of availability of consumption and capital goods in kind – equation (28);

(x) the firms' demand functions for the services of availability of the same commodities in money form – equation (29);

(xi) the equation of the firms' demand for money – equation (30);

(xii) the price–cost equations for consumption and capital goods – equation (31);

(xiii) the supply–demand equations for primary factors of production, services of availability of consumption and capital goods in kind, productive services of capital goods, consumption goods and capital goods – equations (32);

(xiv) the supply–demand equation for the bond – equation (33);

(xv) the supply–demand equation for money – equation (34);

(xvi) the savings – investment equation – equation (35);

(xvii) the individuals' demand function for the bond – equation (36);

(xviii) the firms' supply function for the bond – equation (37);

(xix) the equations implying equality of the rates of net incomes from holding consumption and capital goods in kind as inventories and those from using capital goods in production processes with that from holding the bond; and the equation of the price of money – equations (38);

(xx) the equation for entrepreneurial profit – equation (39).

It was seen in the last chapter that this system of equations contains *five* more equations than the unknowns to be determined, which are:

(i*) the individuals' demands for consumption goods, services of availability of consumption goods in kind, the bond and money;

(ii*) the individuals' supplies of primary factors of production;

(iii*) the firms' demands for primary factors, services of availability of consumption and capital goods in kind and in money form, productive services of capital goods, the bond and money;

6-2

(iv*) the firms' outputs of consumption and capital goods;

(v*) the individuals' and the firms' savings;

(vi*) investments in capital goods for production, and inventory investments in consumption and capital goods;

(vii*) the prices of goods and services, the price of money and the rate of interest;

(viii*) the entrepreneurial profit.

It was also seen that the system includes five equations which are redundant and can be derived from the rest as dependent, so that the unknowns and the independent equations are equal in number. As will be shown in the next chapter, there exists a set of solutions to the system, which gives a monetary general equilibrium.

There are several ways of eliminating redundant equations. We can eliminate one (any one) equation from each of the following five groups of equations: (1) equations (i), (ii), (xiii)–(xv); (2) (xiv)–(xviii); (3) (i), (iii) and (xvii); (4) (ii), (iv) and (xviii); (5) (iii), (v)–(vii). Many combinations are possible, but we are now interested only in the following specific combinations, which may be considered as general-equilibrium-theoretic equivalents of the important, alternative theories of interest so far presented.

(1) In Walras' own system, the bond does not rise to the surface. The reason for this may be either that Walras was simply concerned with an economy where no one could issue bonds, or that he chose to eliminate equations concerning the bond and depicted the remaining equations only. Let us take the first interpretation first, and remove all the current and the past bond variables (i.e. the individuals' demand for the bond, the firms' supply of the bond, and the price of the bond in the current and the previous period) from equations (i)–(xx). Note that the supply–demand equation for the bond, (xiv), and the equation of the price of the bond, an equation included in (xix), of course disappear. Then the budget equation for the firm, (ii), is eliminated from the group of equations (1) above, the firms' supply for the bond, (xviii), from group (2), the individuals' demand for the bond, (xvii), from group (3), and the firms' savings function, (iv), from group (4). The system of the remaining equations is very closely akin to Walras' original system, though not identical with it. However, it must be remembered that Walras' system modified

and interpreted in this way[1] is no more than a special case of our generalized and corrected Walrasian system.

Next, according to the second interpretation, there exist bonds in the economy, but the current bond variables and the equations containing them are eliminated from the system in the following way: First the demand–supply equation for the bond, (xiv), is eliminated from group (1), secondly the equation of the individuals' demand for the bond, (xvii), from group (2), thirdly the budget equation for individuals, (i), which contains their demand for the bond, from group (3), and the equation of the firms' supply of the bond, (xviii), from group (4). Then the rest of the system contains the firms' supply of the bond only in the firms' budget equation (ii), and the bond variables do not appear anywhere else. Therefore, equation (ii) can also be eliminated together with the bond variable. The reduced system obtained in this way, that is the system consisting of equations (iii)–(xiii), (xv), (xvi), (xix) and (xx) only, is very similar to Walras' own system. The number of equations it contains still exceeds the number of the remaining unknowns by one; but one more equation, say (iii), can be eliminated from group (5), as Walras clearly noticed.

There is, however, a difference between the two systems: that is, although the current bond variables have been completely removed, the reduced system still contains the individuals' and the firms' demand or supply of the bond in the previous period, in equations (iii), (iv) and (vi), whereas they do not appear in Walras' own system at all. At this small cost we now obtain a Walras-like model with no current bond variables as a reduced form of the complete, monetary general equilibrium system, not as a special case of it, as was the case in the first interpretation; we are, therefore, enabled to say that Walras' system interpreted in this way is as general as the model presented in the last chapter and, as will be seen later, is equivalent with Hicks' general equilibrium theory of interest, although Hicks, as well as Walras, was not acquainted with this equivalent theorem.

On the basis of the reduced Walrasian system thus obtained, we may conceive of the rate of interest being determined in a number of alternative ways. To see this, the above reduced system is

---

[1] Note that in this system the bond does not exist, but savings are measured in terms of the imaginary perpetuity, E.

further reduced to a two-equation system with two variables by eliminating all the other variables by substitution. First let us partition it into three subsystems: (α) the money equation, (xv); (β) the savings–investment equation, (xvi); and (γ) all the other remaining equations, (iv)–(xiii), (xix) and (xx). Secondly take two variables, say the rate of interest r and the absolute price level ρ, as the parameters of the subsystem (γ); and solve it with respect to the relative prices, outputs of consumption and capital goods, investments in capital goods for production, and inventory investments in consumption and capital goods. We then obtain each as a function of r and ρ, since the subsystem (γ) has enough equations to do so. Finally these functions are substituted into the subsystems (α) and (β); this procedure yields a two-equation system, consisting of the money equation (xv) and the savings–investment equation (xvi), each containing only two variables, the rate of interest and the absolute price level, as the ultimate variables.

This system may be consistent with the following three views about the determination of the rate of interest.

(a) First we may consider a combination of the quantity theory of money with what Keynes called the 'classical' theory of interest and assume that the absolute price level is mainly determined by the money equation and the rate of interest by the savings–investment equation.

(b) Conversely, we may associate the savings–investment equation with the price level and the money equation with the rate of interest. This view might once have been a compromise between two Keyneses, i.e. the Keynes in *A Treatise on Money* and Keynes the liquidity preference theorist in *The General Theory*, before they agreed to the final view that may be summarized as (e) or (f) below.

(c) Or, more generally, we may derive two curves, each describing the rate of interest as depending on the price level (one from the money equation and the other from the savings–investment equation) and consider the intersection of the two to determine the rate of interest and the price level simultaneously. This is no more than an application of the Hicksian idea of *IS* and *LM* curves to the two-equation system in terms of the rate of interest and the price level. Taking r along the vertical axis and ρ along the horizontal axis, the case (a) is found to be an extreme case of (c) with the curve derived from the money equation being vertical and the one from the savings–investment equation horizontal, while the case (b) is the other extreme, where the former is horizontal and the latter vertical.[2]

We may draw a diagram to illustrate the general case (c). Assume that an increase in the rate of interest decreases the demand for money when the price level is kept constant and all other variables are adjusted so that equations (iv)–(xiii), (xix) and (xx) are maintained. A similar effect of an increase in the price level, the interest rate being kept constant, on the demand for money is assumed to be positive. Then the interest curve derived from the money equation traces out an upward-sloping curve in the interest-rate–price-level plane, as Hicks' LM curve does in the interest-rate–income plane. On the other hand, for investment, we may assume that an increase in interest has a negative effect, while an increase in the price level probably gives rise to a proportional increase in investment. For savings, however, these effects are usually uncertain in their directions; savings may increase or decrease when the rate of interest is increased, and it may increase more or less than proportionately when the price level is raised. Therefore, from the saving–investment equation we obtain an interest curve which may be downward- or upward-sloping. On the basis of these two curves it is easy to develop a cobweb dynamics; the stability depends on the relative slopes of the two curves.[3]

In an analogous and alternative way, we may take the rate of interest r and the absolute level of aggregate output Y as the parameters of the subsystem (γ). This substitution of aggregate output for the absolute price level enables us to determine, within (γ), the absolute prices, the relative outputs and investments in capital goods for production in the future and investments for inventory purposes as functions of r and Y. Then, substituting these functions into the money and the savings–investment equation, they turn out to be equations containing r and Y as the ultimate independent variables.

Then we have the following three cases.

(d) First we may assume that the rate of interest is, determined

---

[2] We consider Walras' own theory, summarized in Chapter 8, to belong to group (a) or (c).

[3] The stability will be discussed in more detail in the final part of this chapter.

mainly by the savings–investment equation, and aggregate output mainly by the money equation. This is the case of the classical theory of interest interpreted by Keynes in *The General Theory*.

(*e*) Secondly, the converse of (*d*) is conceivable and economically meaningful. When the speculative motive dominates the income motive in the demand for money, the rate of interest determined by the money equation is almost independent of the level of aggregate output. Also, when aggregate savings and investment are independent of the rate of interest, the savings–investment equation alone can determine the level of aggregate output.

(*f*) Thirdly, more generally, we may follow Hicks in the *Theory of Trade Cycles* and derive the *IS* and the *LM* curve from the savings–investment equation and the money equation, respectively. They each give the rate of interest as a function of aggregate output and jointly determine the rate of interest and aggregate output at their intersection. In the plane with Y and r as the horizontal and the vertical axis, respectively, the *LM* curve is illustrated by a rising curve, while the *IS* curve may be declining or rising. The convergence of cobweb fluctuations, generated by the two curves, towards the general equilibrium given at their intersection depends on the relative steepness of the slopes of the two curves. Case (*f*) includes (*d*) and (*e*) as special cases: The *IS* curve is horizontal and the *LM* vertical in the case of (*d*), while we have a vertical *IS* and a horizontal *LM* curve in the case of (*e*). It is clear that Keynes was concerned with the general case (*f*) in *The General Theory*, but his position was rather nearer to (*e*) than to (*d*).

(II) Let us next turn to Hicks' general equilibrium theory of interest in *Value and Capital*. In his model, savings and investment are not shown explicitly, while equality between the demand for the bond and its supply is counted as one of the conditions for general equilibrium. Such a system can also be derived from our general model, by making the equations involving savings and investment variables redundant. They may be extracted from the general model in the following way. First we eliminate the savings–investment equation, (xvi), from the equation group (2), the individuals' savings equation, (iii), from group (3), the corporate savings equation, (iv), from group (4), and the individuals' savings function, i.e. the second expression of (vi), from group (5). The rest of the system still contains the individuals' and the corporate savings, but they appear in only two places: equations (xvii) and (xviii). We may, therefore, eliminate these equations, together with the savings variables, from the system; and we obtain a system consisting of the following equations: the budget equations (i), (ii); the demand and supply functions for goods, services and money, (v), the first equation of (vi), (vii)–(xi); the price–cost equations, (xii); the supply–demand equations: for goods and services, (xiii); for the bond, (xiv); for money, (xv); the price equations, (xix); and the entrepreneurial-profit equation (xx).

This reduced system may be called a Hicksian system because it differs from Hicks' original only in its assumptions about production. In the latter, diminishing returns to scale are assumed to prevail, so that outputs of consumption and capital goods are given as functions of prices, while in our model they are regarded as independent variables because of the assumed constant returns to scale. But this is a difference of minor importance as far as our present problem is concerned.

This 'Hicksian' system has equations whose number is greater, by one, than the number of unknowns it contains. This is clear because we have not yet eliminated any equation from group (1); as was seen in the last part of the previous chapter, equations of group (1) satisfy Walras' law, so that one of them follows from the rest. In spite of the fact that different decisions as to which equation to eliminate have no effect on the equilibrium of the system, there are at least three candidates for elimination which are of special economic interest. They are: (α) the supply–demand equation for the bond, (β) that for money, (γ) that for the *numéraire*. All the remaining equations are then grouped to form subsystem (δ).

(g) Let us first eliminate the supply–demand equation for the bond. Given the rate of interest, we may solve the supply–demand equation for the *numéraire* and the equations included in subsystem (δ) with respect to prices, outputs of consumption and capital goods and so on, so that they are given as functions of the rate of interest. These are then substituted into the supply–demand equation for money, which in turn can be solved with respect to the final variable, the rate of interest. This is an interpretation of Keynes' liquidity preference theory which was given by Hicks in *Value and Capital*.

(*h*) The above argument holds *mutatis mutandis* if the supply–demand equation for money is chosen to be eliminated. Then the supply and demand for the bond (or borrowing and lending) are reduced to depending ultimately on the rate of interest and, therefore, determine it at their intersection. The loanable fund theory of interest was interpreted in this manner by Hicks in *Value and Capital*.

By the use of the individuals' demand function of the bond, (xvii), that is equation (36) in the previous chapter, and the firms' supply function of the bond, (xviii), that is equation (37) there, we find that the supply of the bond is equated with its demand if and only if the following equation holds:

saving $= 1/(1+r) \times$ the aggregate excess demand for money
$+$ investment.

In this expression the aggregate excess demand for money equals the sum of the households' and the firms' individual excess demands for money *minus* the sum of their individual excess supplies of money. Let the former be denoted by ΔL and the latter by ΔM. Then the above equation may be rewritten as

$$S + \frac{1}{1+r}\Delta M = I + \frac{1}{1+r}\Delta L,$$

where S is aggregate savings and I aggregate investment. This is the same as the usual formulation of the loanable fund theory, except for ΔM and ΔL being discounted.

A further alternative, a variant of case (*c*) above, is obtained by eliminating the supply–demand equation for the *numéraire*. In this case, given the absolute level of prices (or the money price of the *numéraire*) and the rate of interest, subsystem (δ) is solved with respect to the other variables, such as relative prices, outputs and so on. Substituting, we can eliminate these from the supply–demand equations for the bond and money, so that we are provided with a two-equation system which has the absolute level of prices and the rate of interest as the ultimate variables. From this system we can derive two curves, each giving the rate of interest as a function of the price level. The general equilibrium values of the interest rate and the price level are determined at the intersection of the two curves.

(III) In *Interest and Prices* Wicksell was concerned with a pure credit economy with no money.[4] A model very close to this has already been discussed in Chapter 6; it can be reproduced from our present general model with money by simply removing equations and variables concerning money.[5] Alternatively, considering an economy with money and eliminating the supply–demand equation for the *numéraire* commodity *a*, one of the equations in (xiii), from equation group (1), the supply–demand equation for money (xv) from group (2), the budget equations, (xvii) and (xviii), from groups (3) and (4), respectively, and the equation of the individuals' demand for money (vii) from group (5), our general model can be converted into a Wicksell-like monetary model.[6] That is to say, we obtain a reduced system with the equation for borrowing and lending, (xiv), and the savings–investment equation, (xvi), remaining active. These two equations will be considered as jointly determining the rate of interest and the price level; all the other variables (the relative prices, output, investment, the individuals' and the firms' demand for money, etc.) are determined as functions of these two because they have to satisfy the remaining equations.

Following Wicksell, the rate of interest which equates savings and investment is called the natural rate of interest, and the money rate of interest is determined so as to clear the market for the bond. Where the existing quantity of money remains unchanged, the natural rate and the money rate trace out two curves on the interest-rate–price-level plane. The general

<hr />

[4] Wicksell, K., *Interest and Prices*, translated by R. F. Kahn, 1936 (originally published, 1899).

[5] In the model in Chapter 6, note that equations (i) and (iv) do not appear because they have tacitly been eliminated from group (1) and (4), respectively.

[6] Although this model is derived by eliminating some equations involving money variables, it still contains other monetary equations and money variables; so it differs from Wicksell's original pure-credit economy with no money. It is clear that the latter cannot determine the absolute level of prices, because of the absence of money in it (i.e. $\overline{Q}_M = Q_M = \overline{X}_M = X_M = 0$, so that it satisfies Say's law in the sense of Lange; see Chapter 12 below). On the other hand, our Wicksellian reduced system can determine the price level, depending on the existing quantity of money.

equilibrium is established where the two curves intersect; the natural rate of interest equals the money rate.

This is a story about a world where the supply of money is kept constant. When it becomes flexible, we have a completely different version. We have, first of all, to restore equations (xvii) and (xviii) to determine the quantity of money. Adding them and rearranging the terms, we have

$$\text{excess supply of money} = (1 + r) \; (\text{investment} - \text{savings}$$
$$+ \text{excess demand for the bond}).$$

As the supply of money is determined so that the bond market is cleared, this is reduced to

$$\text{supply of money} = \text{demand for money}$$
$$+ (1 + r) \; (\text{investment} - \text{savings}).$$

Suppose now the price level is set at ρ_0 and the money rate of interest at r_0, which is lower than the natural rate. The economy is situated at point a of Figure 2, where the bond market is cleared. Investment will then exceed savings, while, from the above equation, the supply of money is seen to exceed its demand. Then, as will be shown in the next chapter on the quantity theory of money, such an excess supply of money will give rise to a proportional increase in all prices with no effect on the money rate of interest, as well as the real variables such as outputs, consumptions and investments in all commodities, provided that a number of plausible assumptions are satisfied.[7] After the increase in the price level, the economy will be situated at point b, where the demand for money is momentarily equated with its supply, because the price level has been adjusted so as to establish the equality.

However, it is seen from Figure 2 that the rate of interest at point b is lower than that value of the interest rate which clears the bond market, so that borrowing will exceed lending (i.e. the excess demand for the bond will be negative). To clear the bond market, there are two measures available to the banking authorities: one is to increase the rate of interest and the other is to increase the supply of money to meet the excess demand for

[7] These include the assumption that elasticities of expectations are unity: expected prices change *pari passu* with current prices.

borrowing. Suppose now they take the second option. If the quantity of money is increased at the same rate as that at which the price level has risen in the transition of the economy from point a to b, then the excess borrowing (i.e. the excess supply of the bond) will disappear. But, comparing position b after the increase in the supply of money with the initial position a before the increase, we find no change in aggregate real savings and real investment and, hence, no change in the natural rate of interest, because the quantity of money and all prices have changed proportionately. The natural-rate curve, the money-rate curve and the curve of the supply–demand equation of money all shift *pari passu* with the price level, rightwards on the interest-rate–price-level plane (i.e. to their dotted positions in Fig. 2). This is simply because aggregate real savings and real investment and excess demand for the bond are homogeneous of degree zero in prices and the quantity of money, while the demand for money is homogeneous of degree one in the same variables. The discrepancy between the natural and the money rate of interest is not affected by the increase in the quantity of money; in other words, after the increase in the quantity of money, the natural rate exceeds the money rate at point c by the same amount as it did, before the increase, at point a. Therefore, exactly the same process will be repeated until the banking authorities cease increasing the supply of money and change the interest rate. Thus a cumulative movement of prices and money supply will result.

Hicks considered that Wicksell's argument was obscured by his preoccupation with the discrepancy between the money rate and the natural rate. In fact, in a system like Hicks' own (i.e. our reduced system (II)), where an explicit place is not reserved for the equation for savings and investment, the natural rate of interest may be taken as a mysterious concept. Eliminating the equation for money and ignoring the equation for savings and investment, Hicks reproduced a Wicksellian cumulative process in a system like (II) (h) above, which consists of the equation for borrowing and lending and the supply–demand equations for commodities (including the *numéraire*). He found that if all elasticities of expectations are unity, the general equilibrium is neutral, so that the economy can be in equilibrium at any level of money prices.[8] It is true that this interpretation of Wicksell's

[8] See Hicks, *Value and Capital*, pp. 254–5.

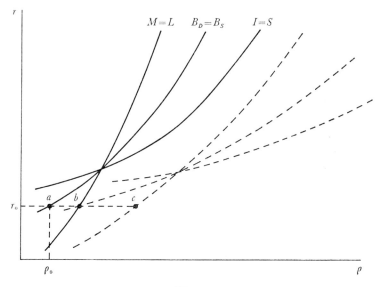

Fig. 2

theory dispenses with the concept of the natural rate of interest. But it is rather unclear whether Hicks kept the quantity of money constant when he derived the conclusion of neutral equilibrium. If he did so, we must say that it is a strange conclusion, which is valid only under Say's law in the sense of Lange. In our above interpretation, unlike Wicksell but like Hicks, we deal with an economy where money is actually circulated, rather than a pure credit economy; unlike Hicks, we clearly assume that the supply of money is increased (or decreased) through an upwards (or downwards) cumulative process. Moreover, in our system (III) the savings–investment equation has a distinct place, so that the natural rate of interest is defined precisely.[9]

We may conceive of a number of other possible systems as well. The Walrasian general equilibrium theory of interest

---

[9] In his *Trade Cycle*, Hicks reproduces the Wicksellian cumulative process on the assumption that the *IS* curve is horizontal. See Hicks, J. R., *A Contribution to the Theory of the Trade Cycle* (Oxford: Clarendon Press, 1950), pp. 139–40. Our formulation does not require such a strongly restrictive assumption and remains valid regardless of the slope of the natural-rate curve. Figure 2 illustrates the case where it slopes more gently than the money-rate curve. The opposite case can be treated *mutatis mutandis*.

which we have presented is so general that it can accommodate all the specific theories of interest so far proposed within it, so that we can compare them consistently

Except the analysis of the Wicksellian cumulative process we have so far mainly been concerned with a static taxonomy which is now complemented with a small piece of dynamics. We do not examine all cases, but concentrate our attention on case (c), the case of Walras' *Elements*, and case (f), the case of Keynes' *General Theory*; other cases can *mutatis mutandis* be discussed in a more or less similar way.

Let us begin with case (c). About adjustment of the rate of interest and the absolute level of prices, Walras wrote: 'Equality between the two sides of the equation [the savings–investment equation] is achieved through an increase or decrease in the price of new capital goods brought about by a fall or rise in i [the rate of interest], according as the demand [savings] is greater than the supply [investment].'[10] 'The price of the service of money [or the absolute price level] is established through its rise or fall according as the desired cash balance is greater or less than the quantity of money.'[11]

In the interest-rate–price-level plane, let us now refer to the two interest curves derived from the savings–investment equation and the money equation as the savings–investment curve and the money curve, respectively. Then, in terms of them, the above quotations may be interpreted as saying (i) that, given an absolute level of prices, the interest rate is determined at a corresponding point of the saving–investment curve, and (ii) that, given a rate of interest, the price level is determined at a corresponding point of the money curve. These Walrasian adjustment hypotheses produce a cobweb (around the point of general equilibrium which is the intersection of the two curves) which is clockwise, provided that the money curve slopes upwards, and the savings–investment curve downwards. The stability of general equilibrium is inconclusive; it depends on the relative steepness of the slopes of the two curves. However, if the rate of interest determined by the savings–investment curve which Wicksellian economists call the natural rate of interest is not much affected by a change in the price level, then the curve is

[10] *op. cit.*, p. 46.
[11] *op. cit.*, p. 327.

almost horizontal and the equilibrium is stable, provided the money curve is sloping upwards.

Case (f) is a general case including (d), the purely 'classical' case, and (e), the purely 'Keynesian' case, as two extremes. From the dynamic point of view, the IS and LM curves of (f) may be looked at in two completely opposite ways. According to the first view, which we call 'classical', given the aggregate output the IS curve determines the interest rate, and given the interest rate the LM determines aggregate output. Therefore the cobweb is clockwise, provided that the IS curve is declining and the LM rising, and the stability depends on the relative slopes. If the IS curve is flatter than the LM, the general equilibrium is stable, and *vice versa*. Between stable and unstable cases, we have a critical case, which generates undamped oscillations of the rate of interest and aggregate output.

According to the second 'Keynesian' view, given aggregate output the curve which determines the rate of interest is the LM instead of the IS; and conversely. Therefore, we have a cobweb which is anti-clockwise, in the normal case of the declining IS and the rising LM curve. The stability again depends on the relative slopes; in this case, however, the equilibrium is stable if the IS curve is steeper than the LM.

Thus a given static diagram of the IS and LM curves is associated with two opposite stability conclusions: where 'classical' economists find an equilibrium to be stable from a certain IS–LM diagram, the 'Keynesians' will conclude instability from the same diagram.[12] Therefore, if both believe stability to exist, they assume different dispositions of the two curves. Case (d) which is obtained by rotating the curves of (e) by $90°$ is stable according to the classical adjustment rule, as is (e) under the Keynesian rule.

Finally, the above Keynesian process may be modified by taking the quantity of money, rather than the interest rate, as the clearing factor of the money market. In this case, we would have a cumulative process, like the Wicksellian one. Concerning commodity markets we have seen that there are two market-clearing hypotheses: Walrasian and Keynesian. The relative prices which are adjusted so as to equate the demands of the corresponding commodities to their respective supplies,

---

[12] This was first pointed out by Kei Shibata, *Criticisms on Hicks' Trade Cycles* (1952), in Japanese.

according to the Walrasian hypothesis, are regarded as constant in the Keynesian regime, where the outputs are the variables clearing the markets. This Keynesian revolution from the price analysis to the quantity analysis (or from the 'flexprice' regime to the 'fixprice') was not complete in *The General Theory*. As far as the money market is concerned, Keynes was a 'price' analyst. He could, like Wicksell, have fixed the interest rate, the price variable of the money market, and assumed that the quantity of money is adjusted so as to clear the money market. The Keynes–Wicksell cumulative movement which would then follow is completely different from the Hicksian cobweb dynamics above.

CHAPTER 11

The quantity theory of money

Money, a fiat paper money, is useless, so that no individual or firm holds it if its market value becomes zero. If this assumption is valid, then no economy can be safe from the possibility that the general equilibrium that is to be established is a peculiar one at which money is reduced to a free good. This has been pointed out by F. H. Hahn.[1] His economy is a monetary economy because money exists, but the equilibrium he pointed out is the same as that in a 'real economy', because the price of money is determined to be zero so that money is annihilated and useless in that state. Therefore, such an equilibrium of a monetary economy may be called a pseudo-monetary equilibrium. It may be compared with a true monetary equilibrium with a positive price of money, which may be established in the same economy.

It will be found that a greater portion of the existing stocks of commodities are stored as inventories in Hahn's pseudo-monetary equilibrium than in the true one, because not only those amounts of commodities which are stored in kind in the latter, but also those stored in money there, have to be stored in kind in the former. Therefore, in the pseudo-monetary equilibrium a smaller proportion of the existing stocks of capital goods can be employed for the production of goods, and a smaller proportion of the current outputs of consumption goods can be consumed, the rest being stocked as inventories, so that it can hardly claim to be a Pareto optimum. In fact, comparing the two equilibria, economic activities, i.e. transactions and productions, would be much smaller and the interest rate would be very much higher in the pseudo than in the true equilibrium. Moreover, the pseudo-equilibrium would be unstable; once the

[1] Hahn, F. H., 'On Some Problems of Proving the Existence of an Equilibrium in a Monetary Economy', in *The Theory of Interest Rate*, Proceedings of a Conference held by the International Economic Association, ed. by F. H. Hahn and F. P. R. Brechling (London: Macmillan, 1965).

price of money takes on a small positive value, individuals and firms want to keep part of their inventories in money. As the price of money is very low, they will need a huge amount of money in order to keep some amounts of commodities in money. The demand for money will exceed the supply, so that the price of money will increase until it finally settles at its true-monetary-equilibrium level.

In Hahn's study it is not entirely clear how the two equilibria are different in the amounts of inventories held in kind. In this chapter, assuming the generalized Walrasian monetary economic system, we are concerned with a similar problem, that is a comparison between a monetary general equilibrium and the corresponding real equilibrium, paying explicit attention to substitution between commodities held in kind and in money form. The correspondence that will be established between the two equilibria is useful, on the one hand, to prove the existence of the true monetary equilibrium that we have so far taken for granted and, on the other hand, to clarify the conditions under which the quantity theory of money is true.

We are then in the position of being able to ask under what conditions and in what sense the classical 'dichotomy' into real and monetary economics should hold true in the generalized Walrasian system. We shall show that under some reasonable assumptions the relative prices of goods and services (in terms of *numéraire a*) and the rate of interest that emerge from the moneyless Walrasian system of capital formation and credit (discussed in Part II above) are identical with those at which a true monetary equilibrium is established in the corresponding system with money. We shall also confirm the quantity theory of money by showing that the money price of the *numéraire* is determined solely by the supply–demand equation for money.

Let us first see how the monetary economy with a given distribution of money among individuals and firms corresponds to a real economy with capital formation and credit. We shall later examine the converse problem; that is to say, we shall be concerned with the problem of constructing a monetary economy which has an equilibrium in common with a given real economy. In the first problem we assume that the general monetary equilibrium model has a set of solutions. But the answer to the second problem will establish, in some way or another, the existence of a monetary equilibrium. Because it has been shown that the Walrasian real model of capital formation and credit has a general equilibrium, and because the monetary economy is so constructed that it has the same equilibrium as the real economy, we obtain the monetary equilibrium simply by substituting equilibrium solutions to the equations of the real economy into those of the monetary economy and then determining the price level so as to equate the demand for money with its supply.

Throughout this chapter, as we confine ourselves to a comparison of monetary and real equilibria, we completely ignore entrepreneurial profit, which vanishes in equilibrium. Apart from this, no special remark is needed; we continue to use the notation which was used in the previous chapters. Let ξ be an economic variable which may be the price or the quantity demanded, supplied, or produced of a good or a service, or the rate of interest. We distinguish by superscript 1 (as ξ^1) its equilibrium value in the system with money (called the monetary equilibrium value) from the equilibrium value of the same variable in the corresponding real economy, which is denoted as ξ^*. On the assumption that the given monetary economy has a truly monetary general equilibrium, we want to show that there is a well defined real economy which is identical with and hence corresponds to the given monetary economy in the sense that they generate the same real equilibrium. We refer to these monetary and real economies as ME and RE, respectively. Then our problem (the first problem) may more rigorously be stated as follows: Let π be the relative price vector in terms of the *numéraire a*, r the rate of interest, X_C and X_K output vectors of consumption and capital goods, and $H_K, H_{C'}, H_{K'}$ investments in capital goods K for production and investments in consumption and capital goods for inventory purposes; then corresponding to any ME, there is an RE such that its equilibrium ($\pi^*, r^*, X_C^*, X_K^*, H_K^*, H_C^*, H_{K'}^*$) is identical with the equilibrium ($\pi^1, r^1, X_C^1, X_K^1, H_K^1, H_{C'}^1, H_{K'}^1$) of the given ME. Thus ME and RE have the same real equilibrium in common; that is to say, in the conversion of the monetary economy ME into the real economy RE, money plays no more than a neutral role.

It was seen in Chapter 9 that in the monetary economy individuals enjoy the services (a sense of security, convenience, etc.) which the availability of consumption goods C and the perpetuity E would provide, partly in kind, as they hold bread, meat, wine, fruit and firewood in their homes, and partly in the form of money, as they hold cash. We denote the latter parts by $N^1_{C'}$ and $N^1_{E'}$, the services of availability that C and E render being referred to as C' and E'. Similarly, the firms keep $\Delta^1_{C'}$ and $\Delta^1_{K'}$ units of the services of availability of consumption and capital goods, C' and K', in money form. Then the supply–demand equation for money can be written as:

$$M \equiv \bar{Q}_M + \bar{X}_M = \frac{p^1_{C'}(N^1_{C'} + \Delta^1_{C'}) + p^1_a N^1_{E'} + p^1_{K'} \Delta^1_{K'}}{p^1_M}, \quad (1)$$

where $\bar{Q}_M$ and $\bar{X}_M$ are the total quantities of money held initially by individuals and firms, respectively; $p^1_{C'}$, $p^1_{K'}$, and p^1_a the equilibrium prices of C', K' and a in terms of money; and $p^1_M = r^1/(1 + r^1)$, where r^1 is the equilibrium rate of interest.[2] Obviously, equation (1) is a reproduction of equation (34) of Chapter 9.

To construct the real economy RE which corresponds to the given monetary economy ME, let those amounts of C', E', K' which are kept in money in ME, i.e. $N^1_{C'} + \Delta^1_{C'}$, $N^1_{E'}$, $\Delta^1_{K'}$, be distributed in *kind* to the individuals and the firms in proportion to their initial holdings of money. The proportions are defined as: $\alpha_i = \bar{q}_{iM}/M$ for individuals i and $\alpha = \bar{X}_M/M$ for the firms. As M equals the sum of all $\bar{q}_{iM}$s and $\bar{X}_M$, we see that the sum of α_is and α equals 1. (We may further divide the firm sector into individual firms with no difficulty.) Also define

$$\bar{n}_{iC'} = \alpha_i(N^1_{C'} + \Delta^1_{C'}), \quad \bar{\Delta}_{C'} = \alpha(N^1_{C'} + \Delta^1_{C'}),$$
$$\bar{n}_{iE'} = \alpha_i N^1_{E'}, \quad \bar{\Delta}_{E'} = \alpha N^1_{E'},$$
$$\bar{n}_{iK'} = \alpha_i \Delta^1_{K'}, \quad \bar{\Delta}_{K'} = \alpha \Delta^1_{K'}.$$

Obviously, we have

$$\sum_i \bar{n}_{iC'} + \bar{\Delta}_{C'} = N^1_{C'} + \Delta^1_{C'}, \quad (2)$$

$$\sum_i \bar{n}_{iE'} + \bar{\Delta}_{E'} = N^1_{E'}, \quad (3)$$

$$\sum_i \bar{n}_{iK'} + \bar{\Delta}_{K'} = \Delta^1_{K'}. \quad (4)$$

With this distribution of C', K' and E' let us next deprive the individuals and the firms of money they hold. Then individual i

[2] For the definition of p_M, see Chapter 9, p. 135.

is provided with $\bar{q}_{iL}$ of the primary factors of production (land and labour), $\bar{n}_{iC'}$ of C', $\bar{n}_{iK'}$ of K', $\bar{q}_{iB}$ of B, $\bar{n}_{iE'}$ of E' and no money, and the firms with $\bar{X}_{C'} + \bar{\Delta}_{C'}$ of C', $\bar{X}_{K'} + \bar{\Delta}_{K'}$ of K', $\bar{X}_{K''}$ of K'', $\bar{X}_B$ of B, $\bar{\Delta}_{E'}$ of E' and no money. However, as the total amounts of C', K', E' which are kept in money are distributed among the individuals and the firms in proportion to the quantities of money they hold, we have[3]

$$\bar{q}_{iM} = (p^1_{C'} \bar{n}_{iC'} + p^1_{K'} \bar{n}_{iK'} + p^1_a \bar{n}_{iE'})/p^1_M, \tag{5}$$

$$\bar{X}_M = (p^1_{C'} \bar{\Delta}_{C'} + p^1_{K'} \bar{\Delta}_{K'} + p^1_a \bar{\Delta}_{E'})/p^1_M, \tag{6}$$

that is to say, the amount of value which an individual loses with the abolition of money is fully compensated for by those C', K' and E' which are newly distributed to him in kind; similarly for the firms.[4] Thus in the real economy, RE, the individuals and the firms have the same purchasing power as they had in the monetary economy, ME.

Suppose now that relative prices and the rate of interest are identical in these two economies, so that $\pi^* = \pi^1$ and $r^* = r^1$. Then in RE the budget equation of individual i may be written as[5]

$$\pi^1_L \bar{q}_{iL} + \frac{\pi^1_{C'} \bar{n}_{iC'} + \pi^1_{K'} \bar{n}_{iK'} + \bar{n}_{iE'}}{p^1_M} + \left(1 + \frac{1}{r}\right) \bar{q}_{iB}$$
$$= \pi^1_L q_{iL} + \pi^1_C d_{iC} + \pi^1_{C'} q_{iC'} + \pi^1_B q_{iB}, \tag{7}$$

subject to which the utility function,

$$u = U(\phi(q_{iL}, d_{iC}) + q_{ia'}, q_{i\bar{C}'}, q_{iB}, 0) \tag{8}$$

is maximized. In (8) the last argument, q_{iM}/ρ^1, is set at zero because of the assumed non-existence of money. The subjective equilibrium determined in this way in RE is denoted by $(q^*_{iL}, d^*_{iC}, q^*_{iC'}, q^*_{iB})$, which is compared with the subjective quasi-equilibrium in ME, $(q^0_{iL}, d^0_{iC}, q^0_{iC'}, q^0_{iB})$, obtained by fixing q_{iM} at zero and maximizing the utility function (8) subject to

$$p^1_L \bar{q}_{iL} + \bar{q}_{iM} + (p^1_a + p^1_B) \bar{q}_{iB} = p^1_L q_{iL} + p^1_C d_{iC} + p^1_{C'} q_{iC'} + p^1_B q_{iB}. \tag{9}$$

---

[3] Multiply both sides of (1) by α_i or α; then we obtain (5) or (6).

[4] Note that $p^1_{C'}/p^1_M = p^1_a + p^1_{C'}$, etc., that is, the sum of the value of one unit of C and the value of the services of availability from it.

[5] Note that $(p_a + p_B)/p_a = (1 + r)/r$.

As (5) holds, individual i experiences no change in his purchasing power between the original monetary economy, ME, and the corresponding imaginary real economy, RE, i.e. the left-hand side of (7) is equal, in real values (i.e., in terms of the *numéraire*), to the left-hand side of (9), provided equilibrium prices $p_L^1, p_C^1, \ldots$ and the rate of interest r^1 prevail. Therefore we have

$$q_{iL}^* = q_{iL}^0, \quad d_{iC}^* = d_{iC}^0, \quad q_{iC'}^* = q_{iC'}^0, \quad q_{1B}^* = q_{1B}^0.$$

As has been seen in Chapter 9, with respect to q_{iL} and d_{iC}, the quasi-equilibrium is identical with the true monetary equilibrium, because of the separability of the utility function and the constant marginal utility of the availability of the *numéraire* a; that is

$$q_{iL}^* = q_{iL}^0 = q_{iL}^1, \quad d_{iC}^* = d_{iC}^0 = d_{iC}^1,$$

q_{iL}^1 and d_{iC}^1 representing the true monetary equilibrium values of q_{iL} and d_{iC} at $p_L^1, p_C^1, \ldots, r^1$. Moreover we can show that the income in RE equals the real income in ME,[6] and that savings and the demand for C' in RE, e_i^* and $q_{iC'}^*$, equal their quasi-equilibrium values in ME, e_i^0 and $q_{iC'}^0$, respectively. Therefore, for individuals as a whole, we have

$$Q_L^* = Q_L^1, \quad D_C^* = D_C^1, \quad Q_{C'}^* = Q_{C'}^0, \quad E^* = E^0, \tag{10}$$

where the capital letters represent the sums of the individual quantities expressed by the corresponding lower case letters over all individuals.

Next let X_C^* and X_K^* be the equilibrium outputs of consumption and capital goods in RE. Then the firms' demands for the primary factors of production, L, and the productive capital services, K'', are determined by the input–output equations:

$$\left.\begin{array}{l} A_{LC}X_C^* + A_{LK}X_K^* = Z_L^*, \\ A_{K''C}X_C^* + A_{K''K}X_K^* = Z_{K''}^*. \end{array}\right\} \tag{11}$$

On the other hand, the services of availability of consumption and capital goods, C' and K', cannot be held in money in RE; they must be provided entirely in kind, so that

$$\left.\begin{array}{l} (B_{C'C} + M_{C'C})\,X_C^* + (B_{C'K} + M_{C'K})\,X_K^* = Z_{C'}^*, \\ (B_{K'C} + M_{K'C})\,X_C^* + (B_{K'K} + M_{K'K})\,X_K^* = Z_{K'}^*. \end{array}\right\} \tag{12}$$

---

[6] The former is $\pi_L^1(\bar{q}_{iL} - q_{iL}) + \pi_{C'}^1 \bar{n}_{iC'} + \pi_K^1 \bar{n}_{iK'} + \bar{n}_{iE'} + \bar{q}_{iB}$, while the latter is $p_L^1(\bar{q}_{iL} - q_{iL}) + p_M^1 \bar{q}_{iM} + p_a^1 \bar{q}_{iB}$. The equality follows from (5).

Where X_C^* and X_K^* are so determined as to equal the equilibrium outputs of C and K in the monetary economy, X_C^1 and X_K^1, we find that the demands for the primary factors and the capital services in RE, Z_L^* and $Z_{K''}^*$, are equal to those in ME, Z_L^1 and $Z_{K''}^1$, while the demands for the services of availability of consumption and capital goods in RE, $Z_{C'}^*$ and $Z_{K'}^*$, are equal to the demands for them in kind *plus* those in money in ME, i.e. $Z_{C'}^1 + \Delta_{C'}^1$ and $Z_{K'}^1 + \Delta_{K'}^1$. Therefore, considering (10), we can easily see that the supply–demand equilibrium conditions for RE,

$$\bar{Q}_L = Q_L^* + Z_L^*, \quad \bar{X}_{K''} = Z_{K''}^*, \quad \bar{X}_{C'} + N_{C'}^1 + \Delta_{C'}^1 = Q_{C'}^* + Z_{C'}^*,$$
$$\bar{X}_{K'} + \Delta_{K'}^1 = Z_{K'}^*, \quad X_C^* = D_C^* + H_{C'}^*, \quad X_K^* = H_K^* + H_{K'}^*,$$

$$(13)$$

are established at

$$X_C^* = X_C^1, \quad X_K^* = X_K^1, \quad H_{C'}^* = H_{C'}^1, \quad H_K^* = H_K^1, \quad H_{K'}^* = H_{K'}^1.$$

In other words, in (13), the conditions for land and labour, L, capital services, K'', consumption goods, C, and capital goods, K, are the same as the corresponding conditions in ME,[7] while the conditions for the services of availability C' or K' are obtained by adding $\Delta_{C'}^1$ or $\Delta_{K'}^1$ to both sides of the corresponding conditions in ME.[8] Also, if the prices of RE are set at the relative equilibrium-prices of ME, i.e., $\pi^* = \pi^1$, then it is evident that the prices π^* satisfy the cost of production equations in RE, because they are identical with those in ME, i.e. equations (18) of Chapter 9, which the prices π^1 satisfy. As the price–cost equations thus hold, the entrepreneurial profit vanishes in RE.

As for the individuals' savings, we have seen that their savings in RE, $\pi_B^1 E^*$, equals quasi-equilibrium savings in ME, $\pi_B^1 E^0$, in terms of the *numéraire a*; we obtain, therefore,

$$\pi_B^1 E^* = \pi_B^1 E^1 + N_{E'}^1,[9]$$

where $\pi_B^1 E^1$ is the true equilibrium savings in ME. On the other hand, the real savings of the firms in RE, $\pi_B^1 F^*$, equals the total value of output, i.e. $\pi_C^1 X_C^* + \pi_K^1 X_K^*$, *plus* the interest on the

---

[7] See equation (32) of Chapter 9.

[8] Note that $N_{C'}^1 = Q_{C'}^0 - Q_{C'}^1$, by definition.

[9] This follows at once from the definitions of $N_{E'}^1$ and π_B^1; that is to say, $N_{E'}^1 = (E^0 - E^1)/r^1$ and $\pi_B^1 = 1/r^1$.

initial holdings of E' and B, i.e. $(\bar{\Delta}_{E'} + \bar{X}_B)$, *minus* the total expenditures on L, C', K' and K'', i.e.

$$\pi_L^1 Z_L^* + \pi_{C'}^1 (Z_{C'}^* - \bar{X}_{C'} - \bar{\Delta}_{C'})$$
$$+ \pi_{K'}^1 (Z_{K'}^* - \bar{X}_{K'} - \bar{\Delta}_{K'}) + \pi_{K''}^1 (Z_{K''}^* - \bar{X}_{K''}).$$

In view of the definition of the firms' real savings in ME,[10] we then find that[11] $F^* = F^1$. Hence,

$$\pi_B^1 (E^* + F^*) = \pi_B^1 (E^1 + F^1) + N_{E'}^1.$$

As the total real savings, $\pi_B^1 (E^1 + F^1)$, in ME equals the total real investment there, that is the sum of investment for production, $\pi_K^1 H_K^1$, and inventory investment, $\pi_C^1 H_{C'}^1 + \pi_K^1 H_{K'}^1$, the above equation implies

$$\pi_B^1 (E^* + F^*) = \pi_C^1 H_{C'}^1 + \pi_K^1 (H_K^1 + H_{K'}^1) + N_{E'}^1. \qquad (14)$$

Finally the relative equilibrium prices, π^1, of ME (hence π^* of RE) satisfy the price equations,

$$\pi_{C'}^1 = \pi_C^1 r^1, \quad \pi_{K'}^1 = \pi_K^1 r^1, \quad \pi_{K''}^1 = \pi_K^1 r^1 + \pi_K^1 \mu, \quad \pi_B^1 = 1/r^1 \qquad (15)$$

which are derived by dividing the corresponding equations of ME, in terms of money, by the price of the *numéraire*, p_a^1.

Walras' theory of general equilibrium of capital formation and credit has shown that an equilibrium is established in the real economy when the input–output equations (11), the inventory equations (12), the supply–demand equations (13), the savings–investment equations (14) and the price equations (15) (as well as the cost of production equations) are all satisfied. It is noted that the savings–investment equation (14) has an extra term $N_{E'}^1$ which does not appear in Walras' original formula. This is the amount of E' which would be reserved in the form of money in the monetary economy; since it should be kept in the form of commodity E when money ceases to exist, savings in RE should be greater than the real savings in ME by the same amount. It is also noted that the equilibrium conditions exceed the variables

[10] $\pi_B^1 F^1 = \pi_C^1 X_C^1 + \pi_K^1 X_K^1 + (p_M^1/p_a^1)(\bar{X}_M - X_M^1) + \bar{X}_B$
$\qquad - \pi_L^1 Z_L^1 - \pi_{C'}^1 (Z_{C'}^1 - \bar{X}_{C'}) - \pi_{K'}^1 (Z_{K'}^1 - \bar{X}_{K'}) - \pi_{K''}^1 (Z_{K''}^1 - \bar{X}_{K''}).$

cf. Chapter 9, p. 146.

[11] Note that $X_C^* = X_C^1$, $X_K^* = X_K^1$, $Z_L^* = Z_L^1$, $Z_{K''}^* = Z_{K''}^1$, $Z_{C'}^* = Z_{C'}^1 + \Delta_{C'}^1$, $Z_{K'}^* = Z_{K'}^1 + \Delta_{K'}^1$. Also note that $p_M^1 \bar{X}_M/p_a^1 = \pi_{C'}^1 \bar{\Delta}_{C'} + \pi_{K'}^1 \bar{\Delta}_{K'} + \bar{\Delta}_{E'}$ and $p_M^1 X_M^1/p_a^1 = \pi_{C'}^1 \Delta_{C'}^1 + \pi_{K'}^1 \Delta_{K'}^1$. Then we obtain $F^* = F^1$ at once.

to be determined by one in number, because the price of the *numéraire* is set at 1. In our RE we have, however, Walras' law,[12] which enables us to eliminate one of the equilibrium conditions, say the supply–demand equation for the *numéraire*, so that we have as many independent equations as we have unknowns to be determined.[13] Considering the fact that π^1, r^1, X_C^1, X_K^1, $H_{C'}^1$, H_K^1 and $H_{K'}^1$ satisfy the equilibrium conditions for the monetary economy at $p_a = p_a^1$, it is seen that they also satisfy the equilibrium conditions for the real economy. Thus we have proved $(\pi^*, r^*) = (\pi^1, r^1)$ and $(X^*, H^*) = (X^1, H^1)$.

The above argument for the identity between the equilibria established in the monetary and the corresponding real economy is based on the assumption that the services of availability of consumption and capital goods and commodity E which are held in money form are perfect substitutes for those held in kind, so that consumers and producers have no preference between them. The inventory coefficients in the real economy are, therefore, simple sums of those in kind and in money in the monetary economy, as is seen in (12). If this assumption is not fulfilled, as is usually the case in reality, the amounts of inventories individuals and firms should keep in the real economy will be different from (probably much bigger than) those they would keep in kind or in money in the monetary economy. If, in spite of this, the same amounts of inventories as are held, in money or in kind, in the monetary economy are provided for individuals and firms in kind in the real economy, then the equilibria to be realized in the two economies will be different with respect to the amounts of goods to be produced as well as those to be traded. However, once we accept the assumption, we find that the same

---

[12] The law is derived by summing up all savings identities for individuals and firms. Taking (2)–(4) into account, it says:

$$\pi_L(\overline{Q}_L - Q_L - Z_L) + \pi_C(X_C - D_C - H_{C'}) + \pi_K(X_K - H_K - H_{K'})$$
$$+ \pi_{C'}(\overline{X}_{C'} + N_{C'}^1 + \Delta_{C'}^1 - Q_{C'} - Z_{C'}) + \pi_{K'}(\overline{X}_{K'} + \Delta_{K'}^1 - Z_{K'})$$
$$+ \pi_{K'}(\overline{X}_{K'} - Z_{K'}) + \pi_B(G - E - F) \equiv 0, \ldots$$

where $\pi_B G = \pi_C H_{C'} + \pi_K(H_K + H_{K'}) + N_E^1$.

[13] In the growth model in Chapter 6, the number of equilibrium conditions exceeds the number of unknowns by three. See Chapter 6, p. 91. Note that in our present model we have already tacitly eliminated two equations concerning the bond, that is, equations (6) and (15) of Chapter 6. Restoring them, the elimination procedure is exactly the same as the one we have already seen.

prices of the services of availability of consumption and capital goods, $\pi^1_{C'}$, $\pi^1_{K'}$, and the same rate of interest, r^1, as those in the monetary economy will be established in the corresponding real general equilibrium system of capital formation, in which inventories C', E' and K' of the total amounts (2), (3), (4) are distributed in kind among individuals and firms in the same proportions as they have money in the monetary economy. The money equation (1) may then be written as

$$M = p^1_a \frac{\pi^1_{C'}(N^1_{C'} + \Delta^1_{C'}) + N^1_E + \pi^1_{K'}\Delta^1_{K'}}{p^1_M}, \qquad (1')$$

and as the fraction on the right-hand side is given, because the rate of interest r^1 in RE determines p^1_M at $r^1/(1+r^1)$, $(1')$ determines the absolute price level or the price of the *numéraire* p^1_a.

We have so far seen that corresponding to a given monetary economy there is a real economy in which the same equilibrium prevails. Conversely, we may examine whether there is a monetary economy (again referred to as ME) which has an equilibrium in common with a given real economy (again RE). To consider this, our second problem, we imagine a real economy with capital stocks $\bar{X}_{K''}$ and inventories $\bar{\bar{X}}_{C'}$ and $\bar{\bar{X}}_{K'}$. Capital stocks K are held entirely by firms, and inventories C' and K' are partly held by firms while the rest are owned by individuals. $\bar{n}_{iC'}$ and $\bar{n}_{iK'}$ denote the amounts of inventories owned by individuals i who have land and labour L of the amounts $\bar{q}_{iL}$, as well (but no bond, so that $\bar{q}_{iB} = 0$), before trade. In this economy with no money, individual i maximizes his utility (8) subject to the budget equation[14]

$$\pi_L \bar{q}_{iL} + (\pi_{C'} + \pi_C) \bar{n}_{iC'} + (\pi_{K'} + \pi_K) \bar{n}_{iK'}$$
$$= \pi_L q_{iL} + \pi_C d_{iC} + \pi_{C'} q_{iC'} + \pi_B q_{iB}. \qquad (16)$$

[14] Note that the left-hand side includes not only the income from owing $\bar{n}_{iC'}$ and $\bar{n}_{iK'}$ but also their value, because individual i may sell them. On the other hand, the individual's demands for stocks of C and K do not appear at all on the right-hand side. This means that in RE the individual sells all the initial stocks, $\bar{n}_{iC'}$ and $\bar{n}_{iK'}$, after having received the income from them, and retains none of them at the end of the period. The purchasing power is held over to the next period in the form of the bond.

Also note that on the right-hand side q_{iB} appears in place of e_i. However, once the former is determined, the latter can easily be calculated by the use of the savings equation: $\pi_B e_i = \pi_B q_{iB} - \pi_C \bar{n}_{iC'} - \pi_K \bar{n}_{iK'}$.

The supplies of land and labour L and inventories C' and K' determined in this way are equal, in equilibrium, to the firms' demands for them, which are determined so as to satisfy the input–output equations (11) and (12); similarly for consumption goods C. In addition to these, demand and supply must be equated for capital goods K and for capital services K''; we thus have

$$\bar{Q}_L = Q_L^* + Z_L^*, \quad \bar{X}_{K''} = Z_{K''}^*, \qquad \bar{\bar{X}}_{C'} = Q_{C'}^* + Z_{C'}^*,\Big\}$$
$$\bar{X}_{K'} = Z_{K'}^*, \qquad X_C^* = D_C^* + H_C^*, \quad X_K^* = H_K^* + H_{K'}^*.\Big\} \quad (17)$$

in equilibrium for RE. The remaining equilibrium conditions are the price-cost equations and the savings–investment equation. We refer to a set of solutions to all these equations as a real general equilibrium[15] and denote it by $(\pi^*, r^*, X_C^*, X_K^*, ...)$.

We can now see that the same equilibrium prevails in the monetary economy, ME, constructed in the following way. Let us take inventories $\bar{n}_{iC'}$ and $\bar{n}_{iK'}$ away from individuals and distribute to them an amount of money equal to the purchasing power of the inventories they had. Then

$$\frac{1}{p_a^*}\bar{q}_{iM} = (\pi_{C'}^* + \pi_C^*)\,\bar{n}_{iC'} + (\pi_{K'}^* + \pi_K^*)\,\bar{n}_{iK'}, \qquad (18)$$

so that the constraint,

$$\pi_L^*\bar{q}_{iL} + \frac{1}{p_a^*}\bar{q}_{iM} = \pi_L^* q_{iL} + \pi_C^* d_{iC} + \pi_{C'}^* q_{iC'} + \pi_B^* q_{iB},$$

is equivalent with (16) when the equilibrium prices and interest rate, π^* and r^*, prevail. Therefore the subjective equilibrium $(q_{iL}^*, d_{iC}^*, q_{iC'}^*, q_{iB}^*)$ in the real economy is seen to be identical with that quasi-equilibrium $(q_{iL}^0, d_{iC}^0, q_{iC'}^0, q_{iB}^0)$ in the monetary economy which we obtain when π and p_a are set at π^* and p_a^*, respectively. We can find the identity relationship between real saving in RE and quasi-equilibrium real saving in ME; that is to say $e_i^* = e_i^0$.

Let $(\tilde{q}_{iL}, \tilde{d}_{iC}, \tilde{q}_{iC'}, \tilde{e}_i, \tilde{q}_{iM})$ be the true subjective equilibrium of individual i in the monetary economy at P^* and r^*

[15] Note that equations concerning the bond are eliminated from the present RE, like the previous one.

where $P^* = p_a^* \pi^*$.[16] Because we assume that the utility functions are separable and the marginal utility of the availability of *numéraire a* is constant, we have $\tilde{q}_{iL} = q_{iL}^0$ and $\tilde{d}_{iC} = d_{iC}^0$ for all i, so that $\tilde{q}_{iL} = q_{iL}^*$ and $\tilde{d}_{iC} = d_{iC}^*$ for all i. Hence the equilibrium conditions (17), except those for C' and K', are satisfied as long as the firms produce the same amounts of consumption and capital goods[17] C and K and make the same investments in capital goods and the same inventory investments in consumption and capital goods in ME as we had in RE.

In ME, individuals keep inventories C' of the amounts $\tilde{Q}_{C'}$ in kind and of the amounts $\tilde{N}_{C'} = Q_{C'}^* - \tilde{Q}_{C'}$ in money. On the other hand, firms keep them in amounts

$$\tilde{Z}_{C'} = B_{C'C}\tilde{X}_C + B_{C'K}\tilde{X}_K$$

in kind and amounts

$$\tilde{\Delta}_{C'} = M_{C'C}\tilde{X}_C + M_{C'K}\tilde{X}_K$$

in money. As (12) holds in RE, we find that $Z_{C'}^*$ in RE equals $\tilde{Z}_{C'} + \tilde{\Delta}_{C'}$ in ME, provided that the same quantities of consumption and capital goods are produced in the two economies, which is assumed throughout the following argument. Now, in switching from RE to ME, we take away the initial stocks of the amounts $\bar{n}_{iC'}$ from each individual i and $\tilde{\Delta}_{C'} + \tilde{N}_{C'} - \sum_i \bar{n}_{iC'}$ from the firms.

Hence from the third equation of (17) we have

$$\bar{\bar{X}}_{C'} - \sum_i \bar{n}_{iC'} - (\tilde{\Delta}_{C'} + \tilde{N}_{C'} - \sum_i \bar{n}_{iC'}) = \tilde{Q}_{C'} + \tilde{Z}_{C'},$$

which is the demand–supply equation for inventories C' in kind in ME. Similarly, the firms keep inventories of capital goods K' of the amounts $\tilde{Z}_{K'}$ in kind and $\tilde{\Delta}_{K'}$ in money on the monetary economy. Taking away the amounts $\bar{n}_{iK'}$ of the initial stocks of K' from each individual i and $\tilde{\Delta}_{K'} - \sum_i \bar{n}_{iK'}$ from the firms in the

---

[16] P^* should not be confused with the equilibrium value of the entrepreneurial profit, which is zero. It represents the equilibrium vector of prices in terms of money.

[17] Since there are no changes in the relative prices of goods and services between the real and the monetary economy, the demands for factors remain unchanged if the same amounts of outputs are produced.

transition from RE to ME, we have from the fourth equation of (17)

$$\bar{\bar{X}}_{K'} - \sum_i \bar{n}_{iK'} - (\tilde{\Delta}_{K'} - \sum_i \bar{n}_{iK'}) = \check{Z}_{K'},$$

because $Z_{K'}^*$ in RE equals $\check{Z}_{K'} + \tilde{\Delta}_{K'}$ in ME. This is the equilibrium condition for inventories of capital goods after the introduction of money.

Thus in the transition from the real to the monetary economy some of inventories C' and K' are taken away from the firms. In compensation let us grant them money of the equivalent amount, $\bar{X}_M$, so that

$$\frac{1}{p_a^*} \bar{X}_M = (\pi_{C'}^* + \pi_C^*)(\tilde{\Delta}_{C'} + \tilde{N}_{C'} - \sum_i \bar{n}_{iC'}) + (\pi_{K'}^* + \pi_K^*)$$
$$\times (\tilde{\Delta}_{K'} - \sum_i \bar{n}_{iK'}) + (1 + \pi_B^*) \tilde{N}_{E'}, \quad (19)$$

where $\tilde{N}_{E'} = \sum_i (e_i^* - \tilde{e}_i^0)/r^*$. As the firms' demand for money amounts to

$$\tilde{X}_M = \frac{1}{p_M^*}(p_{C'}^* \tilde{\Delta}_{C'} + p_K^* \tilde{\Delta}_{K'}),$$

it is seen that the firms will produce the real income[18]

$$\pi_C^* \tilde{X}_C + \pi_K^* \tilde{X}_K + (p_M^*/p_a^*)(\bar{X}_M - \tilde{X}_M)$$
$$= \pi_C^* \tilde{X}_C + \pi_K^* \tilde{X}_K + \pi_{C'}^*(\tilde{N}_{C'} - \sum_i \bar{n}_{iC'}) - \pi_{K'}^* \sum_i \bar{n}_{iK'} + \tilde{N}_{E'}. \quad (20)$$

On the other hand, the firms' real expenditures amount to

$$\pi_L^* \tilde{Z}_L + \pi_{C'}^*(\tilde{Z}_{C'} - \bar{X}_{C'}) + \pi_{K'}^*(\tilde{Z}_{K'} - \bar{X}_{K'}) + \pi_{K''}^*(\tilde{Z}_{K''} - \bar{X}_{K''}).$$

Therefore, their real savings, $\pi_B^* \tilde{F}$, in ME, which are defined as an excess of real income over real expenditure, is seen to be equal to real savings in RE, $\pi_B^* F^*$, *plus* $\tilde{N}_{E'}$;[19] as $\tilde{N}_{E'} = \pi_B^*(E^* - \tilde{E})$ by

---

[18] For the definition of the income of the firm, see Chapter 9, p. 142. In deriving (20), use the price equations: $p_M^* = r^*/(1+r^*)$, $\pi_{C'}^* = \pi_{C'}^* r^*$, etc.

[19] In ME the firms have stocks of C', K' and K'' of the amounts,

$$\bar{X}_{C'} = \bar{\bar{X}}_{C'} - \sum_i \bar{n}_{iC'} - (\tilde{\Delta}_{C'} + \tilde{N}_{C'} - \sum_i \bar{n}_{iC'}),$$
$$\bar{X}_{K'} = \bar{\bar{X}}_K - \sum_i \bar{n}_{iK'} - (\tilde{\Delta}_{K'} - \sum_i \bar{n}_{iK'}),$$
$$\bar{X}_{K''} = \bar{\bar{X}}_{K''}$$

respectively. These, together with $\tilde{X}_C = X_C^*$, $\tilde{X}_K = X_K^*$, $\tilde{Z}_L = Z_L^*$, $\tilde{Z}_{K''} = Z_{K''}^*$, $\tilde{Z}_{C'} + \tilde{\Delta}_{C'} = Z_{C'}^*$ and $\tilde{Z}_{K'} + \tilde{\Delta}_{K'} = Z_{K'}^*$, enable us to confirm the equation asserted.

definition, we have $\pi_B^*(\bar{E}+\bar{F}) = \pi_B^*(E^*+F^*)$. In other words there is no change in total real savings in the transition from RE to ME. Hence the savings–investment equation is satisfied in ME if investments too remain unchanged; i.e. $\bar{H}_i = H_i^*$ for $i = C', K, K'$. Finally we obtain from (18) and (19) the money equation,

$$\bar{Q}_M + \bar{X}_M = p_a^* \frac{\pi_{C'}^*(\tilde{\Delta}_{C'} + \tilde{N}_{C'}) + \pi_K^*\cdot\tilde{\Delta}_{K'} + \tilde{N}_{E'}}{P_M^*}. \qquad (21)$$

As the relative prices π^*, the rate of interest r^* and, hence, $p_M^* = r^*/(1+r^*)$ are determined in the real economy, the money equation (21) determines the price of the *numéraire*, or its inverse, the price of money.[20] We also obtain the proposition of the quantity theory of money to the effect that p_a^* is proportional to the total quantity of money $\bar{Q}_M + \bar{X}_M$ issued. Thus Walras stated: 'We may, therefore, enunciate with what amounts to almost rigorous exactness that: *The rareté or value of the service of money is directly proportional to its utility and inversely proportional to its quantity.*'[21]

Since Hicks' *Value and Capital*, the classical method of dichotomizing the economy into the real and the monetary sector has been discussed by many authors, notably Patinkin. According to them, the real sector contains the equations requiring excess demand of each commodity to be zero, while the monetary sector consists of the supply–demand equation of money. Assuming that excess demands for commodities depend on relative prices only, it has been asserted that the latter are determined in the 'real' sector and that, once they are given, the absolute price level is determined by the money equation. As was pointed out by Patinkin, however, this interpretation of the classical dichotomy is self-contradictory, because the excess demand functions of commodities, which are all homogeneous of degree zero in money prices, imply, because the Walras law holds, that the excess demand function of money is homogeneous of degree one in money prices, so that the absolute level of prices is indeterminate. By admitting that excess demands for commodities depend on initial real money holdings as well as relative prices, a way of escaping from this dilemma has been suggested. But this too

[20] Therefore there exists a set of equilibrium solutions to ME. Note that $\tilde{N}_{C'}$ and $\tilde{N}_{E'}$, as well as $\tilde{\Delta}_{C'}$ and $\tilde{\Delta}_{K'}$, are independent of p_a^*.
[21] Walras *op. cit.*, pp. 328–9. His emphasis.

yields a self-contradiction, because the 'real' sector in this case can no longer be a pure real sector. Real economics, or the theory of value, has to be concerned with the determination of real value of money; therefore, the dichotomy is impossible.

A mistake which is common among participants in the so-called Patinkin controversy is that they simply dichotomize the whole system into the real and the monetary sector without making any adjustment. However, if, by removing money and increasing the initial real endowments, we construct, as I have done above, a real economy RE such that it generates the same equilibrium relative prices and interest rate as the given monetary economy ME (or if we construct, by decreasing the initial real endowments and introducing money, a monetary economy which has the same equilibrium relative prices and interest rate as the given real economy), then we can determine the absolute level of prices by solving the money equation after substituting into the monetary model, ME, the equilibrium relative prices and the equilibrium interest rate of the real model, RE.[22] Since the principle for determining relative prices and the interest rate has been made clear by 'real' economists, monetary economists need not be concerned with the same problem again; they may simply concentrate their attention on the determination of the price level. A division of labour may be possible between economic theorists and monetary specialists which validates the dichotomy in this sense; it is, strictly speaking, entirely different from the one discussed by Patinkin and others.

[22] The real sectors of ME which Patinkin and others were concerned with would differ from the corresponding sectors of RE. For example, the stocks of commodities of ME would be smaller than those of RE. Patinkin substituted solutions to the real sectors of ME into its money equation to determine the price level, while, as we have seen, the proper procedure requires us to substitute the solutions to RE into the money equation of ME.

CHAPTER 12

Say's law

We have so far reformulated and generalized Walras' mathematical model so that it becomes consistent with the view of the capitalist society which he expressed, not in mathematical formulas but in ordinary terms, in various parts of his *Elements*. Drawing a clear distinction between entrepreneurs and capitalists, he wrote: 'In reality, only land and personal faculties are always hired in kind; capital proper is usually hired in the form of money in the market for services. The capitalist accumulates his savings in money and lends this money to the entrepreneur who, at the expiration of the loan, repays the money. This operation is known as *credit*. Hence, the demand for new capital goods comes from entrepreneurs who manufacture products and not from capitalists who create savings.'[1] This view of Walras' is comparable with the one taken by Keynes, who said: 'Any reasonably definition of the line between consumer-purchasers and investor-purchasers will serve us equally well, provided that it is consistently applied...The criterion must obviously correspond to where we draw the line between the consumer and the entrepreneur...Whilst, therefore, the amount of saving is an outcome of the collective behaviour of individual consumers and the amount of investment of the collective behaviour of individual entrepreneurs, these two amounts are necessarily equal.'[2] Thus both agreed with the view that decisions to save are made by individuals such as workers, land-owners and capitalists, and decisions to invest by entrepreneurs or the executives of firms. This independence of saving and investment from each other has been fully taken into account by Keynesians, as they study the determination of aggregate income by using both the savings function and the investment function.

In spite of the clear statement quoted above, however, Walras himself did not develop a Keynesian model. Instead he con-

---

[1] *Elements*, p. 270. Walras' italics.   [2] *The General Theory*, pp. 61–3.

structed a model with completely different effects. He wrote: 'In order to pose the problem of capital formation, we must assume that there are land-owners, workers and capitalists who *save*, that is to say, who do not demand consumers' goods and services up to the total value of the services they offer, but demand *new capital goods* instead for part of this value. We must also assume that over against those who create savings, there are entrepreneurs who produce new capital goods in lieu of raw materials or consumers' goods.'[3] Here he clearly stated that new capital goods are directly demanded by land-owners, workers and capitalists who save, but *not* by entrepreneurs who produce consumption and capital goods. This entirely contradicts what he wrote in the quotation in the last paragraph. However, Walras considered this change to be immaterial. In fact, he wrote: 'Instead of supposing, as we have done hitherto, that the creators of excesses of income over consumption go in person to the market of capital goods to buy new capital goods which they then rent in the market for services to entrepreneurs engaged in industry, let us now suppose that savers lend all or part of the value of these capital goods in *numéraire* to the manufacturers who go in place of the savers to the market for capital goods and buy the new capital goods they want directly. Nothing will be changed in the latter market except that the demand for new capital goods will come from the entrepreneurs and not from the creators of excesses of income over consumption.'[4] He wrote: 'Clearly, from the theoretical point of view it is immaterial to the capitalist and to the entrepreneur whether what the one lends and the other borrows is the capital good itself, new or old, or the price of this capital good in the form of money. It is only from the point of view of practical convenience that the latter arrangement is distinctly preferable to the former.'[5]

But the choice is not a matter of practical convenience unless some restrictive assumption is satisfied. Where capital goods rather than money capital are lent by the capitalists to the entrepreneurs, the demand for capital goods is decided by the capitalists themselves, so that it should be consistent with their decision to save. Therefore, there is no room for an independent aggregate investment function in the model; and the route to

[3] *Elements*, p. 42. Walras' italics.   [4] *Elements*, p. 289.

[5] *Elements*, p. 270.

the Keynesian world is closed. In Walras' model it is assumed that investments in new capital goods and inventory investments in consumption and capital goods are flexible and adjusted so that (i) the selling prices of new capital goods are equal to the ratio of net incomes from them to the current rate of interest as well as their costs of production, and (ii) the total value of investments is equal to total savings.[6] As long as this perfect flexibility or perfect adaptability of investment decisions is assumed and, hence, there is no independent schedule of investment, i.e. no investment function, it is evidently immaterial for a theoretical study whether new capital goods are bought directly by the capitalists themselves or the demand for them is determined by entrepreneurs. Our generalized Walrasian system presented in Chapter 9 is an economy where decisions to invest are made by entrepreneurs, not according to a certain specific investment function but in a perfectly adaptable way. Therefore, in spite of a clear recognition of the role of entrepreneurs, they perform no significant function at all in that model; so it is not surprising that the generalized Walrasian model is non-Keynesian.

This is very much related with the problem of Say's law proposed by Keynes. This law prevails if supply creates its own demand, so that 'the aggregate demand price of output as a whole is equal to its aggregate supply price for all volumes of output',[7] or equivalently, aggregate investment is always smoothly and quickly adjusted and equated to aggregate savings, as if they are both simultaneously decided by the same persons. It is under the assumption of 'perfectly flexible' investment that we have this frictionless adjustment. Thus we may characterise the generalized Walrasian economy as a system satisfying Say's law which, according to Keynes, 'is equivalent to a proposition that there is no obstacle to full employment'.[8] It is indeed reasonable, as we have seen, that the generalized Walrasian model has a full-employment general equilibrium, because of the perfect flexibility of investment as well as of prices.

In an actual economy, however, entrepreneurs decide investments in new capital goods and inventory investments in consumption and capital goods, each according to some rule or an

---

[6] That is to say, in the notation of Chapter 9, prices and investments instantaneously bring about equations (31), (35) and (38) of the same chapter.

[7] *The General Theory*, p. 26.   [8] *op. cit.*

investment function; so Say's law will be refuted there. The state of full-employment general equilibrium which is proved to exist under Say's law will never be actualized in an economy with independent investment functions, except in the lucky case where they generate a state of full-employment equilibrium by chance. The actual economy works under many independent investment functions, and the degree of overdeterminacy which they bring about will correspond with their number. However, we shall confine ourselves in this chapter to the case of the minimum degree of overdeterminacy which Keynes was interested in, that is the case in which a single investment function, the aggregate investment function, is prevalent in the economy. In other words, we are concerned with an economy where the total value of investment, I, is a function of endogenous variables, such as outputs of consumption and capital goods X_C, X_K, prices p_C, etc. and the rate of interest, r; investments in individual new capital goods, H_K, and inventory investments in consumption and capital goods, $H_{C'}$ and $H_{K'}$, are determined so that they are consistent with the aggregate investment function. That is to say, they adjust themselves smoothly and quickly, not to aggregate saving as they do in the generalized Walrasian economy, but to aggregate investment determined in a specific way. Thus we impose an additional condition,

$$p_K(H_K + H_{K'}) + p_C H_{C'} = I(X_C, X_K, p_C, ..., r). \qquad (1)$$

In equilibrium, aggregate investment must equal aggregate saving. But they now have their own laws of determination; there is no smooth automatic adjustment of one to the other. Unless variables $X_C, ..., p_C, ..., r$ take on some special values, aggregate investment is not necessarily equal to aggregate savings, which is decided, independently of aggregate investment, as a function of prices, the rate of interest, the array of individuals' incomes and other variables. Say's law is thus violated as soon as we admit (1).

It is not difficult to see that there is, in general, no full-employment general equilibrium under (1). Let a set of solutions to the system of equilibrium conditions depicted in Chapter 9 (where the above equation (1) is not imposed) be called a Walrasian equilibrium. It establishes the full employment of all factors, land, labour and capital; but there is no reason why the Walrasian equilibrium values of investments, outputs, prices, etc. should satisfy the condition (1). If not, then investments must be adjusted so that (1) holds, because the entrepreneurs decide their investments in individual capital goods according to the consistent aggregate investment plan (1). Such values of investment are incompatible with some of the Walrasian equilibrium conditions; thus the introduction of an aggregate investment function gives rise to overdeterminacy. In general, there exists no general equilibrium satisfying all the Walrasian equilibrium conditions *and* the investment function (1); consequently, in such a system prices and outputs will fluctuate ceaselessly, unless the system is modified so that the movement stops in spite of some equilibrium conditions being violated. In view of the persistent unemployment in the UK economy during the twenties, Keynes proposed a modification: The wage rate remains constant in the presence of unemployment of labour, whereas it increases if the demand for labour exceeds its supply. In conjunction with this hypothesis of downwards rigidity of the wage rate, Keynes replaced the full-employment demand–supply condition for labour by a weaker one to the effect that no positive excess demand for labour should exist in the market. A negative excess demand for labour is perfectly legitimate, so that an unemployment of labour is permissible.

In a state where labour is not fully employed, aggregate income will, of course, not be realized at its full-employment level. Corresponding to this fact, the demand schedules of individuals will be revised, and the actual active and effective demands which are consistent with actual income will be different from those originally aimed at under the assumption that the full-employment income would be realized.[9] Those individuals who are not employed cannot carry out their original plans for purchasing commodities because of the lack of income to buy them; so they must revise their plans. Thus we have to admit that individuals, and firms too, behave according to the principle of

[9] In Chapter 9, the individuals' demand functions were derived by maximizing their utilities subject to their budget constraints. This implies that the individuals plan consumption, saving and holding of cash on an unrealistic, optimistic assumption that their initial endowments produce incomes for them at the market rates if they decide to supply them.

two-stage decision making, as we are concerned with an economy where full employment is not necessarily established.

The economy works in the following way. We negate Say's law and assume that investment demands for goods are determined so as to satisfy the investment condition (1). We consider a general monetary equilibrium system which has the investment function (1) in place of the supply–demand equation of labour, all the other equilibrium conditions remaining unchanged. We assume that in the new system individuals and firms obey the rule of two-stage decision making. It is seen that this system is as determinative as the previous Walrasian system satisfying Say's law (i.e. they have the same number of equations and the same number of unknowns), so that we obtain a set of solutions to the new system. Also, we assume downwards rigidity of the wage rate. Then if the propensity to investment is sufficiently low, the demand for labour is less than the amount of labour which is supplied when the solutions to the new system prevail, so that we have involuntary unemployment of labour. It will persist as long as the wage rate remains unchanged because of its downwards rigidity.

The model thus modified may be called the Walras–Keynes model. In its framework we may discuss the problem of persistent involuntary unemployment which Keynes tackled. There is no reason, on Walras' side, why he should stand opposed to Keynes. In fact, Walras' sociology, viewing the capitalist economy as a society consisting of four distinct classes, workers, land-owners, capitalists and entrepreneurs, should naturally have led him to reject 'Say's law', if he had been given a chance to develop his thought in that direction. It would be unfair to see any past theory as if it were a finished work; this is especially true for Walras because he revised his *Elements* greatly from edition to edition. If we were to regard Walras' *Elements* as definitive, it would perhaps be fair to conclude on the basis of the existing version that Walras' work was either unrelated or antagonistic to that of Keynes. But if we regard it as unfinished, the signs that he was anticipating Keynes, which we can clearly distinguish in the book, should be further emphasized in order to reveal their full implications. In any case, the Walras–Keynes general monetary equilibrium model is a very powerful model, which enables us, on the one hand, to make Walras' analysis free from the hardly acceptable hypothesis of Say's law and, on the other, to re-examine the propositions which Keynes established by macroeconomic analysis, from the point of view of general equilibrium analysis.

Let us next make a few remarks and comments which may help the reader's comprehension. Throughout this Part, we have assumed that all firms have constant returns to scale. However, we can easily generalize the analysis so as to allow for diminishing returns to scale; this has been done for the Walrasian system of capital accumulation and credit without money in Chapter 7. The extension to the system with money is not difficult. As was seen at the end of that chapter, Keynes' straightforward policy recommendations are based on the tacit assumption that industries having diminishing returns to scale play only a negligible role in the economy; otherwise, price effects in various directions prevent us from reaching a clear-cut conclusion, though it is still true that once Say's law is denied and an aggregate investment function is introduced, involuntary unemployment is inevitable, except in some pinpoint cases, even in a system with some or all industries having diminishing returns to scale.

The conclusion we have derived in this chapter is very different from the dominant view of Say's law. We have found that a full-employment equilibrium exists in the (generalized) Walrasian system subject to both Walras' law and Say's law, but that no full-employment equilibrium exists under Walras' law only, because of overdeterminacy due to the introduction of an independent investment function. On the other hand, according to the prevailing view represented by Lange, Patinkin and others,[10] the system of general equilibrium is determinate without Say's law, while it is underdeterminate with Say's law. These writers were concerned with an economy with n commodities plus money; excess demand for each of them (including money) is a function of n prices in terms of money. General equilibrium is defined as a state where all excess demands vanish; we have $n+1$ equations to determine n unknowns

[10] Lange, O., *Price Flexibility and Employment* (Bloomington, Indiana: The Principia Press, 1944); 'Say's Law: A Restatement and Criticism', in O. Lange *et al.* (eds.), *Studies in Mathematical Economics and Econometrics* (Oxford: Pergamon Press, 1942); Patinkin, D., *Money, Interest and Prices* (2nd edition, Scranton Pa.: Harper and Row, 1965).

(prices), but one of the equations can be eliminated as a dependent condition by virtue of Walras' law. Prices are then determined; we have neither over- nor underdeterminacy.

They say that Say's law prevails if excess demand for money vanishes for all values of commodity prices. As excess demand for money identically equals the sum of excess supplies of all commodities multiplied by their respective prices, because of Walras' law, Say's law implies that if excess demand vanishes for each of any $n-1$ commodities, then excess demand for the remaining commodity vanishes too. Under Say's law in Lange's sense there are only $n-1$ independent equilibrium conditions; the condition for money is not an equation which holds only at some particular set or sets of values of unknowns, but an identity which trivially holds everywhere; so it should not be counted among the conditions. We have $n-1$ conditions to determine n prices; the general equilibrium is underdeterminate under Say's law.

Thus, according to the Lange–Patinkin formulation, we have *a* full-employment equilibrium *without* Say's law (exact determinancy) and *many* full-employment equilibria with Say's law (underdeterminancy). Therefore it should have been concluded that there is 'no obstacle to full employment' without the law. On the other hand, according to our formulation, we have *a* full-employment equilibrium *with* Say's law (exact determinacy) and *no* full-employment equilibrium *without* Say's law (overdeterminacy). Hence we conclude that there is an obstacle to full employment without the law. Of course, these opposite conclusions are ascribed to the different respective definitions of Say's law. It is clearly seen that the one which plays a crucial role in establishing the existence of neoclassical full employment and serves as a test for distinguishing Keynesians from other economists is Say's law in our sense; Say's law in Lange's and Patinkin's sense is completely irrelevant in this context.[11] It

[11] More precisely, in contrast with Lange, Patinkin's position is subtle. First, based on Lange's definition of Say's law, Patinkin denies that Say's law is a basic component of the classical and neoclassical position. (See Patinkin, *op. cit.*, p. 193.) Then he later presents a macroeconomic interpretation of the law, according to which the aggregate demand curve must coincide with the 45 degree line (*op. cit.*, pp. 355–7.) As Patinkin seems aware, this version of the law is different from the original one due to Lange; it is, in fact, rather close to our interpretation, because the aggregate demand curve coincides with the 45 degree line if there is no independent investment function and aggregate investment is quickly and smoothly

should also be emphasized that there is no difficulty in discussing Keynesian problems within the (generalized) Walrasian framework, as we in fact have done in Chapter 7. While Say's law (in our sense) is compatible with the Walrasian system, we can equally look for the implications and consequences of over-determinacy due to the denial of the law, assuming the same system.

Finally, for those readers who do not want to be bothered with the complicated, complete, generalized Walrasian model in Chapter 9, let us reproduce, in a simplified, reduced version of the Walrasian model, the reasoning behind our conclusion of exact determinacy of the system under Say's law. Let there be $n-1$ goods and services, in addition to the bond and money, among which m goods are capital goods and m services are capital services; evidently $2m < n-1$. We ignore inventory investments in consumption and capital goods for simplicity, because this is harmless for the present purpose. With Say's law the equilibrium conditions are $n+1$ demand–supply equations for goods and services, the bond, and money; one savings–investment equation; and m price equations to the effect that the rate of net income from each capital good equals the rate of interest. On the other hand the variables are $n-1$ prices, one rate of interest and m investments in capital goods. Although the number of the equilibrium conditions, $m+n+2$, exceeds the number of the variables, $m+n$, by 2, two conditions may be derived from the rest by virtue of Walras' law and the savings identity, stating that aggregate saving consists of savings in the form of the bond, money or investments in capital goods, i.e. the sum of equations (36) and (37) of Chapter 9. Hence, with Say's law (i.e. with no non-trivial investment functions) the number of independent equations is the same as the number of unknowns; so we have exact determinacy. However, without Say's law, the

adjusted to aggregate savings. However, Patinkin did not obtain the same conclusion as ours, because the price mechanism is not explicit in his oversimplified macroeconomic analysis, so that it is obscure whether the whole set of equilibrium conditions is exactly determinative or not with his 'diagonal-cross' version of Say's law.

Say's law in the sense of Lange is not interesting. It allows for money but keeps the excess demand for money constantly at zero; money does not play any significant role. Therefore, the price level is left undetermined in the same way as it is trivially so in moneyless economies.

number of independent equations is greater than the number of unknowns because of additionally introduced investment functions; therefore, some degree of overdeterminacy is inevitable.

Where Say's law holds, investment in each capital good is perfectly flexible, so that any amount of it can be associated with a given rate of net income from that capital good. Suppose that static expectations prevail and the expected rate of net income (or the marginal efficiency) of each capital good equals its current rate. Take investment in a capital good along the horizontal axis and its marginal efficiency along the vertical axis. Then Say's law implies that the marginal efficiency curve is a horizontal line: according as the rate of interest exceeds, equals, or falls short of the marginal efficiency of a capital good, investment in that capital good is zero, indeterminate or infinite, respectively. Keynes replaced the marginal efficiency curve of this sort by a downwards-sloping one so as to enable us to determine the amount of investment at a point where the marginal efficiency equals the interest rate. We may conclude by saying that the constant returns from investment that Say's law presumes are *not* likely to be generally seen in the real world.

PART IV

Time Elements

CHAPTER 13

Capital and money reconsidered

So far, Walras' economics is satisfactory enough; but, looking at it from another point of view, it is found to be far from complete. Unless revisions and reinforcements are made, it cannot deal with those problems which present-day economists usually hope to solve by growth and money theory.

First of all, to produce a commodity takes time between the initial input of factors of production and the final output of their product. Walras of course knew this fact but neglected it. He wrote: 'Production...requires a certain lapse of time. We shall resolve the...difficulty purely and simply by ignoring the time element at this point.'[1] 'We shall resolve the further difficulty apropos of the lapse of time required in the production of new capital goods in the same way that we resolved it in the case of final products, by assuming production to be instantaneous.'[2]

However, this is a drastic simplification. By assuming instantaneous production we ignore a number of important economic problems. The period of production not only significantly differs from zero but also varies with the goods to be produced, e.g. it clearly differs between a definite quantity of cotton yarn and a locomotive, as Marx noticed.[3] Moreover, the production period for a product is not a fixed but a variable number, depending on which method of production is chosen from among those available; therefore, it should be economically decided within the system of general equilibrium, instead of being treated as a purely technological parameter. A widespread replacement of British-made ships by Japanese-made ones could not necessarily be ascribed to a superiority in quality of the latter; a decisive factor might be a substantial difference in the production period

[1] Walras, *Elements*, p. 242.
[2] *op. cit.*, p. 282.
[3] Marx, K., *Capital*, Vol. II (Progress Publishers, Moscow, 1967), p. 232.

which favours the Japanese shipbuilding industry over the British. If this is so, how can we encourage the British ship-builders to choose a method of production involving a shorter production period? Walras' economics cannot answer this question.

Secondly, capital goods are usually durable and are used repeatedly for production over several years; they are subject to wear and tear throughout their lifetime. There are at least two ways of treating durable capital goods: the neoclassical method and the one which I call the von Neumann method. Walras adopted the former, which may be summarized in the following way. A unit of an old capital good at some stage of wear and tear is converted into units of a new capital good of the same kind, such that they are equivalent in their productivity. Assuming that each capital good k evaporates at a fixed rate μ_k in every period in terms of efficiency (so that its productivity decays in a radioactive way), the existing stock of capital good k of the amount $\bar{X}_k$, in efficiency units, will decrease to the amount $(1 - \mu_k) \bar{X}_k$ after one period, and a replacement investment of the amount $\mu_k \bar{X}_k$ enables us to keep the stock of capital good k intact. Thus the neoclassical treatment assumes that old capital goods of various ages are perfectly malleable into the new capital goods; it takes no account of the age-structure of capital. Walras, in fact, wrote: 'This is called the *depreciation (amortissement)* of capital. The amount set aside for this purpose, i.e. the *depreciation charge*, will vary with different capital goods; but once this charge has been levied [and spent on replacing capital goods], all capital goods become rigorously identical with respect to impairment through use, since they all become, as it were, permanent.'[4]

In the case of radioactive evaporation of the efficiency of capital goods, the rate of depreciation μ_k is the reciprocal of the average lifetime of capital good k, T_k.[5] Walras took the depreciation rates as parameters of his system which are exogenously determined by technology; this means that he did not allow for the fact that the firms use capital goods for a longer or shorter period, according to circumstances. For instance, an unexpected rise in the demand for a consumption good *ceteris paribus* tends to

[4] Walras, *op. cit.*, p. 268.

[5] See Morishima, M. and Y. Murata, 'An Input–Output System Involving Nontransferable Goods', *Econometrica*, 36 (January, 1968), p. 86.

prolong the lifetime of a capital good which is needed to produce it, because by virtue of a temporary shortage of that capital good the firm will continue to use those old capital goods of the same kind which would have otherwise been discarded. Similarly a rise in the rate of interest *ceteris paribus* tends to shorten the period during which a capital good serves, because a less productive old capital good is not worth keeping, since the rate of net income from it is less than the new interest rate. Thus the actual economic lifespan of a capital good is not necessarily equal to its physical span and may change in response to exogenous events such as technological inventions, a shift in consumers' tastes, an increase in the supply of money and so on. Walras, however, simply ruled out all these induced fluctuations in the lifetime of capital goods, by making the neoclassical assumption that depreciation rates are all determined outside of the system.

Evidently, new and old capital goods are close substitutes. But they are not perfect substitutes, because, apart from the technological improvements which new capital goods usually embody, new and old capital goods differ in efficiency, since the latter have been worn by use in the past. Also, deterioration in the productivity of capital goods does not advance steadily at a constant rate, as the neoclassical depreciation formula assumes. As we all experience in driving our own cars, the maintenance and running costs are not very great in the earlier stages, but later start to increase at an accelerating tempo until they are finally discarded and replaced by new ones to save money. The quantities of the factors of production combined with an old capital good are thus different from those combined with a new one of the same kind; they are, in the real world, accompanied by different production coefficients, so that they should be treated as different commodities, although they are closely substitutive. A production process which uses capital good k of a certain age leaves, at the end of the production period, outputs from it and the one-year-older capital good k. The latter can be considered as a by-product of the process; from this viewpoint a choice between new and old capital goods is a choice between production processes employing new and old capital goods, respectively, and producing plural products jointly. An old capital good becomes obsolete at a point of time where the production process which uses the capital good of that particular age is found to be unprofitable. The problem of determination of the economic lifetime of durable capital goods is reduced to a part of the general problem of choice of techniques.

In this new formulation of the theory of depreciation, which I call the von Neumann theory, the crucial idea is to distinguish capital goods of different ages from each other as commodities of different kinds.[6] The list of existing commodities is enlarged so as to include old capital goods defined in this way. Once we decide on extending the list, it is easy for us to agree to a further extension, so as to include intermediate products or goods in process in the list. Let us now divide all possible periods of production of commodities by their largest common divisor; the elementary periods defined in this way are of equal length throughout. Insert intermediate products, characterized and distinguished from each other in an appropriate way, at the end of each elementary period. We are then provided with a finite number of elementary production processes, however large it may be, each converting inputs (factors of production, capital goods, intermediate products) into outputs (intermediate or final products, one-year-older capital goods). The problem of determining the production period of a commodity is reduced to a problem of choosing and connecting elementary processes.

This is a very promising approach originally proposed by von Neumann. It is especially powerful in determining the length of the period of production and the economic lifetime of capital goods, both problems argued over by economists of the Austrian school. In my opinion, anyone who wants to solve them has to employ the von Neumann approach or a some kind of variant of it.[7] As these are very important problems of capital theory, any serious capital theory which does not belong to the von Neumann family should be grafted onto the von Neumann stock by reformulating it in an appropriate way. As I have recommended that Marx should have integrated his theory of reproduction with von Neumann's growth model into a Marx–von Neumann model, I propose, in exactly the same manner, to

---

[6] Morishima, M., *Theory of Economic Growth* (1969), pp. 89–97; *Marx's Economics* (1973), pp. 164–78.

[7] Hicks, J., *Capital and Time, A Neo-Austrian Theory* (Clarendon Press, Oxford, 1973).

combine Walras' model with von Neumann's.[8] The Walras–von Neumann model obtained as a result would be as effective and far-reaching as the Marx–von Neumann one. As far as growth problems are concerned, it does not much matter whether one is a Walrasian or a Marxist. To a common question Walrasian and modernized Marxists would give the same answer, in the same way as American and Soviet astronauts behave alike in space.

In spite of this, however, it might be important, from the viewpoint of the history of economic thought or the history of economic analysis, to recognize that Marx's distance from von Neumann was shorter than Walras'. In the case of Marx, there is a chapter entitled 'The turnover of capital' in *Capital*, Vol. II, which I consider one of the most exciting and deeply imaginative chapters, probably the best chapter, in all three volumes. Although it is true that Marx was not fully successful in it, it is also true that he was tackling there the same economic problems as the Austrian economists. He was concerned with the roundabout production processes whereby each commodity results from a sequence of connected activities over a period during which workers operate machines which last for several periods and hence need not be renewed while they are serviceable. In comparison with this view of Marx's, Walras' was very simple; he simply assumed that commodities are produced instantly and machines are permanent, since depreciation charges are levied adequately. Not a chapter or even a paragraph discussing the time structure of production can be found in the *Elements*. We must regrettably say that Walras was far behind Marx in this respect.

The Walras–von Neumann model may be formulated as follows. Let us first extend the list of commodities so as to include intermediate products, I, old capital goods, $\overline{K}$, and old consumption goods, $\overline{C}$.[9] Secondly, the processes of producing consumption and capital goods, C and K, are analysed into elementary processes. In terms of the new lists of commodities and processes the

[8] See my *Marx's Economics*, pp. 164–78, and *Equilibrium, Stability and Growth*, pp. 148–53.

[9] As there are many kinds of intermediate products and old capital and consumption goods, I, $\overline{K}$, and $\overline{C}$ are each sets of indices representing the respective relevant commodities.

matrix of input coefficients and the matrix of output coefficients are defined as A and B, respectively; they are non-negative and rectangular because there is no reason why the total number of goods and services involved should equal the total number of elementary processes. Each column of the output coefficient matrix B may have more than one positive element, because joint production is allowed for. A and B are shown *in extenso* in equations (1) and (2) below.

A column of A, say the first one, represents inputs of land and labour, intermediate products, productive services of new and old capital goods, services of availability of new and old consumption goods, and services of availability of new and old capital goods which are required per unit of operation of elementary process 1. Similarly, the first column of B refers to outputs of intermediate products, new and old consumption goods, and new and old capital goods, produced by operating elementary process 1 by one unit. Let Y_t be the vector of activity levels of the elementary processes at the beginning of the (elementary) period t. The firms' demand functions for factors of production and services of availability of goods in kind (i.e. equations (7) and (8) of Chapter 6 or equations (27) and (28) of Chapter 9) are now rewritten in the following form:

$$
\begin{bmatrix}
A_{L1} & A_{L2} & \cdots & A_{Lm} \\
A_{I1} & A_{I2} & \cdots & A_{Im} \\
A_{K''1} & A_{K''2} & \cdots & A_{K''m} \\
A_{\bar{K}''1} & A_{\bar{K}''2} & \cdots & A_{\bar{K}''m} \\
A_{C'1} & A_{C'2} & \cdots & A_{C'm} \\
A_{\bar{C}'1} & A_{\bar{C}'2} & \cdots & A_{\bar{C}'m} \\
A_{K'1} & A_{K'2} & \cdots & A_{K'm} \\
A_{\bar{K}'1} & A_{\bar{K}'2} & \cdots & A_{\bar{K}'m}
\end{bmatrix}
\begin{pmatrix}
Y_{1t} \\
Y_{2t} \\
Y_{3t} \\
\cdot \\
\cdot \\
\cdot \\
\cdot \\
Y_{mt}
\end{pmatrix}
=
\begin{pmatrix}
Z_{Lt} \\
Z_{It} \\
Z_{K''t} \\
Z_{\bar{K}''t} \\
Z_{C't} \\
Z_{\bar{C}'t} \\
Z_{K't} \\
Z_{\bar{K}'t}
\end{pmatrix}.
\qquad (1)
$$

On the other hand, outputs available at the beginning of period t are results of activities in the previous period $t-1$; note that elementary processes are standardized in such a way that they are all of one period's duration. Thus we have

$$
\begin{bmatrix}
B_{I1} & B_{I2} & \cdots & B_{Im} \\
B_{C1} & B_{C2} & \cdots & B_{Cm} \\
B_{\bar{C}1} & B_{\bar{C}2} & \cdots & B_{\bar{C}m} \\
B_{K1} & B_{K2} & \cdots & B_{Km} \\
B_{\bar{K}1} & B_{\bar{K}2} & \cdots & B_{\bar{K}m}
\end{bmatrix}
\begin{pmatrix}
Y_{1t-1} \\
Y_{2t-1} \\
. \\
. \\
Y_{mt-1}
\end{pmatrix}
=
\begin{pmatrix}
X_{It} \\
X_{Ct} \\
X_{\bar{C}t} \\
X_{Kt} \\
X_{\bar{K}t}
\end{pmatrix}. \tag{2}
$$

The equilibrium conditions between demand and supply (i.e. inequalities (14) of Chapter 6, or equations (32) of Chapter 9) may be written as follows:

$$
\begin{aligned}
&\text{(i)}\ \ \bar{Q}_{Lt} \geqq Q_{Lt}+Z_{Lt}, & &\text{(vi)}\ \ X_{\bar{C}t} \geqq Q_{\bar{C}'t}+Z_{\bar{C}'t}, \\
&\text{(ii)}\ \ X_{It} \geqq Z_{It}, & &\text{(vii)}\ \ H_{K't-1} \geqq Z_{K't}, \\
&\text{(iii)}\ \ H_{Kt-1} \geqq Z_{K''t}, & &\text{(viii)}\ \ X_{Ct} \geqq D_{Ct}+H_{C't}, \\
&\text{(iv)}\ \ X_{\bar{K}t} \geqq Z_{\bar{K}''t}+Z_{\bar{K}'t}, & &\text{(ix)}\ \ X_{Kt} \geqq H_{Kt}+H_{K't}. \\
&\text{(v)}\ \ H_{C't-1} \geqq Q_{C't}+Z_{C't},
\end{aligned}
\right\} \tag{3}
$$

The equilibrium conditions for land and labour (i), for new consumption goods (viii), and for new capital goods (ix) are the same as the previous ones, i.e. the corresponding ones in the set of equilibrium conditions (14) of Chapter 6. Outputs and inputs of intermediate products must satisfy (ii); otherwise elementary processes are not smoothly connected. Inequality (iii) states that the demand for productive services of new capital goods should not exceed the supply provided by those new capital goods which were bought in the last period and are installed at the beginning of the present period. Similar conditions for services of availability of new consumption and capital goods are given as (v) and (vii), respectively. Finally, (iv) requires that the demand for old capital goods, for production or inventory purposes, should not be greater than their supply, while (vi) gives equivalent conditions for services of availability of old consumption goods, to the effect that the sum of individuals' and firms' demand for those services should not exceed their availability. It is noted that these conditions assume, among other things, that there is no investment demand for intermediate products or old capital and consumption goods. It is also noted that they distinguish conditions for old goods, (iv) and (vi), from those for new goods, (iii) or (vii), and (v), so that they enable us to deal with the age structure of capital. As has been recently emphasized by Joan

Robinson, the age composition of capital is one of the focal points of contemporary capital theory.[10]

Walras' equations for determining the production prices of commodities (i.e. (9) of Chapter 6, or (31) of Chapter 9) do not take into account capital gains or capital losses due to price changes. This is acceptable where prices are stationary throughout or no good is durable; except in these totally unrealistic cases, however, they must be revised so as to allow for the effects of a change in prices on costs.

Let us denote, as before, prices of L, C, K, etc. by p_L, p_C, p_K, etc. We write

$$p = (p_L, p_I, p_K, p_{\bar{K}}, p_C, p_{\bar{C}}, p_K, p_{\bar{K}}),$$
$$p^* = (p_I, p_C, p_{\bar{C}}, p_K, p_{\bar{K}}),$$

to which we attach subscript t when we refer to prices prevailing in period t. Let us consider an entrepreneur who has a given sum of money G available for expenditure. He can lend G to someone else for one period at the rate of interest r or spend it on one of m processes. If he chooses the first option he will have the sum $(1+r)G$ at the beginning of the next period; on the other hand, if he chooses the second option, he will have commodities of the amounts:

$$B_{Ii}y_i, \ B_{Ci}y_i, \ B_{\bar{C}i}y_i, \ B_{Ki}y_i, \ B_{\bar{K}i}y_i,$$

at the beginning of the next period, where y_i is the activity level at which he can operate the ith process with the given sum of money; that is, $y_i = G/(p_t A_i)$, where A_i represents the ith column of A. The total value of the commodities he owns in period $t+1$ amounts to

$$p^*_{t+1} B_i y_i,$$

which is compared with the amount from the first option, $(1+r)G$. In equilibrium, these are equal for those processes on which the entrepreneur may spend money, while the former is less

---

[10] Robinson, J., 'The Unimportance of Reswitching', *Quarterly Journal of Economics* (1975), pp. 32–9. Von Neumann himself was concerned only with a state of balanced growth. (See his article, 'A Model of General Economic Equilibrium', *Review of Economic Studies*, Vol. 13 (1945–6), pp. 1–9.) In such a state there is, of course, no problem of the age composition of capital, because it remains unchanged forever. However, by using von Neumann-type models we can discuss how the economy works through time if it is *not* in a state of balanced growth. See my *Theory of Economic Growth*, pp. 89–175.

than the latter for those which are found to be unprofitable. Thus we have[11]

$$p_{t+1}^* B_i y_i = (1+r) G \quad \text{or} \quad p_{t+1}^* B_i y_i < (1+r) G. \qquad (4)$$

Considering the definition of y_i, we have from the above,

$$p_{t+1}^* B \leq (1+r) p_t A, \qquad (5)$$

which is what I call the Walras–von Neumann price–cost equilibrium condition.

For the processes for which (4) holds with equality, we have, after rearranging the terms and removing, for simplicity's sake, the second subscript i from As and Bs,

$$
\begin{aligned}
p_{Ct+1} &B_C + p_{Kt+1} B_K \\
&= p_{Lt} A_L + [\{p_{Kt} A_K + p_{Ct} A_{C'}\} + \{p_{\bar{K}t+1} A_{\bar{K}} + p_{\bar{C}t+1} A_{\bar{C}'} \\
&\quad + p_{It+1} A_I\} - \{p_{\bar{K}t+1} B_{\bar{K}} + p_{\bar{C}t+1} B_{\bar{C}} + p_{It+1} B_I\}] \\
&\quad + [(p_{\bar{K}t} - p_{\bar{K}t+1}) A_{\bar{K}} + (p_{\bar{C}t} - p_{\bar{C}t+1}) A_{\bar{C}'} + (p_{It} - p_{It+1}) A_I] \\
&\quad + r[p_{Lt} A_L + p_{Ct} A_{C'} + p_{\bar{C}t} A_{\bar{C}'} + p_{Kt} A_K + p_{\bar{K}t} A_{\bar{K}} + p_{It} A_I],
\end{aligned}
$$

where $A_K = A_{K''i} + A_{K'i}$ and $A_{\bar{K}} = A_{\bar{K}''i} + A_{\bar{K}'i}$. The left-hand side obviously stands for the value of outputs, while the right-hand side consists of the factor cost (the first term), the user cost (the part in the first pair of square brackets), the capital loss due to price changes (the part in the second pair of square brackets) and the normal profit (or interest) on the total capital including funds for land and labour (the remaining terms). In more detail, the user cost equals the amount of the firm's purchases from other firms (i.e. the part in the first pair of curled brackets), that is A_1 by Keynes' notation, plus the value that the firm's capital equipment at the beginning of the period might have at its end if the firm had refrained from using it (i.e. the part in the second pair of curled brackets), that is Keynes' G', minus the actual value of the firm's capital equipment at the end of the period (i.e. the part in the third pair of curled brackets), that is Keynes' G.[12] Our user cost, $A_1 + G' - G$, ignores Keynes' B', which is the optimum sum to be spent on the maintainance and improvement

---

[11] If there is a process whose $p_{t+1}^* B_i y_i$ is greater than $(1+r) G$, every entrepreneur will concentrate his money on that process and no one will lend money. The interest rate will then increase. This is a possibility which is ruled out in the state of equilibrium.   [12] Keynes, J. M., *General Theory*, p. 66.

of the first capital equipment. It is of course easy to extend our analysis so as to take the processes of maintainance and improvement into account. We would then obtain Keynes' formula of user cost, $A_1 + (G' - B') - G$. In any case it is an important change that while Walras' price–cost equations were static, the Walras–von Neumann conditions (5) give intertemporal interdependence of prices.

Next let us make a few comments on the monetary aspects of Walras' model. As Clower rightly pointed out, Walras did not take fully into consideration the fact that money is the principal means of transaction in the economy.[13] To emphasize this role of money we may assume an abstract economy where money is the sole means of exchange. Barter is impossible; one must pay (or receive) money if one buys (or sells) a commodity. In such an economy, a difficulty may arise if people demand commodities in anticipation of money which they expect to receive from others. For example, person a is going to buy commodity A with the money which he will receive from person b, as a result of selling commodity B to b. Similarly, person b is going to buy commodity B with the money which he will receive from person c, as b is going to sell commodity C to c, and person c is going to buy commodity C with the money which he will receive from person a, as c is going to sell commodity A to a. Money exists in the economy, but we suppose that neither a, b or c has any money. Then it is obviously impossible to settle the above transactions by means of money, because there is no money to circulate within the sub-economy consisting of persons a, b and c. To avoid this kind of perversity we must *either* check whether the economy contains an independent moneyless sub-economy *or* prohibit individuals and firms from demanding a commodity unless they have enough money.

From the theoretical point of view, the second option is more convenient than the first. In monetarization of the growth model we make the elementary period so short that money cannot change hands more than once within it, so that the velocity of circulation of money is at most one. Then, as Clower saw, the budget equation is split into the expenditure constraint and the income constraint. For each individual (or each firm) the former

[13] Clower, R. W., 'A Reconsideration of the Microfoundation of Monetary Theory', *Western Economic Journal*, 6 (1967).

requires that the total value of his (or its) demand for commodities cannot exceed the total amount of money which he (or it) has at the beginning of the period, while the latter states that all the income he (or it) receives during the period has to be kept in the form of money. Then the theory of consumer's demand (or the theory of the firm) becomes more complicated, but such a revision does not cause any substantial theoretical difficulty. Transactions will be smoothly performed, because every demand is backed up with money.

It is important, however, to recognize that the elementary period which is appropriate for the money theory is different from, probably much shorter than, the elementary period for the growth theory.[14] The Walras–von Neumann production processes have to be further divided into stages of shorter duration during which money can change hands only once. As the Walras–von Neumann model already includes a large number of processes, the money model has to be concerned with an enormous multiplicity of processes. This, in principle, does not give rise to any difficulty, but for a practical application the number of processes has to be drastically decreased, to a manageable magnitude. How far it can be reduced without doing much damage to the effectiveness of the model depends on the skillfulness of the applied economist.

Another weak point of Walras' money theory is that his analysis of the role of money as a means of preserving purchasing power for the future is not satisfactory, judged by the present level of the theory of portfolio selection and liquidity preference. It is true that Walras anticipated the Keynesian theory of liquidity preference by deriving the individuals' demand for cash balances (*encaisse désirée*), as well as their savings, from the utility analysis of consumer behaviour. But there is no analysis of risk and uncertainty in the *Elements*; Walras gave no consideration to such organizations as banks, stock markets and futures

[14] Each general equilibrium model is formulated in terms of an elementary period which is proper to that model. For example, in the case of Walras' exchange model it is the period required for one round of *tâtonnement*; in the case of the Walras–von Neumann growth model, it is the standardized production period obtained as the largest common divisor of the production periods of consumption and capital goods and the lifetimes of capital goods; and in the case of the money model it is the period of circulation of money which is the reciprocal of the velocity of circulation of money.

markets. Moreover, as far as firms are concerned, it is no exaggeration to say that their demand for money was left almost entirely unexamined. The coefficients of demand for inventories, which Walras called the coefficients of production made up of the services of availability of commodities required *in kind* for the production of commodities (i.e. $B_{C'C}$, $B_{K'K}$, etc. in Chapter 9), and the coefficients of demand for money, which he called the coefficients of production made up of the services of availability required in money (i.e. $M_{C'C}$, $M_{K'K}$, etc.), were all assumed to be constant, so that the firms' total demands for the services of availability of commodities in the form of money depended simply on the total outputs (see equation 29 in Chapter 9). These show the obvious backwardness of Walras; nevertheless, I would say that it is not very difficult to supplement his general equilibrium theory of money using the recent advanced results of such economists as Hicks, Tobin, Hahn and others.[15]

It has been seen that Walras emphasized the entrepreneur's independent role in deciding on production and investment plans. In his model, entrepreneurs, like Oxfam volunteers, receive nothing for their efforts, so that they cannot survive unless they are, at the same time, land-owners, labourers or capitalists. This is a most unpleasant implication of his model, which he gave only the following excuse: '[U]nder free competition, if the selling price of a product exceeds the cost of the productive services for certain firms and a *profit* results, entrepreneurs will flow towards this branch of production or expand their output, so that the quantity of the product will increase, its price will fall, and the difference between price and cost will be reduced; and, if the cost of the productive services exceeds the selling price for certain firms, so that a *loss* results, entrepreneurs will leave this branch of production or curtail their output, so that the quantity of the product will decrease, its price will rise and the difference between price and cost will again be

---

[15] Hicks, J. R., *Critical Essays in Monetary Theory* (The Clarendon Press, Oxford, 1967); Hester. D. D. and J. Tobin, *Risk Aversion and Portfolio Choice*; *Studies of Portfolio Behavior*; *Financial Markets and Economic Activity*; Cowles Foundation for Research in Economics at Yale University, Monograph 19, 20, and 21, respectively (John Wiley and Sons, Inc., New York, 1967); Hahn, F. H., 'On Transaction Costs, Inessential Sequence Economies and Money', *Review of Economic Studies*, Vol. 40 (October, 1973), pp. 449–62. See also Morishima, M. and others, *Theory of Demand: Real and Monetary* (The Clarendon Press, Oxford, 1973).

reduced.'[16] 'Thus, in a state of equilibrium in production, entrepreneurs make neither profit nor loss. They make their living not as entrepreneurs, but as land-owners, labourers or capitalists in their own or other businesses. In my opinion, rational book-keeping requires that an entrepreneur who owns the land which he works or occupies, who participates in the management of his firm and who has his own funds invested in the business, ought to charge to business expense and credit to his own account [the corresponding – Jaffé] rent, wages and interest charges calculated according to the going market prices of productive services. In this way he earns his living without necessarily making any profits or suffering any losses as an entrepreneur.'[17] 'Equilibrium in production like equilibrium in exchange, is an ideal and not a real state. It never happens in the real world that the selling price of any given product is absolutely equal to the cost of the productive services that enter into that product, or that the effective demand and supply of services or products are absolutely equal. Yet equilibrium is the normal state, in the sense that it is the state towards which things spontaneously tend under a regime of free competition in exchange and in production.'[18] Thus Walras viewed non-zero entrepreneurial profit as a characteristic of a disequilibrium state of affairs. Its permanent existence can be explained only if we allow for disturbing factors which keep the economy out of equilibrium.

This view of Walras' is in clear contrast to the one which we can derive from such subsequent and now popular models of general equilibrium as Hicks', Arrow and Debreu's, and Arrow and Hahn's. These assume that a finite number of firms exist in the economy, each having an entrepreneur or a group of executives at its head. Increasing returns to scale prevail, in each firm, up to a certain level of output and are then transmuted into diminishing returns. Let us assume, for the sake of simplicity, that all the firms producing the same kind of commodity behave in exactly the same way. Let us call the level of output of a firm at which the average cost of production is minimized the optimum scale of production of that firm, and assume that the market demand for each commodity is very large in comparison with the optimum scale of a single firm producing it. If there are, in

---

[16] *Elements*, pp. 224–5. Walras' italics.   [17] *op. cit.*, pp. 225–6.
[18] *op. cit.*, p. 224.

such an economy, sufficient firms for each commodity, then all firms operate at their respective optimum scales. In fact, if there were a big firm which produced a large amount of products at an average cost above the minimum, it would be blocked by a number of smaller firms each of the optimum size. At the optimum output, the average cost equals the marginal cost, which in turn equals the price of the product, so that no firm will earn a positive entrepreneurial profit. On the other hand, if the number of firms producing a commodity is not sufficiently large, the scale of each firm in that industry should exceed the optimum; the marginal cost diverges from the average cost, and a positive entrepreneurial profit will result.

Thus, from this point of view, we might conclude, as Blaug did,[19] that in Walras' system zero profits prevailed in equilibrium, because he postulated that entrepreneurship is a free service, so that there are always sufficiently many firms. The modern general equilibrium theorists mentioned above have abandoned this postulate of Walras' and hold that marginal costs should increase, because of the increasing difficulty of controlling an enterprise.[20] They consider that entrepreneurship is scarce and obtain models with positive equilibrium profits.[21]

Theorists in the mainstream of general equilibrium theory have taken the scarcity of entrepreneurship for granted and have not explained why it should be so. F. H. Knight and J. A. Schumpeter were two notable exceptions;[22] according to them

[19] Blaug, M., *Economic Theory in Retrospect*, 2nd edn, p. 587.

[20] See, for example, Hicks, J. R., *Value and Capital*, p. 83.

[21] However, *either* if the market demand for a commodity is small, *or* if, as Walras postulated, constant returns to scale prevail up to a sufficiently large output (so that the optimum scale of the firm is large), then the smallness of the number of firms is not a sufficient condition for positive profits. In fact, Walras wrote: '[A]lthough the multiplicity of firms conduces to equilibrium in production [with zero profits], such multiplicity is not absolutely necessary in order to bring about this equilibrium, for, theoretically, one entrepreneur alone might do so, if he bought his services and sold his products by auction, and if, in addition, he always decreased his output in case of loss and always increased in case of a profit.' (*Elements*, p. 225.)

[22] Knight, F. H., *Risk, Uncertainty and Profit* (Series of Reprints of Scarce Tracts in Economic and Political Science, No. 16, London School of Economics and Political Science, 1933); Schumpeter, J. A., *The Theory of Economic Development* (Harvard Economic Studies, Vol. 46, Harvard University Press, Cambridge, Massachusetts, 1951).

the main reason why only a limited number of persons can be entrepreneurs is that no one has perfect foresight and the outcome of every economic activity is more or less uncertain and subject to risks. In fact, if everyone knew accurately where opportunities to earn profits were and how he could take advantage of them, then everyone would rush into profitable businesses and profits would disappear. Where people are not evenly endowed with talents, by nature or for other reasons, some of them are better than others at introducing improvements in production, putting inventions into practice, or carrying out innovations in business. The firms which are directed by such able entrepreneurs evidently possess a great advantage over others, so that they will realize a net profit which goes into their entrepreneurs' pockets.[23] Thus entrepreneurial profits are ultimately attributable to uncertainty and, conversely, entrepreneurs themselves produce uncertainty by the innovations which they create. It is no wonder that, having accepted the assumption of perfect foresight, Walras (as well as the mainstream group of modern general equilibrium theorists) could not explain entrepreneurial profits, while he could develop a dynamic theory which examines the sequence of temporary equilibria. Indeed, 'there ought to be an Economics of Risk on beyond the Dynamic Economics'.[24]

[23] 'The innovation is hazardous, impossible for most producers.' (Schumpeter *op. cit.*, p. 134.) A failure in introducing an innovation, of course, causes a loss.

[24] Hicks, J. R., *Value and Capital*, p. 126. It is true that recent writers, notably G. Debreu and R. Radner, have been concerned with uncertainty problems in the general equilibrium framework. But I do not think that they have successfully elucidated the role and behaviour of entrepreneurs.

Index